CREATIVE FINGERPLAYS & ACTION RHYMES

An Index and Guide to Their Use

by
Jeff Defty

Illustrations by
Ellen Kae Hester

ORYX PRESS
1992

The rare Arabian Oryx is believed to have inspired the myth of the unicorn. This desert antelope became virtually extinct in the early 1960s. At that time several groups of international conservationists arranged to have 9 animals sent to the Phoenix Zoo to be the nucleus of a captive breeding herd. Today the Oryx population is over 800, and nearly 400 have been returned to reserves in the Middle East.

Copyright © 1992 by The Oryx Press
4041 North Central at Indian School Road
Phoenix, Arizona 85012-3397

Published simultaneously in Canada

Printed and bound in the United States of America

♾ The paper used in this publication meets the minimum requirements of American National Standard for Information Science—Permanence of Paper for Printed Library Materials, ANZI Z39.48, 1984.

Library of Congress Cataloging-in-Publication Data
Defty, Jeff.
    Creative fingerplays and action rhymes : an index and guide to their use / by Jeff Defty.
        p. cm
    Includes bibliographical references and index.
    ISBN 0-89774-709-7
    1. Finger play. 2. Rhyming games. 3. Finger play—Indexes.
4. Rhyming games—Indexes. I. Title.
    GV1218.F5D44 1992   92-9655
    793.4—dc20   CIP

CONTENTS

LIST OF ACTIVE VERSE

ACKNOWLEDGMENTS

This book would not have been possible without the support and assistance of many people. I am indebted to Howard Batchelor at The Oryx Press for his vision and guidance in shaping the concept for the book; my wife Marina McShane for her support and editorial assistance; my daughter Juliette McShane, who was my final authority on questions of "kid appeal"; and to Brad Parshalle, Elga Brown, Sandra Quigley, and Donna Hill, who read and made many suggestions for the improvement of the manuscript.

I would also like to thank my many teachers and mentors, including Barbara Snow, Bev Bos, Edmond Mignon, Carol Doll, Margaret MacDonald, and especially, the young people who attended Children's Playhouse in Eugene, Oregon, between 1980 and 1986 and who taught me much more than I could have possibly taught them.

I would like to thank T.S. Denison, Inc. for permission to reprint Kathy Overholser's fingerplay "Once there was a Pilgrim" on p. 79 and Mary Jackson Ellis' "Miss Muffet" game on p. 74. Other fingerplays and action rhymes used as examples in this book, unless otherwise noted, are traditional or anonymous. Authorship of fingerplays is difficult to trace because they are so frequently passed through oral traditions. If a fingerplay was found uncredited and unattributed in three sources or more, I have presumed it to be in the "public domain." If an authored verse has been used without attribution and permission, the omission is unintentional; please contact the author through The Oryx Press to correct this in future editions.

PREFACE

Working with young children is not so much imparting a body of knowledge and skills as being a skillful observer who is responsive to the many facets of a child's development and who is able to challenge further where the child is, feelingly and creatively. One needs to be an insider, taking the perspectives of the child, and an outsider, being a part of the child's environment and experience, constantly relating to the child in new ways and growing with the child.

—*Maria Montessori*

INVITATION TO THE DANCE

Some years ago, I attended a workshop with Bev Bos, arguably the country's most inspiring and outspoken advocate of developmentally appropriate practices. At this workshop, she lectured, sang, told stories, and showed slides of her wonderful school, where children are allowed to be children. At one point in her presentation, she made a dramatic pause and held up a sign which read, "If it's not in the body, it's not in the brain!"

These words made a deep impression on me and reverberate throughout the pages of this book. What better way to get language into the body than through the joy of movement expressed in the fingerplay? We are in such a hurry to teach children what words signify that we forget to relish the pure sounds of words with them, sounds that invite spontaneous physical and imaginative play. We also forget that young children are not naturally motivated by adult priorities; they are motivated by fun.

True learning is play in its highest form; it is always its own reward. Far from something that needs to be "reinforced" with praises or prizes, learning through play reinforces itself with the delight it brings. Children experience this delight when rich and playful language is connected to the rhythmic exuberance of the body. Fingerplays and action rhymes are so satisfying to developmental needs and so useful as educational tools that no one who works with young children should be without a "bag of tricks" of active verses. I have used them successfully with many ages and types of groups, as reflected in the scope of this book, which ranges from infancy through the primary grades and encompasses both "normal" and special needs children.

PREFACE

PURPOSE AND PHILOSOPHY

This book is designed to help adults who work with young children find and use active verses suitable for activities, lesson plans, and programs. It is founded on the premise that all learning activities should be based on sound developmental principles. Developmentally appropriate methods support the child-centered curriculum. In such a curriculum, all learning activities are grounded in the child's world and experience. These methods grow out of an understanding of the physical, mental, emotional, and social stages that children pass through as they mature. This approach strives for a balance between activities that children can already confidently perform and those that provide the challenges necessary to nurture their growth.

Young children need a variety of concrete, multisensory experiences to stimulate language acquisition and other types of development. They also need an abundance of fantasy and creative play to internalize and integrate such experiences. In my own work as a preschool teacher, storyteller, and librarian, I have found fingerplays and action rhymes to be ideally suited to these purposes. Unfortunately, information about how to apply our understanding of child development to the teaching of fingerplays has been scant. Nor has there been any good subject access to active verses, which is needed in order to weave them into the content of a curriculum or develop thematic storytimes.

This book will fulfill both needs. The developmental chapters identify what types of active verse are best suited to particular groups, while the Subject Index makes it possible to locate verses on specific themes or subjects. Many examples and ready-to-use activities are offered, all of which have been tested with children. These examples also serve as models for using similar materials accessible through the indexes.

AUDIENCE

While the value of fingerplays and action rhymes is already recognized by preschool teachers and librarians, it is hoped that this work will encourage primary grade teachers to consider adopting it into their curricula as well. There are excellent (though mostly overlooked) opportunities for using active verse with children between the ages of six and eight, a sampling of which is explored in Chapter 7.

New parents will find a wealth of engaging games to play with their babies and toddlers. Chapters 3 and 4 will be of special interest to parents who want to stimulate their children's physical and intellectual growth while strengthening emotional bonds. This book is a foil and a better alternative to the well-intentioned but misguided efforts of parents to make "superbabies" of their offspring. It endorses not premature literacy, but *mature preliteracy*.

Speech and language therapists, special education and E.S.L. teachers, and other adults who work with children with special needs will find this work particularly valuable; many of these people already make use of movement and other physical analogs to reinforce language acquisition. Fingerplays fulfill a strong need for repetition and offer not only new language patterns, but a source of comfort to children who have learning disabilities or are coping with the stresses of learning a foreign language. Chapter 8 is devoted to uses of active verse with special needs children. The Supplemental Bibliography, Chapter 10, lists foreign language materials and audiovisual sources for fingerplays and action rhymes, including records, tapes, filmstrips, and videocassettes.

INDEXES

The indexes, which comprise Part II of this book, list approximately 3,000 unique fingerplays and action rhymes found in 95 sources. Several types of materials were included—fingerplay/action rhyme collections; picture books featuring active verse; and other resources, such as activity books that contain fingerplays and action rhymes. All materials selected are either currently in print or widely available in public libraries (as determined by O.C.L.C. holdings records). A few less common out-of-print sources were indexed when their unique offerings merited inclusion. All of the materials indexed are available through interlibrary loan. The primary goal in the selection process was to offer the widest possible variety of materials that are accessible through public library collections.

PART 1

DEVELOPMENTAL FINGERPLAY AND ACTION RHYME ACTIVITIES

CHAPTER 1

Introduction

DEVELOPMENTAL STAGES

There are many descriptions in this book of what an "average" child is able to do at a certain age. These statements are intended to give the reader a general sense of what to expect and to suggest strategies for child-centered teaching. "Typical" developmental characteristics, however, are not absolute. Some children will appear to be ahead of or behind developmental norms. They may tarry through one stage and rush through another. They may show advanced motor development, but lag in emotional growth. All of these phenomena are normal and common.

Children differ considerably in their rates of development and pass through developmental stages as they are ready to do so, not as some textbook prescribes. What is relatively reliable, however, is the sequence in which developmental tasks are mastered. If a child is unable to perform a task considered to be "developmentally appropriate" for that age, it is not necessarily cause for alarm. Observation and flexible response to the needs of individual children will reward the teacher who is committed to designing the lesson for the child, instead of trying to fit the child to the lesson. Proceed according to the child's demonstrated abilities and build upon strengths. There is nothing to be gained by pushing children beyond their natural limits to the point of frustration. Fingerplays and action rhymes are fun and relaxing; it is counterproductive to turn them into tasks that produce stress.

DEFINITION AND HISTORY OF FINGERPLAYS AND ACTION RHYMES
DEFINITIONS

A **fingerplay** is a verse or rhyme coupled with gestures, movements, or pantomimes of the hands and fingers. It is typically short (four to eight lines), rhymed, and capable of being performed either individually or in a group. **Action rhymes** have essentially the same characteristics, but involve more large muscle movement, such as bending, stretching, jumping, marching in place, or stamping the feet.

The close relationship between fingerplays and action rhymes is reflected in the way they are so often intermixed in collections. One can often find the same verse presented in both forms, or as a hybrid of fingerplay and action rhyme. In some materials, there is obvious confusion as to what distinguishes them. For the purposes of this book, it was necessary to draw the line somewhere, and the following criteria were adopted:

(1) If the rhyme can be performed sitting down and uses primarily the hands, it is defined as a **fingerplay.**

(2) If the performance requires standing up or large body movements, it has been classed as an **action rhyme.**

For the purposes of this work, fingerplays and action rhymes will be referred to collectively as "active verse."

One might see all of these types of rhymes—from passive "tickling rhymes" to complex, interactive play-party games—as part of a spectrum, in which fingerplays and action rhymes play intermediate roles. Lap-time games played with infants teach basic body awareness, such as sensation in the fingers and toes. Toddlers and preschoolers learn to manipulate and coordinate their own movements and, as older children, begin to fit these movements into a social context. Fingerplays are extended to whole-body movements in the action rhyme. The action rhyme, in turn, is extended to a fully social expression in the singing game or drama. The developmental guidelines in this book trace a clear progression through these forms and offer guidance in selecting and using age-appropriate materials. Once again, the reader is urged not to take the age ranges too literally; many children are advanced or delayed for their years, and adjustments must be made accordingly. What is most important is the sequence of these stages and how they relate to each other.

HISTORY OF THE MODERN FINGERPLAY

The term "finger play" appears to have originated in the nineteenth century with Emilie Poulsson's work of that title (1893). Poulsson, in turn, drew heavily on Friedrich Froebel's *Mother-Play* (1873), so termed because the activities in that book were conceived as one-on-one sharing between parent and child. The fingerplay itself was already common folklore; Froebel merely recognized its educational value and adopted it as part of the curriculum for his kindergarten. As Scott (1960) notes:

Many of our traditional fingerplays stem from translations of Froebel, who believed that "children should be children before they are adults," that all education must have a "sense of perception" basis, and that children should be taught from objects in their own setting.

Froebel believed that associations of the sounds and meanings of language with the child's own body were ideally suited to the learning styles of young children. His philosophy was far ahead of the times. In his day, there was no discipline of "educational psychology." Froebel based his work on his own observations and intuitions. Since then, contemporary research in child development has vindicated his basic principles. In the debate over whether young children should be taught by imitation or independent exploration, Froebel's philosophy lends a healthy credence to both approaches. His vehicle—the fingerplay—supports them simultaneously. The verse and its accompanying movements are learned by imitation and repetition, while independent exploration is encouraged through psychological identification, fantasy, and the creation of variations. The expansion of the fingerplay to action rhymes and creative dramatics extends its use further into the exploratory side of learning.

ACTIVE VERSE AS FOLKLORE

Although many teachers and librarians now rely heavily upon printed texts to learn new fingerplays, the source of the texts themselves is usually the oral tradition. This has at least two implications. First, many rhymes have no "definitive" version; a comparison of various presentations reveals local and editorial variations. Even identical texts may have somewhat different scripts for the movement. To get the most satisfying results, it is often necessary to use several sources, taking the best elements of each to assemble a composite version (as has been done with many of the examples in this book). Second, some of the nuances and much of the spirit transmitted through the oral tradition is lost as verses are "frozen" in print; like folktales, they must be lovingly thawed and infused with one's own life experience before they can be enthusiastically given to children. This book, like other books, cannot store or transmit the vitality of the verse; it is up to the users of this guide to discover and impart this vitality themselves.

BENEFITS OF FINGERPLAYS AND ACTION RHYMES
PLAY AND FANTASY

As child-centered activities, fingerplays and action rhymes validate play not only as a learning mode, but as something of value in itself. This is play in its most basic form, without toys, props, or other devices. The child's own body becomes the inexhaustible physical analog for an infinitude of people, objects, animals, and activities, a stage upon which can be played and replayed the dramas of the real world and of the imagination. Even with no other justification, active verses should be played because they are fun and satisfy vital psychological needs. They are for the very young what fairy tales are to older children, a means "by which the child can structure his daydreams and with them give better direction to his life" (Bettelheim 1975).

LISTENING AND ATTENTION SKILLS

Listening skills are sharpened through fingerplays and action rhymes. There is a common misapprehension that young children have "short attention spans." The fact is that when they are engaged, they often exhibit remarkable powers of concentration. The term "attention span" must always be qualified *for what?* It is true that young children have difficulty paying attention to the voice alone because it is abstract, unconnected to concrete objects. Active verse engages the mind by involving the body. The very act of participation will activate the listening ability of young children, who have a strong need for response.

LEARNING TO COUNT

One of the earliest instructional uses of fingerplays was in teaching children to count. Roman children of 50 A.D. played the counting game: "Bucca, bucca, quod sunt hic" (Scott 1960). The ten fingers are the most immediate aids for number concepts available. They are the portable abacuses of every culture. The imaginative act that transforms five fingers into "five little birds . . . frogs . . . bunny rabbits . . . etc." is the first step toward more abstract concepts of arithmetic, such as addition and subtraction. It also empowers the child with new abilities to impose order and control; enumeration and classification begin with this ability to abstract. Finger counting rhymes offer a method of introducing numerical concepts that does not rob children of their enjoyment of numbers. Many such rhymes can be located in the Subject Index under the terms "Counting rhymes" and "Subtraction rhymes."

OTHER CONCEPTS

Fingerplays and action rhymes also offer a gentle method for introducing or reinforcing other basic concepts, such as size, shape, direction, and color. Subject headings have been assigned for all of these ideas and are listed in the Subject Index as subheadings of the term "Concepts." Fingerplays and action rhymes are particularly effective for teaching spatial relationships because such concepts are easily demonstrated with physical movement. The association with the body provides a concrete analogy for abstract concepts. Developmentally delayed learners will especially benefit from the physical reinforcement of difficult concepts and may more easily grasp whole/part relationships with the aid of a fingerplay or action rhyme.

SEQUENCING

One of the most basic human thought processes is the ability to think sequentially. This skill is so fundamental to other types of learning that it is often taken for granted. It is, however, a learned ability and must be acquired through practice. Sequential thinking is aided by rhymes that proceed in an orderly sequence. Order is reinforced not only through mnemonics of meter and rhyme, but by the flow of physical movements that mirror the language. As the child is gradually led from simpler to longer and more complex active verses, this sequencing ability is strengthened and refined. Patterns of cause-and-effect are presented in a palpable and developmentally appropriate way. Fingerplays offering simple, sequential "building blocks" are an excellent introduction to storytelling, plotting, and predicting the outcome of a sequence of events.

PERCEPTUAL-MOTOR DEVELOPMENT

Fingerplays and action rhymes also build coordination, dexterity, and strength, both in small and large muscle groups. The bending, stretching, and twisting motions in many action rhymes develop and coordinate whole body movement. In addition, there are strong correlations between perceptual-motor abilities and other types of growth, such as intellectual, emotional, and social development. Hand-to-eye coordination and fine muscle development of the fingers are essential pre-reading and pre-writing skills.

It is interesting to watch children of different ages perform a verse such as "The eensy weensy spider." The degree of coordination required to make the spider climb "properly" is actually rather high, but younger children delight in their own efforts. The developmental stages of gross and fine motor skills are described in this book, which will aid adults in selecting and teaching active rhymes of appropriate complexity to various ages.

MUSIC AND DANCE

The performance of active verse complements music and movement activities, teaching fluency and rhythm. A natural sense of *phrase* and *cadence* emerges through the recitation of verse. The marriage of movement to the rhythms of the spoken word disciplines the body and frees the vocal mechanism for uninhibited singing. Young children often provide their own melodies for fingerplays they have learned, or may chant the words in a half-sung, half-spoken voice. These tendencies should be encouraged, as they help build bridges between speaking, singing, and creative movement.

SELF-ESTEEM

A positive self-image is one of the most basic building blocks of all learning. It is significant that active verses are performed without props; children learn that their minds and bodies contain a whole world of possibilities. They learn that they are valuable persons in and of themselves. (Many fingerplays have this theme built into their content.) As young children develop a repertoire of active verses, they take great pride in performing them and teaching them to others.

SOCIALIZATION

In a day care setting, where there is a steady influx of "new arrivals," the older children can be enlisted to teach newcomers the school "repertoire" of active verse. This not only establishes a sense of belonging for the new children, but it also gets the others to play with them right away. Fingerplays are also a delightful way of doing something "separately, together," which can ease the transition from individual to interactive play.

TRANSITIONAL "RITUALS"

Fingerplays and action rhymes supply routines that are comforting to young children, who need to know what to expect throughout the day. Chapter 4 includes a discussion and some examples of how to use fingerplays as transitions between activities and how to encourage cooperation during unpopular times of the day, such as cleanup or nap. Fingerplays useful for signaling special times of the day can be found in the Subject Index under a number of different headings, including "Activities—Cleaning up," "School—Circle time," "School—Lining up," "School—Nap time," "School—Snack time," and "Storytime."

BEHAVIOR AND GROUP MANAGEMENT TOOL

Besides easing transition times and serving as meaningful rituals, fingerplays have a variety of uses in managing groups of children. A fingerplay is often the perfect way to refocus the children's attention when emotional tension, restlessness, or boredom makes other activities impossible. In a circle- or storytime setting, where the children are expected to sit together and pay attention, fingerplays and action rhymes are often used to help them "get their wiggles out." More importantly, it gives them a greater stake in the activity and honors their active contribution. If the planned activity is a sharing time, fingerplays help release inhibitions. Fingerplays are also excellent time-fillers, good for moments when the group is together but has to wait a few minutes for a scheduled activity to begin.

SPEECH AND LANGUAGE THERAPY

There are many ways to use active verse to improve speech and language. Fingerplays can be used to give children practice with sounds that are difficult for them. They can also be used to build comprehension, active vocabulary, listening skills, and the conceptual base upon which language development rests. The motivation is built into the "exercise": fingerplays are fun and stimulate children to challenge themselves so they can participate. Chapter 8, which focuses on children with special needs, will give some examples of how to use fingerplays and action rhymes for speech and language improvement.

ENGLISH AS A SECOND LANGUAGE

As all E.S.L. teachers are aware, physical gestures and pantomime are extremely important cues for learning a foreign language. Fingerplays and action rhymes have built-in physical analogs that convey and reinforce the meanings of the words in the verse. The use of meter helps children gain fluency in speech, and rhymes are valuable as memory aids. Fingerplays have been used with great success with Spanish-speaking children. Some suggestions for incorporating active verse into E.S.L. programs are offered in Chapter 8.

MULTICULTURAL EDUCATION

The multicultural character of fingerplays is reflected in this book by the presence of verses in Arabic, French, German, Italian, Japanese, Russian, Spanish, Tagalog, and Turkish. Even if a native speaker or bilingual teacher is unavailable, these verses still present an excellent opportunity to introduce foreign languages and world cultures. An early awareness of the languages and folklore of other countries and cultural groups enriches the child's world and helps foster attitudes of tolerance and an appreciation of cultural differences. The very fact that other cultures share the tradition of the fingerplay promotes a sense of commonality, which is essential for developing a tolerant attitude. An appreciation of differences comes through hearing and learning to form the unusual sounds of other languages and in references to cultural differences in the content of the rhyme.

INTRODUCTION TO POETRY

Finally, fingerplays and action rhymes serve as an introduction to poetry for young children; the appealing features of rhythm and sound are punctuated physically as well as vocally. Not only do the movements help children remember the rhyme, they also generate a positive effect that forms the basis of a lifelong enjoyment of poetry. Because of this, it is important that we select the very best active verse for young children, to offer them poems that celebrate the beauty and diversity of language and that touch their own experiences most closely. Chapter 2 offers guidelines for evaluating active verse as literature.

LINKING ACTIVE VERSE TO OTHER ACTIVITIES
FINGERPLAYS AND THE FLANNELBOARD

Fingerplays are easily linked to other storytelling forms, such as the flannelboard. Louise Binder Scott's *Rhymes for Fingers and Flannelboards* (1960), for example, offers verses in both formats, a useful way of beginning with a "known" and moving into new territory (either from fingerplay to flannelboard or vice versa). The visual format of the flannelboard is particularly useful for reinforcing sequences. It also provides another means of hands-on participation, as children enjoy the opportunity to re-enact a flannelboard story or fingerplay after it has become familiar to them. They can also use the flannelboard figures to experiment with alternative sequences.

MUSIC

As mentioned earlier, music is a natural extension of the fingerplay or action rhyme. In fact, several of the best-known active verses are traditionally performed with tunes, such as the "Eensy Weensy Spider" and "I'm a Little Teapot." Tom Glazer has set many well-known verses to music, and his three books (1978, 1980, 1983) have full musical scores for each fingerplay and action rhyme. A complete list of "Musical rhymes" appears under that heading in the Subject Index. Here again, one may use fingerplays to introduce music and singing, or use the tunes as an aid to learn the verses. Generally speaking, a verse that is set to music is more quickly learned and permanently retained by children.

PUPPETRY AND DRAMA

Active verse can also be a stepping stone to puppetry and creative dramatics. As a first exercise in puppetry, individual fingers become objects or characters in the verse. "Where is Thumbkin?" (see p. 120) is an ideal fingerplay for this purpose. When the verse has been learned, the fingers and thumbs are transformed into puppets by painting faces on them. They are then animated with the same motions (hiding, coming out and bowing, then running back to hide again). This gentle approach can help avoid a common mistake in introducing puppetry to children: beginning with too much paraphernalia. I have seen teachers attempt to start preschoolers with hand puppets and a stage that hides the puppeteer. This ignores the fact that preschool-aged puppeteers do not distinguish themselves from their characters. Allowing them to begin with the puppets as extensions of their own bodies and then gradually removing the puppeteer from the stage is a more natural way to proceed.

Drama, likewise, should not begin on a stage with costumes, but with simple interactive exercises. Active verse provides a good starting place. When children are comfortable with fingerplays and action rhymes, the door to interactive games is opened. (See p. 22 and p. 75 for activities to extend active verse to drama.) There are no hard and fast rules to determine when children are ready for full-fledged dramatic activity; this is a judgment on the part of the activity leader. If some children are reluctant to participate, suggest that they form an "audience" to enjoy the performance of the others. Some children may seem only barely attentive, yet actually take in quite a bit of what is going on. Allow them to observe and learn in their own way. If forced to participate, they may develop a negative attitude that will only prove counterproductive.

REFERENCES

Bettelheim, Bruno. *The Uses of Enchantment: The Meaning and Importance of Fairy Tales.* New York: Random House, 1975, p. 7.

Froebel, Friedrich. *Mother-Play and Nursery Songs: Poetry, Music and Pictures for the Noble Culture of Child Life with Notes to Mothers.* Translated by Fannie E. Dwight and Josephine Jarvis. Boston: Lothrop, Lee & Shepard Co., 1873, 1906.

Glazer, Tom. *Do Your Ears Hang Low? Fifty More Musical Fingerplays.* Garden City, NJ: Doubleday, 1980.

———. *Eye Winker, Tom Tinker, Chin Chopper: Fifty Musical Fingerplays.* Garden City, NY: Doubleday, 1973, 1978.

———. *Music for Ones and Twos: Songs and Games for the Very Young Child.* Garden City, NY: Doubleday, 1983.

Poulsson, Emilie. Finger *Plays for Nursery and Kindergarten.* New York: Dover, 1971 (reprint).

Scott, Louise Binder. *Rhymes for Fingers and Flannelboards.* St. Louis: Webster, 1960, p. 2.

CHAPTER 2

Evaluating, Selecting, and Teaching Active Verse

EVALUATING FINGERPLAYS

Because young children are only beginning to develop their own tastes, it is precisely during these formative years that we should most strive to provide them with the best literature available. Fingerplays and action rhymes—taken as a whole—are not comparable with the best quality children's poetry. Active verse still lacks some respectability, although in recent years it has gained more attention and credibility. Tastefully selected and appealingly illustrated books by well-known authors such as Marc Brown, Sara Hayes, and Joanna Cole have highlighted some of the best material in the genre. This can only have a positive effect on the future of the literature. In the meantime, we should be looking at the texts of fingerplays with the same critical eye we lend to other children's poetry.

The qualities of good children's poetry are not fundamentally different from those of good verse for adults. The language of children's verse is simpler and more concrete, but many of the same litmus tests apply to both children's and adult verse; some of these tests follow.

Do you like the verse yourself? One simple guideline that will weed out many inferior rhymes is to only choose verses that you appreciate. This is a matter of personal taste, of course, but because the verse is presented orally, it is important that it is presented sincerely. It's hardly possible to garner enthusiasm for something one does not personally enjoy. This test also weeds out many contrived or "cute" sounding rhymes that have no particular staying power.

It's no accident that this same criterion is always mentioned at storytelling workshops in reference to tale selection. The core that animates the oral tradition is personal sharing of whatever gift is given: story, poem, song. We should choose only those materials in which we ourselves believe.

Does the verse bear repetition? This is particularly important for active verse because it must be repeated often in order to be learned. Is there something in the sound of the language that makes children want to hear and say it again? Remember that their tolerance for repetition is already generally higher than ours; in fact, repetition is a basic early childhood need. This means that the "repeatability" of a verse is to be judged by their standards, not ours.

Is the imagery or action strong? If the poem seems bland or flat, look for something better. There should be some exciting language—either action or imagery, or both—to enliven and propel the verse forward. While few fingerplays contain this much richness, consider as a paradigm the Mother Goose rhyme "Ride a Cock-Horse to Banbury Cross," which packs a variety of delightful images into four lines:

> Ride a cock-horse to Banbury Cross,
> To see a fine lady upon a white horse,
> With rings on her fingers and bells on her toes,
> She shall have music wherever she goes.

The poem evokes both sight and sound. The images are strong and come in pairs. We are immediately called to adventure with the invitation to ride a "cock-horse" to a mysterious destination, "Banbury Cross." Here we have a visual treat: "a fine lady upon a white horse." Is she a queen, a Gypsy, or some elegant woman? (The poem probably referred to Lady Godiva.) Her feet must be bare because we see the "bells on her toes." There's something very eccentric and audacious about this fine lady, and we feel compelled to follow her. As we do, the poem shifts to auditory images, evoking the jangling sounds of the "rings on her fingers and bells on her toes," tuneful language that makes us want to hear the poem again.

Does the verse have a compelling rhythm? "Ride a Cock-Horse" is also an example of a verse with a compelling rhythm. In fact, it so perfectly matches the bouncing rhythm of horseback riding that it makes an outstanding "knee-bouncer" for babies or toddlers. Such harmonious marriage of rhythm and content is rare in fingerplays, but is worth seeking out to share with children because it provides an outstanding introduction to poetry. The subject heading "Mother Goose rhymes" indexes some other fine folk poems that are traditionally performed as knee-bouncers, fingerplays, or action rhymes.

Active verses frequently have strongly accented rhythms, such as the following (for complete text of this fingerplay, see p. 114):

‾　∪　∪　‾　∪　　‾　∪　　∪　∪　‾
Three little monkeys jumping on the bed

‾　∪　‾　∪　‾　　‾　‾
One fell off and broke his head...

Here, once again, the bouncing rhythm of the verse is ideally suited to the content and action, even to the last verse where an accusing finger shakes to the rhythm of "No more monkeys jumping on the bed!" In such a case, a strict, metrical performance of this rhythm seems justified because it fits the poem and makes the verse easier to chant as a group. Be careful, however, not to inadvertently train children in the "sing-song" habit of reciting poetry, where every accent is exaggerated and every line is followed by a measured pause. These habits are devastating to the oral interpretation of metered verse. Choosing rhymes with a variety of rhythms and avoiding the sing-song voice will open children's ears to the diverse possibilities of rhythm, rather than attuning them to the monotony of rote chanting.

What kinds of rhyme are used? Rhyme is one of the elements of poetry that brings delight to children. Young children enjoy rhymes so much that it is possible to hold their attention by simply reading entries out of a rhyming dictionary. The purposes of rhyme in fingerplays go beyond pure entertainment. Rhymes lend a sense of musical harmony, a characteristic vocal flavor to the verse. They make the cadences sweeter and more satisfying. They also make the poem more predictable and easier to learn.

Rhyme schemes for fingerplays and action rhymes are usually simple; the most common forms are AABB and ABAB. A number of questions relate to the interest and quality of the rhyme: Are the rhymes natural, or do they sound forced? Are the rhymes exact? If not, does this detract from the verse? Are the rhymes all at the ends of lines, or are there internal rhymes and assonances? Consider this fingerplay, for example:

> Clap, clap hands, one, two, three,
> Put your hands upon your knees
> Lift them high to touch the sky
> Clap, clap hands and away they fly.

Although there is an inexact rhyme between the first and second lines, it does not impede the forward movement of the verse. The internal rhyme in the third line (high-sky) suddenly quickens the tempo of the poem, giving the last line a delightful buoyancy. Try saying the verse aloud substituting "up" for "high"; the poem loses its giddy momentum and much of its fun.

What is the tone of the verse? Tone has two separate, but related aspects. One is the literal sound of the verse, affected by the qualities discussed above and other characteristics, such as assonance (characteristic vowel sounds) and alliteration (repetition of a consonant sound). The other aspect of tone has to do with the authorial voice of the poem and its relationship to the audience. Is the verse narrated in first, second, or third person? Is this voice appropriate? Is the tone sincere, or does it preach or trivialize? This last question is particularly important because a false note can destroy a poem's credibility with children. The next section will discuss two particularly undesirable characteristics in tone: sentimentality and didacticism.

QUALITIES TO AVOID IN ACTIVE VERSE
SENTIMENTALITY AND DIDACTICISM

J.D. Salinger defined sentimentality as "giving a thing more tenderness than God gave it." Some fingerplays are spoiled by the author's attempt to sentimentalize childhood. This sentimentalization adds nothing from the child's point of view. It merely indulges an adult nostalgia for lost childhood innocence and freedom from responsibility.

Didacticism is another common flaw in fingerplays because so many have been contrived for "educational" purposes. While this attempt is not necessarily disastrous, it often produces verses that are little more than rhyming lectures. The worst offenders in this category are verses that attempt to teach behavior, moral values, or safety. (Some of these can be found in the Subject Index under the headings "Behavior" and "Safety.") When the first line is, "I try to listen and obey" (Cromwell & Hibner 1983) or "Only one can talk at a time" (Karay 1982), one can be sure that what follows isn't much better.

LITERARY RUBBISH

The fingerplay and action rhyme literature is a curious mixture of genuinely good verse cluttered with an appalling assortment of literary rubbish. My personal quest for the worst published fingerplay has tentatively concluded with this unfortunate text (Patrick 1987):

Breakfast is good.	rub tummy
Breakfast makes me grow.	stand on tiptoes; reach arms high
Breakfast helps me think.	touch head
So, I eat breakfast every day.	pretend eating

Not only is this verse hopelessly didactic, there is no music in it; it is language without play. It simply dies on the tongue, rather than inviting a dance. Although it addresses the idea of nourishment, it provides none itself.

One need only glance through a single fingerplay collection to note the disparity of quality among the rhymes. This does not reflect a lack of discrimination on the part of selectors; fellow teachers and librarians often complain about bad fingerplays. It is hoped that the increased ability to compare texts by means of the index in this book will help weed out the inferior verses in publications of the future. A willing and deserving audience is there to accept them.

RACISM AND SEXISM IN FINGERPLAYS

Many of the best-known fingerplays are thirty or forty years old. Not surprisingly, one does come across blatantly sexist or racist verses. While this insensitivity can at least be historically understood in older collections, it is inexcusable in newer materials. Individual adults who plan to use fingerplays must exercise their own judgment and apply community standards in evaluating the gender or racial bias in materials.

Gender Bias

There are certainly some very clear-cut cases of gender-role stereotyping in fingerplays. Consider, for example, the images offered in this contemporary verse (Karay 1982):

> My daddy is big. My daddy is strong,
> And his steps are big and long.
> My mother is a lady, so dainty and nice,
> When Daddy steps once, my mother steps twice . . .

Be particularly careful of verses gathered under the heading of "Families." So many of these fingerplays assume a two-parent household where the father works and the mother stays home, such as in "Jimmy's House" (Patrick 1987, 75):

> . . . Here is the mother who cares for the house
> And the daddy who works every day . . .

M.C. Pugmire, a supervisor of Child Development Labs at Ricks College, notes that in her 12 years as a single parent, she has yet to come across a fingerplay about a single-parent family (Pugmire 1980). With the exception of one such poem offered by Pugmire herself, my own search for such materials from 1980 to date has been equally fruitless. Even with the increasing number of "nontraditional" households, the fingerplay literature has generally failed to respond with verses that reflect and validate other family structures.

Other instances of gender bias may be subtler, but equally damaging. Fingerplays on "Careers" or "Community helpers" may dictate or suggest gender. Fortunately, many of these can be easily updated. "Ten brave firemen" can just as well be "Ten brave firefighters." It may require a little creativity to substitute "mail carrier" for "postman" and adjust the rest of the line for rhythm, but it is worth the effort if the verse is otherwise sound.

Some traditional verses may be only marginally sexist; whether this should be ignored or the verses altered or discarded is a matter of judgment. A popular traditional knee-bounce rhyme begins like this:

> This is the way the ladies ride,
> Nimble-nimm, nimble-nimm.
> This is the way the gentlemen ride,
> A-gallop-a-trot, a-gallop-a-trot . . .

When the rhyme reaches the boisterous "butcher boy," he rides "tripperty-trip" headlong into the ditch. Parents and care-givers will have to decide for themselves: is this traditional rhyme just a charming ditty or the beginning of a harmful stereotype?

Racial and Ethnic Bias

Material transmitted through oral traditions changes with the times. In the familiar "Eeny, meeny, miney, moe" counting-out rhyme, the line, "Catch a nigger by his toe" has been almost universally replaced by, "Catch a tiger by his toe." When the source of the fingerplay is written, however, the verse becomes insulated from change, and care must be taken that such material is not a prisoner of its time.

There are a number of fingerplays listed in the Subject Index under the heading "Indians of North America." There may be stereotypes built into some of these verses that are best avoided. Fingerplays containing blatantly racist terms were not indexed in this book. One such verse appears in a book that is often used as a reference work (Delamar 1983):

> . . . Two little Injuns fooling with a gun,
> One shot the other, then there was one . . .

Not only does this verse employ a racial slur, it implies that Indians are thoughtless or careless. Such negative stereotypes should be scrupulously avoided.

With the current interest in multicultural education, it is certainly desirable to offer young children images of indigenous and nonwhite cultures. From this point of view, it appears acceptable to teach verses in which Indians wear head dresses, paddle canoes, and creep soundlessly through forests. At the same time, each of these images can become a stereotype in the absence of some exposure to genuine Native American culture. A useful test for any multicultural material is to imagine that there are representatives from that culture in the room. Can you offer the song, story, or fingerplay without any qualms, or is there a twinge of doubt about its integrity? When in doubt, it might prove useful to ask the advice of a representative of the culture in question.

TEACHING FINGERPLAYS AND ACTION RHYMES

Although longer and more involved fingerplays may need to be broken up and taught in parts, many verses are short enough to be learned after only a few repetitions. The following guidelines, reflecting my experience and the advice of Grayson (1962), Scott (1984), Colville (1973), and others, will help make the learning quick and enjoyable. These guidelines apply generally to all ages; various age-specific refinements will be offered in the chapters that follow.

Memorize and master the fingerplay yourself before attempting to teach it. This may seem obvious, but it is surprising how often adults will try to teach a fingerplay by reading it out of a book. Do your homework at home and leave the book behind when teaching fingerplays. Memorizing the verse and practicing the movements so that they are fluent and natural will free you to make eye contact with the children as you perform the verse with confidence and enthusiasm. It hardly inspires confidence when an adult needs a crutch to remember verses children are expected to learn. Getting the book out of the way also emphasizes the social and playful qualities of the fingerplay; it is something done together as an end in itself, rather than just another lesson.

Make sure the children can see you clearly. Invite them to mirror your movements from the beginning. The children can begin learning the fingerplay the first time they hear it. Be sure to give them plenty of time to observe and imitate your movements. Give a lot of encouragement for participation, but don't try to correct or refine movements at this point. When teaching a fingerplay that specifically calls for motions of the right or left hands, reverse your own movements to match those expected of the children. The concept of left and right is difficult enough for young children. It is unreasonable to expect them to grasp the idea that left and right are relative to the direction they face. Although it may feel peculiar to call out "left" and move your right hand, it is actually more effective as a means of getting children to identify which hand is which.

Repeat the verse line by line, inviting children to echo each phrase. Use the movements to punctuate significant words. One can also use the device of leaving out the last word of each line, which the children will gleefully supply. Turn the learning process itself into a game. Once you have used a method that works, it will transfer to other verses, and the children will pick up new material much faster.

Find opportunities to repeat the fingerplay often and in different settings. Frequent repetition is the key to fingerplay mastery. One needn't wait for "circle time" to do fingerplays or action rhymes. They can be used as a break during other activities, during playtime as a door to imaginative games, or as a way of calming and focusing children who feel restless standing in a line. Because fingerplays require no materials or equipment, they are among the most portable of all learning activities.

When the fingerplay or action rhyme has been mastered, encourage variations. Observations of young children at play have shown that once they have mastered a skill, they will spontaneously create their own variations to test and extend their mastery; it adds pleasure to the play and provides intrinsic rewards for learning. An example would be a child who has learned to go down the slide and then begins to introduce all kinds of complications and variations, such as twisting, bumping, and going down backwards. Miller (1973) calls this variation-making behavior "galumphing."

As with other types of play, fingerplays and action rhymes provide many opportunities for galumphing. Say the rhyme faster or slower. Use exaggerated inflections; whisper, shout, or sing the verse. Make the movements larger or smaller. Substitute the children's names for names in the verse. If an animal is featured, try changing the animal. Use the fingerplay or action rhyme as a pattern to create new verses. This teaches creative thinking and the subtle and useful concept of variations on a theme. A sequence or pattern learned through one fingerplay will shorten the learning curve for other similar verses. An established pattern can also become a vehicle for generating new fingerplays. (See p. 79 for a description of this process.)

Use music and visual aids to strengthen the learning process. In general, children learn musical fingerplays and action rhymes much faster than those that are merely spoken. The vehicle of music adds a buoyancy to the verse and pleasurable associations that aid in assimilation. Some teachers sing all of their active verse, whether a melody was given or not. Children often improvise melodies to fingerplays they have learned or use other familiar tunes to carry the words of the verse. One teacher used an opaque projector to trace oversized copies of the diagrams illustrating hand movements in Marc Brown's *Finger Rhymes* (1980). These were colored by the children and hung on the walls as reminders of the sequences of movement in several of the verses. Picture books, finger puppets, and flannelboards are also useful visual aids for reinforcing fingerplays. The use of these tools is discussed in Chapter 6.

Other audiovisual sources for active verse, such as records and cassettes, filmstrips, and videotapes, are listed in the Supplemental Bibliography (Chapter 10). These should be used to enhance, rather than replace, live performance. They are also useful for adults as models of how to perform the rhymes in an engaging and enthusiastic manner. Particularly instructive in this regard are videotapes by Mary Clever and Marc Brown. These can be used either with a group of children or with adults who wish to learn how to work with active verse in a group.

Keep the "play" in fingerplay. Be encouraging and offer praise for participation, but let the fingerplay be its own reward. A number of studies of intrinsic and extrinsic motivation (Lepper et al. 1973) have shown that if external rewards are offered for intrinsically satisfying activities (i.e., they are fun to do), children's responses to the activity will be less creative and complex. (They will do less galumphing on their own.) If the teacher's goals are too narrowly focused on learning concepts or building motor coordination, there may be a temptation to offer extrinsic rewards for the performance of the rhyme. On the contrary, even when these goals may be the underlying rationale for the selection of particular verses, it is wise to "forget" this rationale when offering the fingerplay to children. When motivated by their own enjoyment, they are likely to learn more than you intended to teach them in the first place.

Get parents involved. Like other kinds of learning, the work done with fingerplays at school or the library multiplies in value when reinforced at home. When Froebel adopted the "mother play" for his kindergarten curriculum, it was not intended as a replacement for active verse at home, but as an extension of parent-child play. Repetition with a parent not only helps children master the verse; it enhances the value of the activity through parental sanction and participation. It also helps integrate active verse into their lives, so artificially fragmented by the arrangements for care and schooling made for them by adults. A community bond between home, school, and library grows through shared folklore, and this bond in turn builds the child's sense of security, belonging, and self-esteem. When a common body of songs, books, fingerplays, action rhymes, and other games is shared among these institutions, children are immersed in an environment in which the various adults in their lives are cooperatively guiding and nurturing them.

Unfortunately, what Froebel originally learned from parents must now be taught to them, as many oral traditions—including storytelling and fingerplay—have eroded or passed into the keeping of specialists. Here are several strategies for getting active verse into the home:

- *Print a short handout or booklet* of fingerplays that have been introduced at school or in the library storytime. Include texts of fingerplays in newsletters or on book marks. Better yet, make a cassette tape that can be cheaply duplicated and either given or loaned out.
- *Ask children to teach the fingerplays* they learn to friends and family members. Encourage them to "show off" what they have learned. Preschool aged children, in particular, thrive on this. Eight-year-olds are also fond of performing songs or action rhymes at home for whoever will listen and watch.
- *Model fingerplay and action rhymes activities for parents* in the storytime, at drop-off and pick-up times, or at open houses. Because most active rhymes require less than thirty seconds to perform, such demonstrations can be informal and brief. If you perform the rhyme along with the child, it models good teaching methods for the parents, who will also enjoy seeing their children demonstrate what they have learned.

DEGREES OF DIFFICULTY

It is recommended that one begin with simple fingerplays and only gradually introduce more complex rhymes. The level of difficulty of a fingerplay can be judged according to several criteria. Length is one important determinant. In the beginning, look for very short verses, preferably four lines or less. They should present only a very few ideas in simple language that the children can readily repeat. The accompanying movements should also be simple and easily mastered.

When the simpler rhymes have been mastered, longer and more difficult fingerplays and action rhymes can be attempted. Directions and diagrams for hand movements vary considerably in clarity; if a motion appears too complicated or irrelevant to the text, it should be adapted or omitted. This will become easier with practice. Actions can also be expanded into whole-body movements or made interactive. For example, the fingerplay "Here's a Cup" can be extended into a social experience by dividing the group into pairs and having each child take a different role:

Here's a cup,	**one child makes circles with thumb and index finger of each hand**
And here's a cup,	
And here's a pot of tea.	**partner makes fist and extends thumb for "spout"**
Pour a cup,	
Pour a cup,	**pouring motions**
And have a drink with me.	**first child offers one cup to partner, both pretend to drink**

If the rhyme and motions are already familiar as a "single player" fingerplay, the transition to this more interactive form will be easy and natural. Methods of adapting fingerplays and action rhymes to group activities will be further explored in Chapter 4.

Once children have mastered and delighted in a few fingerplays, they will be eager to learn new verses. Once fingerplay activity has been established as a familiar ritual, it can serve as a springboard to new territory, such as puppetry, drama, and storytelling.

REFERENCES

Brown, Marc Tolon. *Finger Rhymes*. New York: Dutton, 1980.

Colville, M. Josephine. *The Zoo Comes to School: Finger Plays and Action Rhymes*. New York: Teachers Publishing Division, Macmillan, 1973.

Cromwell, Liz, and Dixie Hibner. *Finger Frolics: Fingerplays for Young Children*. Livonia, MI: Partner Press, 1983.

Delamar, Gloria T. *Children's Counting-Out Rhymes, Fingerplays, Jump-Rope, and Bounceball Chants and Other Rhythms*. Jefferson, NC: McFarland, 1983.

Grayson, Marion, and Nancy Weyl. *Let's Do Fingerplays*. Washington, DC: Robert B. Luce, Inc., 1962.

Karay, Hanne. *Let's Learn with Finger Plays: A Collection of Finger Plays, Action Verses, and Songs for Early Childhood*. Bowling Green, KY: Kinder Kollege Press, 1982.

Lepper, M.R., D. Greene, and R.E. Nisbett. "Undermining Children's Intrinsic Interest with Extrinsic Rewards: A Test of the Overjustification Hypothesis." *Journal of Personality and Social Psychology*, 1973. Vol. 28: 129-37.

Miller, S. "Ends, Means and Galumphing: Some Leit-Motifs of Play." *American Anthropologist*, 1973. Vol. 75:87-98.

Patrick, Jenett. *Gingerbread Kids: Super Easy Activities to Help Young Children Learn*. Livonia, MI: Partner Press, 1987.

Pugmire, M.C. Weller. *ABC Way to an Effective Fingerplay*. Rexburg, ID: Ricks College Press, 1980. p.4.

Scott, Louise Binder. *Rhymes for Learning Times: Let's Pretend Activities for Early Childhood*. Minneapolis: T.S. Denison, 1984.

CHAPTER 3

Active Verse for Infants

DEVELOPMENTAL CONSIDERATIONS

The first year of life is full of developmental milestones, but a detailed description of them is beyond the scope of this book. There are many works that offer month-by-month accounts of the average infant's growth, such as Caplan's *The First Twelve Months of Life* (1971), which is highly recommended. For our purposes, a general overview of the baby's development during the first year will help orient us to the kinds of active verse that are most beneficial.

SENSORY-MOTOR LEARNING

The first year is dominated by what Jean Piaget termed "sensory-motor" learning. During this first stage of development, the baby's nervous system evolves rapidly. The parts of the brain that organize sensation must be stimulated repeatedly in order for the child to integrate tactile, auditory, and visual sensations into meaningful patterns. As Scott (1987) notes, there are three basic requirements for healthy sensory-motor integration:

1. touching and other gentle, *tactile stimulation,* to develop the connections between the central and extended nervous systems;

2. *vestibular stimulation,* which is movement that develops a sense of orientation to gravity;

3. *proprioceptive stimulation,* which involves movement of the joints and large muscles.

PHYSICAL DEVELOPMENT

The basic physical sequence of infant development is marked by the development of the tonic neck reflex, the ability to hold the head erect, sitting, creeping and crawling, standing, and finally, walking. The ages at which these developmental tasks are mastered vary considerably, but the sequence is fixed. Physical development is highly dependent on the three types of stimulation mentioned on the previous page and can be nurtured through games that will be described in this chapter.

EMOTIONAL DEVELOPMENT

Healthy emotional development during the first year necessitates both bonding and basic trust. Bonding, the instinctive and mutual attachment of parent (or surrogate parent) and child, begins at birth, but is nurtured through contact, holding, and nursing. Basic trust is the infant's sense of security about getting basic needs met. The first half-year is the most critical period for the growth of these two fundamental emotional needs. There is some debate as to what child rearing practices best meet these needs, but there is a decided swing away from the "early independence" philosophy, which advocates sequestering infants in cribs or allowing them to cry without response.

LANGUAGE DEVELOPMENT

Infant language development is harder to track because much of it is passive. The first sounds that babies make are reflexive rather than intentional. Babbling does not typically begin until about the sixth month, and even then, much of it is pure play and practice with sounds rather than a deliberate effort to communicate. Babies nevertheless do communicate in a great variety of ways. Mothers and fathers quickly learn to distinguish a cry of protest from a cry to feed, and infants develop a rich repertoire of signals that enable them to get their needs met.

MENTAL DEVELOPMENT

Two milestones of cognitive development deserve our special attention. The first is the distinction between self and other. Very young infants do not distinguish their bodies from the environment that surrounds them. The discovery of their own hands and feet comes prior to any recognition that these "belong" to them. The second cognitive milestone, object permanence, is a kind of abstraction, an advanced concept of infancy not likely to develop until the sixth month or beyond. Until then, objects and other people only "exist" for the baby when they can be seen or touched. As soon as they are removed from the child's field of vision, they become "nonexistent."

NURSERY RHYMES AND GAMES

Every culture has nursery rhymes of some kind. It was probably an early discovery that the human voice, combined with some kind of rocking or bouncing movement, was soothing and pleasurable to babies. Adults have a natural impulse to want to play with their babies, and as a result, most cultures have developed a rich folklore of nursery rhymes, lullabies, and infant games that are orally transmitted from one generation to the next; grandmothers are the great experts on these matters.

These nursery songs and games take predictable forms, even cross-culturally. Babies respond well to sounds, particularly voices, within a short time after birth. Auditory faculties develop much faster than visual perception. The infant's first toy is its own body, an object of intense fascination. Not surprisingly, the best first games to play with babies use the voice and the body. They are presented (roughly) in developmental order, beginning with rocking and tickling rhymes, and concluding with some variations on the perennial favorite of peek-a-boo.

ROCKING RHYMES

Cradle the baby in your arms and gaze into its eyes. Eye contact is extremely important throughout infancy. It establishes trust and enables the adult to watch for signals from the infant that will help regulate the activity to the child's rhythms and needs. A gentle bounce at about the rate of the mother's own heartbeat is just about ideal; it is best not to rock any faster because the child is attuned to this tempo from being in the womb. Matching it brings the infant to equilibrium; exceeding it may bring on anxiety or unease.

Softly chanting a nursery rhyme or singing a lullaby is soothing and pleasurable for both adult and child. It strengthens bonding and provides vestibular stimulation. Lullabies such as "Hush Little Baby, Don't Say a Word" and "Rock a Bye, Baby" have persisted because their rhythms and simple melodies lend themselves so well to rocking and repetition. Norah Montgomerie (1967) has collected a number of rocking rhymes, including this traditional verse from Great Britain:

> Diddle-me-diddle-me-dandy-O!
> Diddle-me-diddle-me-darlin.
> If I ever bake a sugar cake,
> I'll bake little baby a parkin.

FINGER- AND TOE-COUNTING RHYMES

Somewhere about the fifth or sixth week, the baby discovers its hands. The hands are the baby's first toy, the most fascinating objects of infancy. Babies often spend lengthy periods watching their hands as they grasp and release and move back and forth. There is also some considerable exploration of the hands through mouthing and sucking. Not long after discovering the hands, an awareness of the feet will emerge. At first, the hands are perceived as whole units that can only grasp and release. Development of individual sensation in the fingers and toes comes gradually. Starting at about three or four months, this can be aided by finger- and toe-counting rhymes, the most famous of which is "This Little Piggy Went to Market" (for full text, see p. 120). There are many others, such as the old English rhyme that follows. As you say the rhyme, wiggle each of baby's toes in succession, starting with the little toe (just the opposite of "This Little Piggy"):

> This little cow eats grass,
> This little cow eats hay,
> This little cow looks over the hedge,
> This little cow runs away,
> And this BIG cow does nothing at all
> But lie in the fields all day!

Use exaggerated inflections of the voice to emphasize the different "cows." Although it may feel embarrassing at first, extreme vocal modulations can attract and hold the baby's attention and add pleasure to the game. The silly names for the toes in the following rhyme nearly force the voice to follow with an extreme dip in pitch:

> Wee Wiggie,
> Poke Piggie,
> Tom Whistle,
> John Gristle,
> And Old Big Gobble, Gobble, Gobble!

More of these kinds of rhymes can be located under the subject heading "Games—Toe-Counting Rhymes." Most of them can be played either upon the fingers or the toes. One can also use many counting rhymes for this purpose, so an ample supply is available through the Subject Index under "Counting Rhymes."

Frequent stimulation of fingers and toes has short- and long-term benefits. Not only is it good for sensory-motor integration, it helps later with walking and in the first steps toward gaining fine motor control. Toe-counting rhymes can be continued throughout infancy and even into the toddler years, where the child will point to his or her own fingers and toes as the rhyme is recited.

FOOT-PATTING RHYMES

Foot-patting rhymes are good as lap-time games, or at changing or bath time. They provide gentle stimulation of the soles of the feet that is pleasurable and amusing to infants. A number of Mother Goose rhymes are traditionally played as foot-patting games, such as this familiar verse:

> Shoe a little horse,
> Shoe a little mare,
> But let the little colt
> Go bare, bare, bare.

Tap the soles of the baby's feet alternately as you say this rhyme. A little tickling on the words "bare, bare, bare" is a nice variation.

"This Old Man" makes a wonderful foot-patting rhyme. On the words, "This old man came rolling home," roll the baby's feet around in circles. The baby will look forward to this part of the verse each time it comes around and may anticipate it with smiles. An elementary kind of sequencing is being taught through such games. Use the rhythm to create both anticipation and surprise.

TICKLING RHYMES

Tickling games are pure fun, but they also serve vital developmental needs. As Montagu (1971) has demonstrated, the stimulation of the skin contributes to sensory-motor integration. Babies will smile and giggle as long as the game is pleasurable, but it is wise to watch for signs of overstimulation. If the baby begins to frown or fret, discontinue the game. One of the best-known tickling rhymes is "Round and Round the Garden":

> Round and round the garden,   hold baby's hand, palm up, trace circles with index finger
> Like a teddy bear.
> One step, two step.   slowly "walk" up baby's arm
> Tickly under there!   rush up to armpit and tickle

One effective device built into many tickling rhymes is a rapid change of tempo. Babies love suspense and surprises, so vary not only the rhymes, but the way they are paced. Here's another tickling rhyme with ample room for variation:

> Slowly, slowly, very slowly,   start at feet, let fingers slowly walk up baby,
> Creeps the garden snail.   fill voice with suspense
> Slowly, slowly, very slowly,
> Up the wooden rail.

Quickly, quickly, very quickly,   speak quickly, in a high-pitched voice

Runs the little mouse.   tickle about the tummy with circular motions

Quickly, quickly, very quickly,

Round about the house.

PAT-A-CAKE AND CLAPPING GAMES

Pat-a-cake is a good game to play starting at about four or five months. A good way to play is to sit in front of a mirror with the child in your lap; then you can see the child's expressions. Work the child's hands to perform the actions of the rhyme. Beyond "Pease Porridge Hot" and "Pat-a-Cake, Pat-a-Cake, Baker's Man," there is a wealth of material that can be used, including clapping rhymes that older children perform independently. This one works well with babies:

(to the tune of "Row, Row, Row Your Boat")

Clap, clap, clap your hands   begin very slowly, clapping baby's hands

As slowly as you can.   together rhythmically

Clap, clap, clap your hands   clap baby's hands very quickly

As quickly as you can.

Roll, roll, roll your hands . . .   action follows text

Shake, shake, shake your hands . . .

Pat, pat, pat your head . . .

Some jump-rope rhymes also make good pat-a-cake games. This adaptation of a jump-rope rhyme is a very active game for baby:

Handy, pandy,   clap, clap

Jack-a-dandy,   clap-clap-clap

Loves plum cake   put baby's hands to mouth:

and sugar candy.   left, right, both-both-both

He bought some at

the grocer's shop,   clap, clap, clap-clap-clap

And out he came,   lift baby suddenly

hop, hop, hop!   bounce baby three times

LEG-WAGGING RHYMES

These games provide healthy exercise for gross motor development. Alternate leg flexes condition the child's crawling reflex to alternate strokes and strengthen the leg muscles for standing and walking. These exercises can be started at six weeks to two months. Any rhymes with a "see-saw" rhythm will work; here's one from Mother Goose:

> See-saw, sacradown,
> Which is the way to London town?
> One foot up and one foot down,
> That is the way to London Town.

When the child is a little older and prefers a more active game, try this traditional leg-wagging rhyme, but on the last line, lift the baby up suddenly:

> Leg over leg,
> As the dog goes to Dover,
> When he comes to a wall,
> Jump! He goes over!

FACE-TAPPING RHYMES

The face is an object of great fascination for infants. Newborns will stare intently at faces within a one-foot field of vision. Studying the features of the human face appears to have a vital developmental function that is not yet well understood. Once babies reach three or four months of age, they are increasingly interested in their own faces.

Face-tapping rhymes develop awareness of the infant's own facial features. Babies who are ready for this kind of play will respond with smiles and laughter. Sit face to face with the baby on your lap. Touch each part of the face in succession as the rhyme suggests:

Knock at the door.	tap baby's forehead
Peep in.	point to eyes
Lift up the latch.	push up tip of nose
Walk in.	"walk" fingers on lips
Chin chopper,	tap chin rhythmically to end of verse, going faster and faster
Chin chopper,	
Chin, chin, chin!	

Here's another one, which adds the variation of tickling at the end:

Brow, brow, binky;	tap brow
Eye, eye, winky;	point to eyes
Nose, nose, nebbie;	tap end of nose
Cheek, cheek, cherry;	pat cheeks
Mou, mou, merry;	trace around lips
Chin, chin, chebbie;	tap chin
Catch a fly, catch a fly,	tickle down
Catch a little fly!	

KNEE-BOUNCE RHYMES

Knee-bounce rhymes are vigorous games, to be played when the baby is wide awake and full of energy. The baby is held by the armpits on the adult's knees and bounced up and down in time with the verse. Sometimes there is a "whoops!" at the end of the rhyme, where the adult pulls his or her legs apart and lets the baby drop through the hole (still supported by the armpits, of course!). After the rhyme has been repeated many times, the baby will look forward to that moment with great anticipation, flexing his or her legs out to cushion more of the landing. Here is a perennial favorite:

Trot, trot to Boston,	bounce child on knees in "trotting" tempo,
Trot, trot to Linn,	gradually go faster
Watch out, little boy /girl,	
Don't fall in!	let child slip through legs on "in!"

One can also substitute the child's name for "little boy" or "little girl." In fact, it is a good idea to look for ways to personalize all kinds of play rhymes. Traditional material keeps its vitality through change, not stasis, and personalizing the old rhymes creates unique and valuable "family folklore."

The galloping rhythms of knee-bounce rhymes are derived from horseback riding, which is usually reflected in the content as well (many, if not most are about horses or riding). Many of these rhymes are of British origin. One might speculate that they may have been used to condition young children to the rigors of riding at an early age. Whatever their use traditionally, they are wonderful games for infants and bear plenty of repetition. One should only take caution not to overstimulate a child with too much vigorous bouncing at one time. Play in front of a mirror and watch the child's face for any signs of tiring or annoyance. At the first sign of displeasure, do something different.

Knee-bounce rhymes can be done starting at about four months and continued through toddlerhood. (Preschool children—even though they may seem "too old" for it—still enjoy this game and can play it beyond the endurance of most adults. A group of them will wear you out quickly, so try the same rhymes using stick horses or galloping in a circle, with an "all fall down" at the end; it's good fun for the children and less wear and tear on the teacher.)

Mother Goose abounds with knee-bouncing or "jig-jogging" rhymes. Many of these existed for generations as oral literature before they were ever written down. They were not meant to be "read" to children, but played with them. Adults who have not learned these rhymes through an oral tradition need to commit them to memory, so that their full attention can be placed on the child. There is a place for reading Mother Goose aloud to children when they are older. For infants and toddlers, however, Mother Goose rhymes are richest as pure oral literature, to be learned by heart and played as games. This favorite knee-bouncer is a fine example. Once again, the vigor of the bounce and the duration of the game should be measured by the child's enjoyment.

> To market, to market,
> To buy a fat pig,
> Home again, home again,
> Jiggety-jig!
>
> To market, to market,
> To buy a fat hog,
> Home again, home again,
> Jiggety-jog!

Some knee-bounce rhymes are sung to traditional melodies. Jane Yolen's *Lap-Time Song and Play Book* (1989) is an excellent source for all kinds of lap games and includes musical notation for these melodies.

PEEK-A-BOO

Peek-a-boo is a favorite game of babies in their fifth or sixth month. It requires a fully developed facial memory—the ability to recognize and remember familiar faces—as well as the concept of object permanence—the understanding that a thing continues to exist when it is out of sight. It may also signal the beginning of a sense of humor, as the baby delights in the "trick" upon the adult, as soon as the game can be reciprocated.

It is, of course, the physical game of peek-a-boo that the child responds to. The simplest version is to put your hands over your face and then suddenly remove them, exclaiming "peek-a-boo!" One can also hide behind furniture or a garment. To switch roles, the adult then covers the child's eyes and pretends to look surprised at the "peek-a-boo." Eventually, the child will cover his or her own eyes and choose when to pop out.

Peek-a-boo can be played with or without a rhyme, but some special words give added pleasure, and most cultures have created short verses to go along with the game.

Here is one simple peek-a-boo game. Cover your face with both hands. As you say, "peek, peek, peek . . . " open and close the hands just a little, building the suspense for the final "peek-a-boo!" where the hands fly open. Vary the game by changing the number of teasing "peeks" or starting slowly and building speed:

> Peek . . . peek . . . peek . . . peek
> Peek . . . peek . . . peek . . . peek
> Peek-a-boo!

When the child is crawling, peek-a-boo games can make use of doors and furniture for hiding. In this rhyme, the child hides behind a chair or door:

> Peek-a-boo, peek-a-boo,
> Who's hiding there?
> Peek-a-boo, peek-a-boo,
> (Sarah's) behind the chair [door]!
> [substitute child's name]

A source for some other traditional peek-a-boo rhymes is Scott (1987), who includes peek-a-boo games in French, Japanese, and Hindi. The sounds of foreign languages are rich aural experiences for babies, who are still responding to language primarily as sound. Parents and caregivers should not hesitate to use them for fear of confusing the child. Exposure to a diverse palette of vocal sounds encourages the child to be experimental with babbling, where these sounds are practiced playfully. This is helpful in creating a language-rich environment. The association of vocalized sounds with objects and other referents is a separate developmental step, not to be hurried.

This is not to say that we should avoid meanings, even with infants under six months. Because infants learn to understand before they learn to speak, we should give as many clues to the meanings of words as possible: tone of voice, facial expression, and gesture. Playing a face-tapping game may not have the immediate effect of teaching infants the names of facial features, but by naming and associating words with the baby's own body, the stage is set for the "explosion" of language that takes place when the child is about two years of age.

REFERENCES

Caplan, Frank. *The First Twelve Months of Life: Your Baby's Growth Month by Month.* New York: Grosset & Dunlap, 1971.

Montagu, Ashley. *Touching: The Human Significance of the Skin.* New York: Columbia University Press, 1971.

Montgomerie, Norah, comp. *This Little Pig Went to Market: Play Rhymes.* New York: Franklin Watts, 1967.

Pearce, Joseph Chilton. *Magical Child: Rediscovering Nature's Plan for Our Children.* 1st ed. New York: Dutton, 1977.

Ra, Carol F. *Trot, Trot, to Boston: Play Rhymes for Baby.* New York: Lothrop, 1987.

Scott, Anne Leolani. *The Laughing Baby: Remembering Nursery Rhymes and Reasons.* South Hadley, MA: Gergin & Garvey, 1987.

Yolen, Jane, ed. *The Lap-Time Song and Play Book.* San Diego: Harcourt, Brace, Jovanovich, 1989.

BOOKS ON INFANT DEVELOPMENT

Brazelton, T. Berry. *Infants and Mothers: Differences in Development.* New York: Delacorte Press, 1971.

———. *What Every Baby Knows.* Reading, MA: Addison-Wesley, 1987.

Cohen, M., and P. Gross. *The Developmental Resource: Behavioral Sequences for Assessment & Program Planning.* Grune & Stratton, 1979.

Fischoff, Andi. *Birth to Three: A Self-Help Program for New Parents.* Eugene, OR: Castalia, 1986.

Miller, Karen. *Ages and Stages: Developmental Descriptions & Activities, Birth Through Eight Years.* Marshfield, MA: Telshare Publishing Company, 1985.

Roiphe, Herman. *Your Child's Mind: The Complete Book of Infant and Child Mental Health Care.* 1st ed. New York: St. Martin's/Marek, 1985.

CHAPTER 4

Active Verse for Toddlers

DEVELOPMENTAL CONSIDERATIONS

T he 18 to 36 month age of toddlerhood is a time of explosive mental and physical growth. Most speech and language experts consider this to be the most concentrated period of language acquisition. It is an ideal time for "language play" and a rich opportunity to use active verse to stimulate the child's innate drive for self-expression. Following are some observations on the developmental characteristics of toddlers. (For more in-depth information see the bibliography of "Books on Toddler Development" on p. 42.)

SOCIAL AND EMOTIONAL DEVELOPMENT

Toddlers are naturally egocentric. Having discovered the world that exists apart from them, they see it as existing for their own pleasure and gratification. There is nothing "wrong" with this orientation; it simply is. In the social scheme, the other is not quite yet a person; toddlers may quite innocently treat their peers as objects and inadvertently hurt one other through physical exploration. Developing some sensitivity and respect for others is the primary social challenge of this age.

There is little truly social play among toddlers; they are more likely to engage in parallel play, playing alongside, but not really with, other children. Engrossed in their own worlds, they may ignore peers completely or interact only to take a toy that they want. Their preference for interaction is still one-on-one with an adult they trust. A great deal of patient guidance and gentle correction are necessary, especially since toddlers are so easily frustrated. Tantrums are common and may be brought on by minor irritations.

Toddlers frequently assert their independence and take great pride in their abilities to do things for themselves. They are striving to define themselves as individuals. The toddler's emerging self-concept begins with an awareness of the physical body and its capabilities and extends to the world of objects circumscribed by the child's needs and desires.

Daily routines are a part of this self-definition, and toddlers may become very unhappy when their routines are disrupted. Routines should be liberally supplemented with "rituals": meaningful repetitions that bring order and connection to the day's events. Implicit in the ritual is the assurance that the world is stable and that the child's needs will be met. This is particularly important in a group setting, where the child is removed from the familiar home environment. The need for routines and rituals is strong and continues through the preschool years.

GROSS AND FINE MOTOR SKILLS

As soon as a child learns to walk, a new repertoire of movement becomes possible, and new coordination skills must be practiced. There is a strong drive among toddlers to develop and use their trunk and limbs in new ways, so it is not surprising that there is relatively less development of fine motor skills during this time. Instead, they are preoccupied with large muscle activities such as climbing, jumping, and running.

At the same time, hand-eye coordination is developing to the point where simple puzzles (e.g., those with single shapes) and a variety of manipulatives become useful learning tools. Wrist rotation develops during this time and can be stimulated with such activities as screwing lids on and off of jars. There is little sense of right- or left-handedness at this age, and independent motion of the two hands is rare until about age three. Fingers tend to work together, as do arms and legs. The independent movement of the two hands increases dramatically toward the end of toddlerhood. By the age of two-and-one-half, toddlers' overall coordination is much improved. They can walk on tip-toes, stand on one foot, and jump with both feet.

SPEECH AND LANGUAGE DEVELOPMENT

The once prevailing psycholinguistic theory of language development had very little to say about toddlers' use of language because the "language explosion" of vocabulary typically takes place at the end of this period. Functional or pragmatic theories account much better for the expressive abilities of toddlers, who use sounds, gestures, and some single words in a wide variety of ways to greet, label, request, answer, protest, imitate, express feeling, and demand attention.

Nonsense sounds and babbling continue but become more elaborate as the child learns to form some of the more complex sounds associated with his or her native speech. The first single words are often nouns or greetings and are usually delivered with some physical punctuation, such as pointing. By the end of toddlerhood, most children are using two or three word phrases to express themselves.

The passive vocabulary (words the child understands but does not use) enlarges, and the ability to follow simple verbal directions develops considerably during this period. At two-and-one-half years, the average child knows about 200 to 300 words. Imitation, however, is still the primary means of learning more complex behaviors.

Two-year-olds enjoy hearing short stories and rhythmic verse over and over again, and they like to hear it exactly the same way each time. This desire for uniform repetition should be indulged, however unappealing for adults. Like other daily rituals, the repetition is comforting, and a surprising amount of new learning may be taking place that is unapparent to the adult observer.

MENTAL DEVELOPMENT

Toddlers are still largely immersed in the "sensory-motor" stage of intellectual development, but this period signals the transition to "concrete operations," which will dominate the preschool years. This means that tactile and physical teaching methods are still better than verbal directions, though it is important to talk about the activity while it takes place, for example: "You've found the hole where the puzzle piece goes, and now you're putting it in." This descriptive talk connects the learning to language and strengthens cognition.

Spatial concepts such as "up and down" and "front and back" can be understood by the age of two-and-one-half, but "in and out" and "over and under" are more advanced and should not be expected of toddlers. Number concepts are usually limited to singular and plural: even though toddlers can be trained to recite numbers, they lack the means to understand the concept of number. They may also begin using words for quantity (e.g., "big and little") but possess only the most rudimentary ability to judge relative sizes or quantities.

Sequencing abilities are just developing during these years. The toddler is so absorbed in the present that past-present-future patterns have little meaning. There is much more concern with objects than relationships among objects. The first relationship they will explore, though, is cause-and-effect. Toddlers enjoy experimenting and will set up tests to "see what happens." Unfortunately, this is sometimes interpreted as pure destructiveness, as their experiments often involve breaking things.

Attention spans for other people's agendas are short, although toddlers may stay focused for lengthy periods on self-chosen activities. They are easily distracted and may seem at times to wander almost aimlessly from one pursuit to the next. The attempt to coerce engagement beyond a child's natural limit will only result in frustration—for both parties. Social skills such as turn-taking are nonexistent and should not be expected or coerced.

SELECTING ACTIVE VERSE FOR TODDLERS
LIMITATIONS

In selecting fingerplays for toddlers, it is best to choose verses that are quite short: four or five lines is usually about maximum. Longer fingerplays can be adapted by using the first few lines only. One can add text gradually as the child's attention span lengthens. In this way, a rhyme can grow with the child.

Most toddlers will imitate movements before they echo speech. After a number of repetitions, they may begin to join in on selected words or silently mouth syllables. This shows that they are making connections between movements and words. Encourage and repeat, but do not press them or expect too much. Their low tolerance for frustration must be kept in mind. Keep the sharing very light and playful. Above all, stay flexible. If a planned activity isn't working, drop it and try again some other time.

Toddlers' limited fine motor skills must be taken into consideration. Simplify hand motions. Choose large body movements over detailed manipulations of the fingers. The "climbing" motion of the "eensy weensy spider" requires considerable coordination and the opposing motion of the wrists, which is way beyond the range of most toddlers. The rhyme can be performed with a simpler movement, such as raising both hands while opening and closing the fists or slowly creeping the fingers upward.

Unfortunately, there are books that recommend developmentally unsuitable fingerplays for toddlers. Nichols' *Storytimes for Two-Year-Olds* (1987), for example, is seriously flawed in this respect. She recommends rhymes that require the five fingers to be held up in succession, a formidable and frustrating task for most two-year-olds. Readers need to cultivate their own instincts about developmental appropriateness, guided by observation and study of the various stages.

"PASSIVE" RHYMES

Toddlers still love to be bounced upon the knee, and these games can be continued with vigor. More sophisticated finger counting rhymes are possible with toddlers, including this favorite:

Johnny, Johnny, Johnny, Johnny	start with pinky and touch one finger for each "Johnny"
Whoops! Johnny, Whoops!	slide finger down child's index finger on first "Whoops!" then back up on second "Whoops!"
Johnny, Johnny, Johnny, Johnny	keep tapping fingers in this pattern, the faster, the better

In some books, it is recommended that the child's name be substituted for "Johnny." That's fine for some names, but I know at least one parent who really struggled with this and finally gave up; her daughter's name was "Aurora." If you really want to make it move, try "Willy."

EXTENDING GAMES FROM INFANCY

Many of the passive games of infancy, such as knee-bounce rhymes, can be made more interactive. The game of peek-a-boo can be turned into a fingerplay with a rhyme such as this:

(The adult recites the verse, while the child performs movements.)

Jack-in-the-box,	child makes a fist, thumb inside
Jack-in-the-box,	
Sits so still.	
Won't you come out?	adult whispers to hand
Yes, I will!	thumb suddenly pops out, adult jumps back in surprise

Painting a face on the thumb turns the rhyme into an elementary finger puppet play, which toddlers like to repeat. The adult should remember to act surprised every time. An exaggerated expression of surprise is good for a hearty belly laugh or two because toddlers enjoy knowing the "secret" that the adult is only pretending. The delight in this unspoken secret is the beginning of acting and imaginative play, and two is the ideal age to begin cultivating a sense of drama.

DAILY ROUTINES AND HOUSEHOLD TASKS

Dramatic play centered around the ordinary routines of the day—such as waking up, dressing, eating, and going to bed—is also of great interest to two-year-olds. Here's one simple fingerplay that makes an especially good "transition" rhyme to naptime or bedtime:

This little boy	Lay index finger of one hand ("boy")
is just going to bed.	in other palm ("bed")
Down on the pillow	
he lays his head.	
He wraps himself	
in the covers tight,	Fingers close over for covers
And this is the way	
he sleeps all night.	

If you like, repeat the verse substituting "this little girl" for gender balance. This is a nice fingerplay for twos because it calls for simple independent action of the hands, which they are just learning. When it has been mastered, add the refinement of using the thumb as a "pillow." (See illustration at right.)

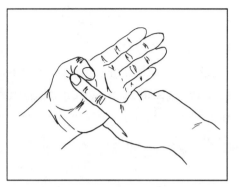

Toddlers love "helping" around the house (or school) and will eagerly imitate such daily routines as cooking, cleaning, and sewing. This fingerplay is a perennial favorite among toddlers:

Mix a pancake,	**motions follow verse**
Stir a pancake,	
Pop it in the pan;	
Fry the pancake,	
Toss the pancake,	
Catch it if you can.	

The stirring motion, performed with either or both hands, is a natural developmental task for this age group, as is the tossing and catching motion. Other fingerplays and action rhymes feature opportunities to pantomime sweeping, dusting, sewing, or washing. Some of these are listed in the Subject Index under the heading "Helping." Offset any implicit gender bias (e. g. , "I help my mother . . . ") by substituting words as needed, so daddies do housework, too.

PARALLEL MOTION

Symmetrical or parallel movements should be preferred to differing gestures on the right and left sides, which will be difficult for toddlers to manage. What is done on the left side should also be done on the right, although these motions needn't occur simultaneously. One fingerplay that works well with toddlers and illustrates this point is "Two Little Blackbirds":

Two little blackbirds	**hold up pointer fingers**
sitting on a hill,	
One named Jack,	**show one finger**
One named Jill.	**show the other finger**
Fly away, Jack!	**move one hand behind back**
Fly away, Jill!	**move the other hand behind back**

Come back, Jack!	bring hand from behind back
Come back, Jill!	bring the other hand out

Alternation of right and left is essential to the climbing or swimming motions of the arms and legs, where the limbs are alternately extended and retracted. Toddlers need to learn this alternating motion to develop some of the large muscle coordination discussed earlier.

MUSIC

Use as many musical rhymes as possible. Melody soothes and invites and may help a reluctant child feel comfortable about joining in. Chanting or intoning the words of a fingerplay will get a toddler's attention with an almost magic power. Fingerplay activity can be considerably prolonged when the verses are sung rather than spoken.

Tunes for fingerplays can either be made up, "borrowed" from familiar songs, or found in special collections (where a melody has been notated, an asterisk (*) appears after its source in the indexes). Tom Glazer has set many fingerplays to music, and those contained in *Music for Ones and Twos* are highly effective for toddlers (Glazer 1983). Here is a face-tapping rhyme that Glazer has set to music in *Eye Winker, Tom Tinker* (1978):

Eye Winker,	point (with both hands) to eyes
Tom Tinker,	point to ears
Nose Smeller,	point to nose
Mouth Eater,	point to mouth
Chin Chopper,	tap chin rhythmically to end
Chin Chopper, Chin Chopper,	
Chin Chopper, Chin.	

As noted with the variation "Brow, brow, binky" (see p. 30), this rhyme can be done passively with ones, as a face-tapping game. As children get older and the rhyme becomes familiar to them, they will want to join in, either by pointing to their own features or to yours. You can help by guiding their hands and gradually leading them to independent action. Two-year-olds delight in their ability to point to the right feature at the right time, which strengthens their self-concept and need for independence. "I have ten little fingers" (p. 119) is another excellent rhyme for these purposes. It emphasizes the "I can" of which toddlers are so proud.

SELF-CONCEPT

Many other self-concept rhymes are listed in the Subject Index under the headings "Body Parts" and "Self-Concept." These verses address the child's need for self-definition while emphasizing symmetrical movements of the hands. They also supply and reinforce basic vocabulary on the subject of greatest interest to this age: "all about me." Here is another example:

Creeping, creeping,	slowly creep hands up sides
To my head.	place hands on head
Down again, down again	bring hands down
Put them all to bed.	fold hands in lap

This rhyme also introduces the concept of "up and down." While it is best not to try to teach spatial concepts before the preschool years, the implicit lesson in this case is handled lightly and passes as a case of "environmental" language learning. Toddlers who are ready will passively absorb developmentally appropriate concepts without conscious attempts on the part of adults to reinforce them. What we are aiming for is a language-rich environment that does not overstimulate or frustrate.

MOTHER GOOSE

The ones and twos are a golden age to introduce Mother Goose rhymes, many of which have traditional or added movements (such as "Peas porridge hot"). Lap games, such as knee-bouncing, toe-counting, face-tapping, and tickling rhymes, are wonderful one-on-one activities that will be enjoyed throughout the toddler years. As noted above, children of this age love the sounds and rhythms of sing-song rhymes, and as long as they are going to be repeated frequently, it is best to choose verses with staying power. The Subject Index includes a heading for "Mother Goose Rhymes," and most of these work nicely with toddlers.

TEACHING ACTIVE VERSE TO TODDLERS

The general suggestions for teaching fingerplays offered in Chapter 2 apply here, but with toddlers, it is best to work one-on-one or to have an adult help each child form the individual "shapes" of the fingerplay as it is being taught. The goal is to move at the child's pace to independent performance, and the most effective route is to have the adult helper physically guide each child's hands. The children will protest this guidance as soon as it is no longer necessary by pulling their hands away or acting fussy. Then they are ready to either try it themselves or move on to some other activity. Conducting shorter sessions in which everyone is "still having fun" is preferable to prolonging the activity beyond natural, observed limits.

Frequent repetition is essential at this age, so it is good to enlist the help of parents. Send fingerplay texts home with them and encourage them to learn and do the verses with their children. Many parents never got much of this themselves as children, so they will need a lot of support and encouragement to get going, but once they do, they usually find it very satisfying. (See p. 20 for ideas to get parents involved.)

REFERENCES

Glazer, Tom. *Eye Winker, Tom Tinker, Chin Chopper: Fifty Musical Fingerplays.* Garden City, NJ: Doubleday, 1973, 1978.

———. *Music for Ones and Twos: Songs and Games for the Very Young Child.* Garden City, NJ: Doubleday, 1983.

Nichols, Judy. *Storytimes for Two-Year-Olds.* Chicago: American Library Association, 1987.

BOOKS ON TODDLER DEVELOPMENT

Ames, Louise Bates, and Frances L. Ilg. *Your One-Year-Old: The Fun Loving, Fussy, Twelve to 24 Month Old.* New York: Delacorte Press, 1982.

———. *Your Two-Year-Old: Terrible or Tender.* New York: Delacorte Press, 1976.

Cohen, Jean Pierre. *Childhood, The First Six Years: A Parenting Manual for Your Child's Most Crucial Formative Years.* Englewood Cliffs, NJ: Prentice-Hall, 1983.

Harris, Robie H., and Elizabeth Levy. *Before You Were Three: How You Began to Walk, Talk, Explore and Have Feelings.* New York: Delacorte Press, 1977.

Miller, Karen. *Ages and Stages: Developmental Descriptions & Activities, Birth Through Eight Years.* Marshfield, MA: Telshare Publishing Co., 1985.

White, Burton. *Parent's Guide to the First Three Years.* Englewood Cliffs, NJ: Prentice-Hall, 1980.

CHAPTER 5

Active Verse for Preschoolers

Those who have the privilege of watching children grow through the years between three and five witness profound physical, mental, and emotional changes. These years have rightfully been deemed the "formative years" for it is here that the foundations of the individual are laid: the basic personality, a sense of self-esteem, and lifelong attitudes about learning and working with others. Because distinct phases of development take place, the following discussion on developmental aspects is subdivided by age.

THREE-YEAR-OLDS
Emotional and Social Development

By the age of three, parallel play has begun to give way to interactive play, generally with one other person at a time. Three-year-olds are also beginning to learn to treat others as people. They may have a rudimentary sense of turn-taking, although they need lots of guidance and reinforcement in its practice.

The three-year-old appears more emotionally stable than the toddler, less willful, and better able to compromise. Because they are so eager to please, many adults find three-year-olds charming and generally a pleasure to be around. With progress toward toilet training and independent dressing and eating, care-givers spend less time managing the child's physical welfare. This means that more adult-child interaction can take place in learning and play time, and threes enjoy and look forward to this interaction.

Language Development

Threes are also much better at communicating their needs and feelings as their language skills blossom. Verbal expressions begin to replace physical aggression during conflicts, but peacemaking skills must be patiently and constantly reinforced.

Three-year-olds like the sounds of language, especially silly sounds. They delight in making exaggerated animal noises, using the customary English sound-words "moo," "baa," "meow," "woof," "cock-a-doodle-doo," and so forth.

An average child at the age of three-and-a-half knows about 1,200 words, enough to convey a wide range of experiences and emotions. They may also know and try to use words they don't have the conceptual faculty to understand. Rather than ignoring unfamiliar words, they will attempt to assimilate them into their own understanding, distorting pronunciations if necessary. It is a good age for rhythmic verse, abundant nonsense, and play with the sound of language. Plays on meanings are lost on three-year-olds, who are very literal-minded; puns and other word play start to make sense to five- and six-year-olds.

PHYSICAL DEVELOPMENT

Much of the "clumsiness" of the toddler years has disappeared. Threes move with more grace and self-assurance. Their sense of balance has improved, enabling them to practice such advanced gross motor skills as climbing with alternate movement of the legs. Threes will watch and attempt to imitate the large body movements of older children. They enjoy acting out animal movements and throwing objects at targets.

Movements of the hand are not yet finely controlled. Three-year-olds commonly grip crayons or paint brushes with the fist and draw or paint with large movements of the arm and forearm. They will need to build muscular strength in the hand before some of the subtler motor control of the fingers can be practiced and mastered. They are, however, able to hold up their fingers in succession, a skill that they are proud of displaying as they hold up three fingers to indicate their age (without understanding the concept).

PHYSICAL-LINGUISTIC CONNECTIONS

One interesting behavior of two- to four-year-olds is their tendency to announce their intentions before executing certain movements—to literally describe what they are doing, are about to do, or have already done out loud (e.g., "Evan stand up go to door," or "Sara kick the ball"). This was considered a cute mannerism until early childhood researchers (Luria 1961; Curran & Cratty 1979) identified the behavior as preprogramming and reflection; the child uses vocal utterances to rehearse, track, and reflect upon the sequences of movements he or she intends to make. These and other researchers have also demonstrated a correlation between speech and language disorders and motor impairment. An intimate developmental connection between language and physical movement strongly suggests that linking the two in structured activity as well as play can help reinforce both areas of growth.

MENTAL DEVELOPMENT

Around the age of three, children enter a stage of cognitive development that Piaget termed "pre-operational." This means they know that words represent objects and ideas and have a basic sense of cause-and-effect relationships, but are as yet unable to manipulate words or ideas independently of the things they symbolize. Three-, four-, and five-year-olds may still retain beliefs in "magical" explanations and distinguish poorly between fantasy and reality.

Fundamental concepts such as color, size, and shape can be introduced to three-year-olds. Of these, color seems to be the most abstract and difficult to learn. Numbers and letters can be recited by rote, but they will not be understood until much later. Most early childhood specialists do not advocate teaching numbers and letters to three-year-olds, because they can learn to use them much more quickly at a later age. Many concepts of time also tend to be too abstract for three-year-olds. While they may be able to grasp the idea of "morning, afternoon, and night" or "yesterday, today, and tomorrow," the days of the week and months of the year are little more than words to them. They will just start to notice the seasons this year, so it is a good time to talk about the changes in nature associated with the seasons: falling leaves, snow, flowers, heat, and the greening of trees.

FOUR-YEAR-OLDS
PHYSICAL DEVELOPMENT

Many four-year-old children practice gross motor coordination skills almost constantly. They seem to want to run everywhere. They also like to jump over things, challenge themselves with physical obstacles, and even hop in place while they carry on conversations. The constant "lining up" enforced in some school situations displays a total ignorance of this developmental need. The child who wiggles "excessively" may develop gross motor coordination much faster than the tightly controlled "good child" who does not move as much.

Unlike toddlers and even threes (who are relatively more conservative in this respect), fours have been known to take daring physical risks, much to the chagrin of their parents and care-givers. They need plenty of opportunities to take these risks within a margin of safety that their caretakers can accept.

Fine motor coordination is also being practiced extensively during these years. Handling crayons, paintbrushes, puzzle pieces, small blocks, and other manipulatives provides a physical foundation for pre-writing skills. In the handling of implements for drawing or writing, one witnesses a progression from the early "fist" grip to the five-year-old's opposing grip of thumb and forefingers, permitting more precise movements. Scribbling styles are indicative of this progression. The fist grip only permits circular and zig-zag movements, performed mostly with the whole arm. The subtler movements required for forming letters and numbers develop later.

LANGUAGE DEVELOPMENT

Having gained much fluency in language, four-year-olds enjoy talking and playing with language and sound. Their physical exuberance may be echoed in their speech, which easily grows loud and excitable. Adults may be annoyed with the constant stream of "whys" from four-year-olds—especially when they may be used as an attention-getting device, but respectful responses nurture an inquisitive mind and build a foundation for problem-solving skills.

Four-year-olds especially enjoy language that is full of action, silly or exaggerated, or that describes exciting or outrageous things. They also delight in playing with the sound of the voice: shouting, whispering, or speaking with exaggerated high or low pitches.

Speech improves rapidly during this year. The consonants m, n, b, p, t, d, k, g, w, and h have usually been mastered (roughly in that order). The more difficult consonants and diphthongs r, l, s, z, sh, j, ch, f, and v will need more practice.

MENTAL DEVELOPMENT

Four-year-olds are eager to learn. Concepts can be expanded to include more spatial relationships, shape, and color. Fours love to count and sort things by categories. They are able to take a collection of objects and sort first by color, then by shape, then again by size. The imagination exerts a powerful influence over their lives. The world of make-believe becomes extremely rich and detailed. Four-year-olds are interested in stretching their limits as far as possible, and their world of fantasy has no limits whatsoever.

EMOTIONAL AND SOCIAL DEVELOPMENT

This is likely to be a gregarious age; fours actively seek playmates for almost every endeavor, especially physical activity. They should already know the basic rules about getting along with others, but they will also be testing their own power during this time and may willingly break these rules in acts of self-assertion. Behavior can become quite aggressive, both physically and verbally, particularly among boys, who see physical aggressiveness modeled by male Saturday morning TV "superheroes."

Language used to describe emotional states is extreme; fours either "love" something or "hate" it. They may appear to have an exaggerated or dramatic emotional response to many things, but this response is also short-lived.

FIVE-YEAR-OLDS
EMOTIONAL AND SOCIAL DEVELOPMENT

Many adults find the age of five to be the most pleasant of the parenting or teaching years. The unbounded energy of the previous year has been contained or drawn inward. Fives are in less of a hurry to do everything, more cooperative, and once again eager to please. They develop a genuine sense of group belonging and learn to play and work more effectively in groups. Friendships are less jealously guarded; they can switch playmates without "breaking off" friendships. Although they may have a rebellious period midway through this year, they generally understand and respect limits better than they did at age four. Rational explanations for these limits are now much more meaningful, since it is possible to appeal to the welfare of the group or to the principle of fairness as an ultimate reason for a rule.

A sense of family and belonging are crucial to fives. They need to have important jobs, to receive approval for their accomplishments and their increased independence. They may become shy in unfamiliar surroundings, less sure of themselves than fours. It is a time when the self-concept needs strengthening through praise and encouragement.

PHYSICAL DEVELOPMENT

While some gross motor skills such as galloping or skipping may be extensively practiced and mastered during this year, fives seem less physically active, more subdued than they were a year ago. They are certainly more economical with their energy and less "explosive." The arms are more often held closer to the body, the whole posture more self-contained. This is not to say that fives do not need plenty of exercise through physical play; they still enjoy running, jumping, throwing, and riding bicycles and tricycles. Creative movement activities can be made far more social: "partner" games and dances are often effective.

Considerable growth takes place in hand-eye coordination and fine motor control. Although visual acuity is still not fully mature, fives become gradually capable of detailed beading, lacing, and tying and have more serenity and the longer attention span required to practice these quiet and intricate movements. A sense of right- or left-handedness may clearly emerge during this year. Writing is of great interest to fives, who are proud of their ability to write their own name.

MENTAL DEVELOPMENT

By the age of five, sequencing abilities have become fairly advanced. The average five-year-old can tell a story with a beginning, middle, and end, fully connected by a logical sequence of events. The fundamental concepts of size, shape, color, and temporal sequence are generally in place. In Piaget's scheme, they are still "pre-operational"; they can attach words to objects, but they cannot yet manipulate concepts independently. The distinction between fantasy and reality may still be blurred. Fives often retain "magical" beliefs, including animism (everything is alive) and anthropomorphism (attributing human characteristics to things or animals). For this reason, dramatic play is enriching and engaging.

Fives make significant strides in the development of memory. They are able to remember longer strings of words, images, and movements. For one thing, because they are using longer sentences themselves, they can retain whole phrases with less difficulty.

SPEECH AND LANGUAGE DEVELOPMENT

Fives enjoy talking. Some, in fact, may talk almost constantly, but we must keep in mind that at this age there is still little distinction between thinking and speaking; they may be only thinking out loud. Fives develop rich vocabularies and the ability to understand and create complex sentence structures. They use more relational words and adjectives and learn to make compound sentences. A five-year-old child who is delayed in the area of language may also have underdeveloped conceptual skills, particularly in the area of sequencing.

The five-year-old has mastered most of the sounds of the English language, with the likely exceptions of *s, r, th*, and *l* (which may not be accurately produced for another year or two). The ability to pick up other languages by imitation is at a peak during the years of five through eight.

FINGERPLAYS AND ACTION RHYMES THROUGH THE PRESCHOOL YEARS

The ages of three to five are the recognized "golden years" for fingerplays and action rhymes. It is here that many children's experiences with active verse begin—and end (how that experience can be extended is the subject of the following chapters). Preschool and day-care teachers have kept much of the material alive in the oral tradition and are frequently the authors of fingerplay collections; I have learned most of the fingerplays in my personal "permanent" repertoire directly from other teachers. This may explain why such a large proportion of the fingerplay literature is designed for this audience.

In many situations, three-, four-, and five-year-olds are grouped together. While some of the developmental aspects of each age suggest different types of fingerplays and action rhymes, it is not always practical to separate them. Fortunately, there is a wealth of material that can be used with the whole group. However, some active verse that works with five-year-olds may demand too much of the younger children; a number of guidelines for identifying this kind of material are discussed in the following pages.

ACTION RHYMES FOR PRESCHOOLERS

The verses easiest to use with mixed groups of preschoolers are action rhymes incorporating whole-body movements. The following verse is ideal for a rainy day, when the children are confined indoors and feeling restless:

Around and about,	make circles with arms
Around and about,	
Over and under,	hands glide up, then down
And in and out.	push out with hands, retract
Run through the meadow,	run in place
Swim in the sea,	mime swimming
Slide down a mountain,	use hands to mime sliding down
Climb up a tree!	climbing motions with arms

Busy four-year-olds will eagerly repeat this verse many times in succession. A variation that adds interest is to begin in slow motion and gradually build up speed until a brisk tempo is reached. The last time through, end the verse like this:

Around and about,	rapid circular motions with arms
Around and about,	
Around and about,	
All pooped out!	everyone falls to the floor

Be sure that everyone has plenty of "elbow room" for verses like these. Particularly as the tempo accelerates, some children may get so caught up in the movement that they may not be too aware of others around them. Four-year-olds need about twice as much space as their three- and five-year-old neighbors.

Some other action rhymes suitable for three- to five-year-olds are "Head and shoulders, knees and toes" (p. 116); "Reach for the ceiling"; "Ride with me on the merry-go-round"; "Clap your hands and stop your motion"; and the perennial favorite singing rhyme, "The wheels of the bus go round and round" (p. 121). Sources for these rhymes are listed in the First Line Index. Directions for the movements in many of these action rhymes are implicit in the words. It is not necessary to teach the text to the children. The action is more significant, and the children will learn to follow the motions quickly if they are not expected to remember the words. Remember, too, that the three-year-olds may not be able to learn such long verses. Think of these rhymes as "Simon Says" games; you can even try to "fool" the group by slowing down and speeding up. This helps children focus their attention and teaches them to follow directions.

FINGERPLAYS FOR "TRANSITION" TIMES

Many child-care providers make use of "ritual" fingerplays to signal transition times in the day, such as snack time, clean-up, naptime, and circle time. In general, preschool-aged children find daily routines comforting, but young children are also frequently less able than adults to immediately "shift gears" from one activity to the next. A verse that is spoken and performed together does several things. First, it focuses the attention of the group. Children who are absorbed in play often need more than the sound of the teacher's voice to disengage. The announcement is not only verbal; it is physical. Secondly, it discourages rebellion because *the children themselves are making the announcement.* Even if the adult has chosen the timing, when the children announce the change themselves, they are far less likely to resist it. This fulfills the paradoxical needs of being guided—receiving direction—and acting independently. Thirdly, it signals the content of the forthcoming activity and gives the children some idea of what to expect next. The following ritual fingerplays were used routinely in a small preschool as transitions to the indicated activities:

Snack Time

Peanut sat on a railroad track,	pretend to hold peanut between thumb and index finger
His heart was all a-flutter.	pat chest
Around the bend	circle with arm
came Number Ten:	show ten fingers
Choo-choo	mime pulling on whistle cord
—peanut butter!	umpire's motion of "Safe!"

Clean-Up Time

Busy little finger people.	flutter fingers rapidly
Who will put the toys away?	clench both fists

50

"I will, I will,
I will, I will, I will,"   **show five fingers, one at a time**
All the finger people say.   **show all ten fingers**

Lining Up

Lining up is an unfortunate necessity, but in some schools, there's entirely too much of it. Though the sight is prized by many adults, there is nothing more stiff or unnatural looking than a group of preschoolers standing rigidly in line with their hands to their sides. When forced into formation, the average child rebels and starts to push and shove. When there is something fun to do, however, these behaviors can be avoided. If the line becomes a train, for example, it becomes a very different experience.

Choo-choo-choo-choo,   **swish palms together rhythmically**
The train is sounding fine.   **tap three children to line up**
Choo-choo-choo-choo,   **swish palms**
The cars all get in line.   **tap three more children**

(repeat until the whole group is lined up)

To get children to walk quietly in line, try the following action rhyme as a "tip-toe" march. It's especially effective if the children can "sneak up" on someone who pretends to be unaware of their approach (perform in a whisper).

The Indians are creeping,   **tip-toe in march time**
Ssh! Ssh! Ssh!   **raise finger to lips**
The Indians are creeping,
Ssh! Ssh! Ssh!
They do not make a sound
As their feet touch the ground.
The Indians are creeping,
Ssh! Ssh! Ssh!

Nap Time

This first rhyme is a reminder to children to put their shoes under their cots; the second rhyme helps them get settled down into bed.

Before I jump into my bed,   **make one fist "jump" up and land in the other palm**
Before I dim the light,   **pretend to turn out light**
I put my shoes together,   **put hands together**

51

So they can talk at night	pump thumb and fingers of both hands together to mime "talking"
I'm sure they would be lonesome	frown
If I tossed one here and there,	toss hands to right and left
So I put them close together,	put hands together
For they're a friendly pair.	

"Come little children,"	wave, as if to call someone
Calls Mother Hen.	
"It's time to take	
Your nap again."	
And under her feathers	fingers of one hand creep underneath the other
The small chicks creep,	
And she clucks a song	
Till they fall asleep.	rest head on hands, close eyes

COUNTING RHYMES

One of the types of fingerplays that occurs cross culturally is the counting rhyme. Because our decimal numbering system is clearly derived from the ten fingers, it is natural that rhymes and games using the fingers to count would arise. Some 262 of these rhymes are listed in the Subject Index under the heading "Counting Rhymes." There is no reason not to begin doing these with three-year-olds, who are just able to hold up their fingers one at a time. We should not presume, however, that simply because they can say the names of the numbers in succession that they understand the concept of number at this age. There is a vast difference between being able to recite the cardinal numbers in their proper sequence and using them in enumeration and comparison. (A child might be able to "count" nine blocks in each of two groups—one of which is arranged in two rows, the other of which is in one long line—but when asked "which group has more?" the child is likely to point to the group laid out in a single line.)

Five-Finger Rhymes

Begin with five-finger rhymes. Many of these are modeled after "This Little Piggy Went to Market." They use ordinal, rather than cardinal numbers, but their primary value is the practice they provide in holding up the fingers one at a time, a skill needed for all other counting rhymes. Here is a good five-finger counting rhyme that children enjoy doing:

The first little pig	hold up thumb
danced a merry, merry jig.	
The second little pig ate candy.	add index finger
The third little pig	add middle finger
wore a blue and yellow wig.	
The fourth little pig was dandy.	add ring finger
The fifth little pig	
never grew very big,	point to pinky
So they called him	
Tiny Little Andy.	

For a nice visual treat, top off this rhyme by reading Don and Audrey Woods' *Piggies* (1991).

Subtraction Rhymes

There are an abundance of rhymes which begin "Five little . . . ." Unfortunately, some of these sound forced or contrived, so be selective. Many of them are "subtraction rhymes" (use this heading in the Subject Index). In this type of rhyme, the counting proceeds backwards, starting with the largest number:

Five little fishes	hold up all five fingers; bend them down, one by one,
were swimming near the shore,	starting with the thumb
One took a dive,	
then there were four.	

Four little fishes
were swimming out to sea,
One went for food,
then there were three.

Three little fishes said,
"Now what shall we do?"
One swam away,
and then there were two.

Two little fishes
were having great fun,
But one took a plunge,
and then there was one.

One little fish said,
"I like the warm sun."
Away he went,
and then there were none.

Ten-Finger Rhymes

There are also subtraction rhymes starting with ten, which are more suitable for the five-year-olds. (They tend to be somewhat too long for younger children.) Five-year-olds will be able to handle "Ten Little Indians" in reverse order, but fours may find this baffling.

Ten-finger rhymes present difficulties for three-year-olds, who are still developing independence of the hands and may have difficulty forming asymmetrical combinations.

Counting in Foreign Languages

Five-year-olds love to learn to count in foreign languages, and fingerplays are an expedient teaching method. This traditional Spanish rhyme introduces the number sequence in an appealing verse:

La Mariposa (The Butterfly)

hold up appropriate number of fingers as numbers are counted

Uno, dos, tres, cuatro, cinco,	(One, two, three, four, five,)
Cogi una mariposa de un brinco.	(I caught a butterfly.)
Seis, siete, ocho, nueve, diez,	(Six, seven, eight, nine, ten)
La solte brincando otra vez.	(I let him go again.)

Cinco Pollitos (Five Little Chickens)

Cinco pollitos   show five fingers
(Five little chickens.)
Tiene mi tía;
(my aunt has)

Uno le canta,   **show index finger only**
(one sings for her)
Otro le pía,   **raise middle finger**
(Another peeps.)
Y tres le tocan   **show five fingers**
La chirimía.
(and three play the flute for her).

Give the numbers special emphasis with your voice. There are several ways to teach children the meanings of the words. One way is to simply perform the verse in English (as noted in the first of the two rhymes above). This is fine, as long as rhythm and rhyme aren't too strained in the translation. Another method uses picture cards identifying key words in the verses, held up in succession as the fingerplay is slowly repeated. In the second example above, one card could show the five little chicks; a second would show one chick singing; a third would picture a chick peeping ("pa, pa" makes a nice sound-word); and the last card could show three chicks playing flutes or hand pipes. These visual cues not only teach the meanings of the foreign words, but reinforce the sequence of the rhyme.

"Eins, zwei, Polizei" (see p. 94) (Scott 1960, 47) teaches numbers in German, just as "Un, deux, trois, j'irai dan le bois" (Scott 1960, 40) demonstrates counting in French. These are exceptional self-esteem builders, as young children take pride in their ability to recite in foreign languages. (It may also teach them a skill their parents lack; fives especially enjoy the opportunity to teach their parents something new.)

Counting rhymes can be tied into many other subjects, so while the focus of the children's interest might be directed toward the content of the rhyme, the number sequence continues to be reinforced.

CONCEPT RHYMES

A variety of concepts can be taught and reinforced through active verse. The Subject Index lists rhymes suitable for this purpose as subheadings under "Concepts" and includes such categories as "color," "fat and thin," "open and shut," "opposites," "right and left," and "shapes," to name a few.

Kinesthetic Learning

Fingerplays provide a physical or kinesthetic "hook" for ideas that may be abstract and difficult to teach. Sometimes teachers make the mistake of relying exclusively on visual perception for learning various concepts. Take shape, for example. We want children to be able to identify shapes by sight, but it does not follow that visual methods alone are the best learning vehicles. In fact, since children's tactile sense is (physiologically) more fully developed than their eyesight at age three, it makes sense to teach shapes by "feel" as well as sight. Having children handle, manipulate, and trace the shapes of blocks are effective and developmentally appropriate methods of teaching shape. The following rhyme teaches shapes by tracing them in the air and can be performed either as a fingerplay, using the index finger to "draw" the shapes, or with broader gestures as an action rhyme:

Draw a circle, draw a circle,	trace circles in the air
Round as can be;	
Draw a circle, draw a circle	
Just for me.	point to self
Draw a square, draw a square,	trace square
Shaped like a door;	
Draw a square, draw a square	
With corners four.	show four fingers
Draw a triangle, draw a triangle,	trace triangle
With corners three;	show three fingers
Draw a triangle, draw a triangle,	
Just for me.	point to self

Match the rhythm of the drawing motions to the flow of the words. Several "definitions" are implicit in the text: circle = round; square = four corners; triangle = three corners. The association with a door adds an operational definition using a familiar object. When performing this rhyme with four-year-olds, let the actions be vigorous and exaggerated; play with tempo and loudness. With fives, try refining the tracing action to small motions of the index finger, or possibly holding an imaginary pencil. Fives may wish to do this rhyme more slowly and carefully. They are more likely to pay attention to the accuracy of the shapes they are drawing, unlike the younger children, who may be focused on the movement alone.

For a more active variation, use masking tape to mark out each of the three shapes on the floor (they should be large enough so that the whole group can stand on the perimeter). The children then walk, skip, run, or jump around each shape in turn. A (rotating) leader can be chosen to call out which shape—and type of movement— will be next.

Specific Concepts—Narrowing the Scope

A good rhyme for teaching concepts has a limited scope; it should not embrace too many ideas at once. The following rhyme might be acceptable as a kind of "review," but contains too many concepts to be useful for teaching any of them singly:

This is high,	**stretch hands over head**
And this is low,	**bend and touch floor**
Only see how much I know.	
This is narrow,	**put hands close together**
This is wide,	**hold hands at arms' length**
Something else I know besides.	
Up is where the birds fly free,	**point up**
Down is where my feet should be.	**point down**
This is my right hand, as you see,	**hold up right hand**
This is my left hand, all agree.	**hold up left hand**
Overhead I raise them high,	**raise hands over head**
Clap 1, 2, 3,	
And let them fly.	**clap hands and flutter hands away**

Specific Concepts—Colors

Because fingerplays can only refer to objects of a certain color, they are somewhat less useful as teaching tools for color concepts. Here is where a visual aid—such as a finger puppet glove or the flannelboard—complements and enhances the rhyme. Here is an Easter rhyme that teaches both colors and numbers. It can be done using egg-shaped paper finger puppets (with or without faces) which are colored as indicated in the rhyme. The children begin with all of the eggs on their fingers and then take them away one by one, as the rhyme indicates:

Five little Easter eggs lovely colors wore.
Mother ate the blue one, then there were four.

Four little Easter eggs, two and two, you see;
Daddy ate the red one, then there were three.

Three little Easter eggs, before I knew,
Sister ate the yellow one, then there were two.

Two little Easter eggs, oh what fun!
Brother ate the purple one, then there was one.

One little Easter egg, see me run!
I ate the last one, and then there was none.

The same rhyme could also be easily done on the flannelboard, or with an egg carton containing five real colored eggs. If real eggs are used, the activity can integrate arts and crafts (dyeing the eggs), language arts (learning and performing the rhyme), and snack (eating the result!).

Specific Concepts—Size

The Subject Index lists a number of fingerplays reinforcing the concept of size. The following fingerplay is well conceived in that it (1) deals with only two concepts— size and number; (2) makes the size comparisons using the same type of object; and (3) selects as this object an item that is an everyday part of the child's world and is easy to represent.

A great big ball,	make a circle with hands over head
A middle-sized ball,	make a circle by touching fingers and thumbs of both hands together
A little ball I see.	make circle with thumb and index finger
Let's see if we can count them:	
One, two, three.	repeat motions above

QUESTIONABLE CONCEPTS FOR THE PRESCHOOL YEARS
RIGHT AND LEFT

Many early childhood specialists recommend leaving this concept until kindergarten. There are several reasons for this. For one thing, a sense of right- or left-handedness often does not clearly emerge until the age of five. More importantly, however, until the age of five, most children are not developmentally ready to grasp the concept because it involves "concrete operations." Even when children can correctly identify their own right and left hands, the relativity of the concept will probably not sink in until years later. In Chapter 2, it was recommended that when "right" and "left" were mentioned in a verse, the teacher facing the group should reverse right and left so that the group all moves in the same (absolute) direction. Whether the concept is taught at all is up to individual preschool teachers. In my experience, the attempt to teach the concept to preschoolers is not worth the time it takes.

TELLING TIME

There are fingerplays and action rhymes designed to help children learn to tell time (using an analog clock face). It is difficult, although possible, for many five-year-olds to learn this skill. Even so, while they may be able to "tell" the time, they will not understand that the divisions of the clock face have different meanings for the hour, minute, and second hands. The amount of time needed to master the task falls sharply at the age of seven or eight, because at this age children can begin to grasp the principle of the analog clock. Like so many other "tricks" we can train young children to do, the performance of the task may not reflect a genuine understanding. The fact that it can be imitated at a younger age does not necessarily mean that it should be taught. For the preschool years, morning, afternoon, and night seem to be the only times children really need.

ACTIVE VERSE FOR DEVELOPMENTALLY APPROPRIATE LANGUAGE ARTS

The developmentally appropriate preschool emphasizes the spoken language. It creates and sustains a language-rich environment through everyday communication, guidance in giving words to feelings, conflict resolution, dramatic play, reading aloud, singing, and performing fingerplays and action rhymes.

As David Elkind (1987) has ably demonstrated, the "superbaby" philosophy, which has prompted parents and teachers to push preschoolers into reading and writing, has backfired; many of the early readers fall behind in later years because social skills were neglected or because the children could not sustain their parents' ambitions over the years. Many children who are prematurely pushed into academics eventually rebel and regress, either in the near future or as adolescents.

Active verses are a healthy foil to the superbaby mania. They teach grammar; build vocabulary, fluency, and listening skills; and develop the ear for rhythm and rhyme. Used in concert with reading aloud, storytelling, and story creation (the adult notates the child's stories), a solid pre-reading foundation can be established that will serve both immediate and long-range literacy goals.

COMPLETION GAMES

Preschoolers love to make rhymes and enjoy supplying a rhyming word at the end of a line. Try this subtraction verse, leaving out the last word of each stanza, but leading with the voice to the missing words; the children will eagerly fill in the blanks.

hold up appropriate number of fingers as verse progresses

Five little snowmen, knocking at my door.
One melts away, then there are . . .

Four little snowmen, playing with me.
One melts away, then there are . . .

Three little snowmen, playing with you,
One melts away, then there are . . .

Two little snowmen, playing in the sun.
One melts away, then there is . . .

One little snowman, when the day is done.
He melts away, then there is . . .

USING FINGERPLAYS TO INVITE DIALOGUE

The fingerplay can elicit many kinds of verbal exchange that enhance children's communication skills. After teaching the children a new fingerplay, the teacher can ask who, what, where, when, and why questions. Here's a simple rhyme that can be used in this way:

This is my turtle.	make a fist, extend the thumb
He lives in a shell.	hide thumb in fist
He likes his home very well.	nod head up and down
He pokes his head out	thumb pops out
when he wants to eat,	wiggle thumb
And pulls it back in	hide thumb in fist
when he wants to sleep.	

Here are some examples of questions that can be directed to children after they have learned the rhyme:

1. Where does the turtle live?
2. Does he like his home?

3. When does he poke his head out?
4. What does he do when he wants to sleep?
5. Why does he hide in his shell?

These questions all have brief answers derived directly from the fingerplay, but once the conversation has been started, more open-ended questions can follow, such as, "Have you ever seen a real turtle?" or "What do you suppose he likes to eat?"

CIRCLE TIME

The first structured group experience for most children is the preschool circle time. The democratic shape of the circle suggests equality and turn-taking; there are opportunities for both listening and sharing, and an effective circle time encourages and sets limits for participation. Fingerplays, songs, and games involve everyone, maintain group focus, and provide an enjoyable experience that helps form positive attitudes toward group activity.

OPENING RITUAL

We have already noted the value of active verse in managing transitions from one activity to the next. Because circle time requires special cooperation, it is important to set the right tone and to capture the attention of the group right at the beginning. A fingerplay or action rhyme is an ideal opening ritual. (See the section on "Opening and Closing Rituals" on p. 67 for a full explanation and examples.)

THE CALENDAR

Although the concept of a monthly calendar cannot possibly mean much until children reach the age of five or six, it is frequently used in the circle time to identify the day of the week, the month, and—for some strange reason—the date. Date is such an abstract and irrelevant concept that it is remarkable how much attention it receives in preschools across the United States. There is no evidence to suggest that preschool-aged children can understand the concept at all. Ask preschoolers what month it is, and you're just as likely to get an answer of "spring" or "Tuesday" as "April." Ask them the date; five minutes after the end of circle time, it is just as likely to be "Wednesday" as "the 23rd."

The calendar concepts they seem best able to grasp are days of the week and season. There is an identifiable rhythm to the week—which includes the contrast between school and weekend days—and even three-year-olds can appreciate the cycle. Putting names to the days of the week seems to be a defensible developmental practice. Seasons, similarly, bring palpable physical changes that young children can easily identify: cold and snow for winter; flowers for spring; hot, sunny days for summer; and changing leaves for autumn. Even here, we must be careful about what we presume they understand. One four-year-old appeared to understand the seasons perfectly until one unseasonably warm day in December, when he exclaimed, "It's hot; today is summer!"

Nevertheless, the concept of season is worth teaching, and there are many fine fingerplays that celebrate the seasonal cycles of nature. The Subject Index lists about 120 rhymes about seasons. Here are several examples:

Autumn

Leaves are floating softly down.	float hands down, turning them side to side
They make a carpet on the ground.	put hands flat on floor
Then swish, the wind comes whistling by,	move arms from one side to the other
And sends them dancing to the sky.	hands flutter up into air

Winter

Here's a great big hill,	hold one arm out to side
With snow all down the side.	flutter fingers over arm
Let's take our speedy sleds,	place palm on shoulder
And down the hill we'll slide!	slide hand down arm

Spring

This is the way the flowers sleep,	make two fists
Through the winter long.	
This is the way the flowers grow	slowly open hands
When they hear the robin's song.	raise arms

Summer

A little boy went walking	"walk" fingers
One lovely summer day,	
He saw a little rabbit	raise index and middle fingers of other hand
That quickly ran away.	"hop" rabbit behind back
He saw the shining river	make wave motions with both hands
Go winding in and out,	

| And little fishes in it | wiggle index fingers up and down |
| Were playing all about. | |

Weather

Another favorite circle time activity is to talk about the day's weather. This is usually done by questioning the children about what kind of day it is outside—wet or dry, warm or cold, calm or windy. This is a good lead-in to a fingerplay about the weather. The Subject Index contains 140 rhymes about the weather, including verses on wind, rain, frost, snow, clouds, and storms. It is recommended that a few contrasting verses about the weather become a part of the "core repertoire" of the group. Here's an example of a fingerplay to be used on a rainy day:

Pitter, patter falls the rain,	flutter fingers down
On the roof and window pane.	put hands on head for roof, put hands out with
	palms flat for pane
Softly, softly it comes down,	flutter fingers down
Makes a stream that runs around.	put palms together and make winding motions
Flowers lift their heads and say:	cup and outstretch hands
"A nice cool drink for us today."	

CIRCLE GAMES AND OTHER ACTIVITIES

There are numerous circle games suitable for preschool age children, and though a few are listed in the Subject Index, the topic is somewhat outside the scope of this book. Many three-year-olds are still too young for circle games and may feel intimidated and reluctant to participate. For these children, it is best to have a separate circle that focuses on parallel play, such as fingerplays. Most fours, on the other hand, are eager for a rousing game of "Duck-Duck-Goose" and thrive on the excitement of active, movement-oriented circle games.

The cooperative fives may actually prefer a quieter circle game, such as "Farmer in the Dell." They are also more willing to wait their turn, so this is a golden age for games with "one in the middle." An excellent source for singing and play-party games is Marc Brown's *Party Rhymes* (1988). Like Brown's fingerplay books, it uses easy-to-follow pictorial diagrams that can serve as reminders to both adults and children.

Flannelboard, puppetry, and drama activities using active verses will be discussed in the next chapter. (See pp. 73–76.) A diversity of presentation methods helps to accommodate different learning styles and individual tastes. By balancing the familiar and everyday with the new, circle time can provide both security and expanding horizons.

HOLIDAYS

The preschool year is marked by the changing of seasons and the major calendar holidays. School bulletin boards rotate a predictable display: January—snowman, February—pink hearts, March—green shamrocks, and so forth. Though it betrays a certain lack of imagination, as long as all traditions are equally respected, there is nothing wrong with this arrangement (except in the infant and toddler room, where it is meaningless). In fact, structuring the year around seasonal highlights and traditional holidays provides a natural and comforting rhythm to the year. Children are not only socialized into holiday rituals and traditions, but they also gradually gain perspective about calendar time, which is difficult to grasp. An expanded ability to think in temporal terms does not come until about the age of seven, but younger children can appreciate the changes and tides in the calendar year qualitatively.

Fingerplay collections abound with holiday rhymes. The Subject Index lists about 300 such verses. Which holidays are to be celebrated—and in what manner—is entirely dependent on the individual school, but there is a wide selection of material in the indexes and teachers should have no trouble identifying appropriate rhymes.

The best focus for a seasonal rhyme is a physical object that uniquely identifies the holiday, a pumpkin on Halloween, for example:

I am a pumpkin,	hold arms over head in a circle
big and round.	
Once upon a time	
I grew on the ground.	point at floor
Now I have a mouth,	
two eyes, a nose.	point to mouth, eyes, nose
What are they for,	
do you suppose?	point to forehead, frown
When I have a candle	
inside shining bright,	hold up index finger
I'll be a jack-o-lantern	
on Halloween night.	put thumbs in armpits, as if to brag

Similarly, the turkey is a common focus for Thanksgiving fingerplays, including this brief verse, which plays on the "gobble, gobble" sound that children find so delightful:

The turkey is a funny bird,	make a fist, extend thumb
His head goes wobble, wobble.	wag thumb back and forth

He only knows a single word:
Gobble, gobble, gobble.   **wag thumb on "gobble"**

For a more elaborate turkey, place the fist against the palm of the other hand, with fingers spread wide for feathers. (See illustration at right.)

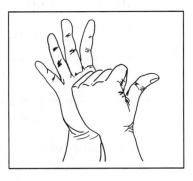

Holiday rhymes are good for focusing some of the excited energy around holidays and turning it to a useful purpose. While teachers prefer to keep them seasonal, the children may be eager to repeat many of them at odd times of the year. In some preschools, rhymes like "Five little pumpkins sitting on a gate" may become perennial favorites and are likely to be requested at any time of the year. Rather than attempt to resist their demands ("I'm sorry, Michael, we don't say that rhyme until October"), why not indulge them? It may offend some adult sense of order, but—like singing "Jingle Bells" in June—repeating children's favorite holiday fingerplays in the off-season is fun and makes a refreshing break from routine.

Holiday rhymes are listed in the Subject Index for April Fool's Day, Christmas, Columbus Day, Easter, Fourth of July, Groundhog Day, Halloween, Hanukkah, May Day, Memorial Day, Mother's Day, New Year's Day, St. Patrick's Day, Thanksgiving, and Valentine's Day. A thoughtful observer of the preschool holiday calendar might note that the meanings of these holidays are beyond the grasp of most young children. What young children really relate to are the trappings of the season: Santas, colored eggs, menorahs, shamrocks, hearts, and turkeys. These objects and shapes are more concrete than the abstract concepts (e.g., "freedom," "thankfulness," and "redemption") that they are meant to symbolize. Some holiday verses sermonize on these abstract ideas, and such verses are better left to older children or abandoned altogether. All of these qualities are more effectively taught by daily adult modeling. In the meantime, do holiday verses because they are fun; use the symbols as "markers" to map out the calendar year. Let the meanings grow as children are able to understand them.

OTHER SPECIAL DAYS

It's also nice to have fingerplays to mark other days of distinction, such as birthdays. A special rhyme for birthdays personalized with the child's name not only gives special honor to that child, but also becomes another thread in the social fabric that binds the group. It is a reminder that birthdays are something we all share, though they fall on different days. This simultaneous sense of belonging and being a unique individual is an important developmental value that is served by these kinds of rituals. This birthday rhyme can be used for any child, on any birthday:

Today is _____'s birthday,	supply child's name
Let's make him (her) a cake;	
Mix and stir, stir and mix,	mixing and stirring motions
Then into the oven to bake.	mime putting cake into oven
Here's our cake	
so nice and round,	trace circle with finger tip
We frost it pink and white;	"frost" palm with a finger
We put _____ candles on it,	show age with fingers
And light the birthday light.	mime lighting candle

REFERENCES

Brown, Marc Tolon. *Party Rhymes*. New York: E.P. Dutton, 1988.

Curran, J., and B.J. Cratty. *Speech and Language Problems in Children*. Denver, CO: Love Publishing Co., 1979.

Elkind, David. *Miseducation: Preschoolers at Risk*. New York: Alfred A. Knopf, 1987.

Grayson, Marion. *Let's Do Fingerplays*. Robert B. Luce, Inc., 1962.

Luria, A.R. *The Role of Speech in the Regulation of Normal and Abnormal Behavior*. London: Pergamon Press, 1961.

Scott, Louise Binder. *Rhymes for Fingers and Flannelboards*. St. Louis: Webster, 1960.

Wood, Audrey, and Don Wood. *Piggies*. New York: Harcourt Brace Jovanovich, 1991.

BOOKS ON DEVELOPMENTAL STAGES OF PRESCHOOLERS

Ames, Louise Bates, and Frances L. Ilg. *Your Five-Year-Old: Sunny and Serene*. New York: Delacorte Press, 1979.

———. *Your Four-Year-Old: Wild and Wonderful*. New York: Delacorte Press, 1976.

———. *Your Three-Year-Old: Friend or Enemy*. New York: Delacorte Press, 1976.

Cohen, Jean Pierre. *Childhood, the First Six Years: A Parenting Manual for Your Child's Most Crucial Formative Years*. Englewood Cliffs, NJ: Prentice-Hall, 1983.

Craig, Grace J. *Child Development*. Englewood Cliffs, NJ: Prentice-Hall, 1979.

The Growing Years: A Guide to Your Child's Emotional Development from Birth to Adolescence. The New York Hospital-Cornell Medical Center, Department of Psychiatry. New York: Atheneum, 1988.

Healy, Jane M. *Your Child's Growing Mind: A Parent's Guide to Learning from Birth to Adolescence*. 1st ed. Garden City, NY: Doubleday, 1987.

Singer, Dorothy G. *A Piaget Primer: How a Child Thinks*. New York: New American Library, 1978.

CHAPTER 6

Active Verse for Storytimes

OPENING AND CLOSING RITUALS

Many storytellers who work with preschoolers use "ritual" fingerplays to open or close the story hour. They become ritual fingerplays through repetition. After two sessions or more, the children come to expect the rhyme. There are several important functions of ritual fingerplay in story hour:

1. It brings the group to immediate focus. Before any audience can become engaged, there must be some common focus. An active verse invites attention and focus, rather than demanding it.

2. It is useful in setting a tone for the story hour, which combines listening and appropriate response. While this tone needn't be solemn, it should evoke respect for both teller and audience. This sense of mutual respect can prevent many behavioral problems from arising, even with so-called difficult children.

3. It sets the story hour apart as a special time and place, unique from the rest of the child's experience. The words "Once upon a time . . ." or "Long, long ago . . . " have a similar function. They invoke a sacred time, full of fantasy and wonder, which is set apart from ordinary time. An opening ritual for storytime invites children to safely enter time and space that belong to them, just as a closing ritual helps make the transition back into the ordinary world.

4. It brings the children together as a group. For many young children, preschool storytime is their first group experience. While the youngest may be too shy or lack the social skills necessary for a fully interactive group experience, they begin to gain confidence in a group by having enjoyable social experiences. Active verses allow children to participate in parallel group activity. When they become completely comfortable with

this type of participation, they can be gently guided toward more interactive activities.

5. It gives sanction to the active participation of each child. By inviting children to participate, the storyteller validates children's needs for self-expression, particularly physical expression. The idea that three- to five-year-olds should sit quietly and utterly motionless for half an hour flies in the face of everything we know about their developmental needs. They internalize literature through active involvement as well as passive listening.

6. It provides a gentle means of behavior management. There are, of course, times during the story hour where we are asking the children to simply listen. Fingerplays and action rhymes help "get the wiggles out" before the children are expected to sit quietly. It's not a matter of active participation versus passive listening, but a question of balancing the role of the audience to meet their needs. Children need cues to know what is expected of them, whether that means joining in or listening quietly. Active verses can be used to validate and cue both behaviors. Here's an opener which meets all of the criteria above:

Sometimes my hands are at my side;	hands to sides
Then behind my back they hide.	hands behind back
Sometimes I wiggle my fingers so,	wiggle fingers
Shake them fast,	shake fingers fast
Shake them slow.	shake fingers slow
Sometimes my hands go	
"Clap, clap, clap!"	clap hands
Then I rest them in my lap.	hands in lap
Now they're quiet as can be,	put fingers to lips
Because it's storytime, you see.	hands in lap, nod slowly

This rhyme attributes something of an independent life to the hands—as if they were wayward children—and this has a certain benefit for behavior management. The hands do things, like hide or clap, and it is the child who brings them under control. This shifts the responsibility for enforcement from the adult, who no longer needs to police behaviors so much, to the children themselves, who take responsibility for keeping their hands under control. It often takes only a subtle shift in perspective to obviate the need for overt discipline during the story hour.

WIGGLES WORKOUT

It is common practice to take a break for a stretch about midway through the story hour. For these occasions, the storyteller should be equipped with a variety of fingerplays and action rhymes to help "shake the wiggles out." There are some three dozen such rhymes listed in the Subject Index under the heading "Wiggles." Some are very simple, such as this popular fingerplay:

I wiggle my fingers,   **actions follow text**
I wiggle my toes,
I wiggle my shoulders,
I wiggle my nose.
Now the wiggles are out of me,   **whisper last two lines, cupping hand to mouth**
And I'm as still as still can be.

If the group is really antsy, a more vigorous action rhyme may be necessary, such as the following. Be sure to vary the tempo and volume for interest.

My hands upon my head I place,   **actions follow text**
On my shoulders, on my face,
On my knees, and at my side,
Then behind me they will slide.
Then I raise them up so high,
'Til they nearly reach the sky.
Now I clap them—1, 2, 3,
Then I fold them silently.

STORYTIME "THEMES"

The most traditional and widely adopted structure for the library preschool storytime is the "thematic" format. A storytime is said to be "about" bears, trains, winter, or St. Patrick's Day. Themes may have value in helping children organize and verbalize their responses, or in relating books to their experience. They are also a convenience to the storyteller, who must make meaningful transitions in the storytime. The Subject Index will be of value to storytellers who wish to find active verses on specific themes to enhance storytimes.

At the same time, it should be recognized that the adult preoccupation with themes has little developmental basis, at least with children under the age of five. Until that age, their abilities to abstract and categorize their experiences are limited, and the themes we spend so much time preparing have less significance (to them) than we imagine. The primary reason for themes is to reassure adults that this is, indeed, an educational experience.

Unfortunately, storytellers who choose a theme and then search for relevant books and fingerplays often satisfy themselves with mediocre material. It is better to begin with an outstanding book, song, or fingerplay and then to ask, How might this relate to other quality literature for this age group? It may take more time to develop a "theme" in this more organic manner, but the results are superior. For some fine examples of how to apply this process, see Margaret Read MacDonald's *Booksharing: One Hundred One Programs to Use with Preschoolers* (1985), which uses a "pearl-growing" approach to thematic storytimes. Another fine source for theme-integrated storytimes is Carolyn Cullum's *The Storytime Sourcebook* (1990), which includes a suggested fingerplay for every theme.

There are many themes for which it may be impossible to find a good fingerplay or action rhyme that is "relevant." In such cases, it is better to use a good fingerplay that has no special relevance to the theme. The children will forgive you more easily for the "digression" than for offering something you both know is second-rate.

Another fixed idea that bears reexamination is the storyteller's avoidance of repetition. Adult culture is preoccupied with variety and newness; as a result, we feel compelled to offer unique programs that do not overlap materials. We do this in spite of the fact that young children often request stories they have heard before. Fingerplays and action rhymes are not just literature; they are rituals, meant to be repeated and to become part of a shared experience that grows between adult and child. Favorite books and stories can serve the same function. The storyteller who desires to meet children's authentic developmental needs will not be afraid to repeat literature of all kinds with storytime groups, in spite of the appearance of lacking a large repertoire.

FINGERPLAYS AND ACTION RHYMES IN THEMATIC STORYTIMES

With these caveats in mind, let us consider the question of how to relate active verse to other types of literature. Subjects are an obvious connection. A storytime devoted to the life cycle of moths and butterflies might include this fingerplay, which compares the butterfly's pupa to a child's bed:

"Let's go to sleep,"	lay fingers of one hand in palm of other hand
the little caterpillars said,	
As they tucked themselves	
into their beds.	bend fingers down to palms

They will awaken by and by,	slowly unfold fingers
And each one will be	
a lovely butterfly.	flutter hands up into air

This fingerplay does not require independent movement of the fingers, so it is easy to perform and quite accessible to a new group. It makes a nice introduction to a book like *Aldita and the Forest* (Catterwell 1989), which carries the transformation motif one step further by having the butterfly become the butterfly orchid.

A similar fingerplay describes how moths spin cocoons. The analogy to the child's bed is maintained by comparing the cocoon to a blanket:

Fuzzy wuzzy caterpillar	creep index finger along arm
Into a corner will creep.	
He'll spin himself a blanket,	spin hands around one another
And then fall fast asleep.	head rests on hands, eyes closed
Fuzzy wuzzy caterpillar	open eyes and stretch
Wakes up by and by,	
Stretches his lovely wings,	stretch
Then away the moth will fly!	put thumbs together, wave hands

(The last lines traditionally read: "To find his wings of beauty /Changed to a butterfly." Like a number of other fingerplays, songs, and stories, this perpetuates the early childhood educator's myth that butterflies emerge from cocoons. Eric Carle's *Very Hungry Caterpillar* (1976) notwithstanding, the fact is that only moths actually spin cocoons. Butterflies emerge from a chrysalis or pupa.)

If more activity is needed in the storytime, the fingerplay can also be easily adapted into an action rhyme, as follows:

1. Children squirm on the floor, like caterpillars.
2. The caterpillars stop wiggling, yawn, and fold their hands as pillows.
3. They close their eyes and quietly snore.
4. As they are touched on the head, one by one, they sit up and stretch their wings.
5. Moths fly around the room.

After giving directions for the action—and perhaps demonstrating it—the storyteller speaks the verse and controls the pace of the game. Children love to repeat dramatic action rhymes such as these, so do not hesitate to do it several times before moving on to something else. The children will be refreshed and ready to listen to the next story after they have had a chance to participate actively in the storytime.

ACTIVE VERSES AS TRANSITIONS

Fingerplays and action rhymes can also provide nice transitions between books. A storytime that takes "The Wind" as its theme could feature Ets's *Gilberto and the Wind* (1963) and use the next action rhyme as a transition to *The Wind Blew*, by Pat Hutchins (1974).

The wind came out	
to play one day.	begin crouched, suddenly stand
He swept the clouds	sweeping motions with arms
out of his way.	
He blew the leaves	
and away they flew.	fluttering motions with fingers
The trees bent low	bend at waist, arms extended
And their branches did too.	
The wind blew the great big	
ships at sea.	bend up, sweeping motions
The wind blew my kite	
away from me.	raise hand to brow, look up

This rhyme ties together the idea of the wind as a not-always-friendly playmate with the concept that the wind can blow many things. A natural follow-up question is: "What else could the wind blow?" Nearly every child in the group will want to contribute something, so leave plenty of time for sharing. They will come up with a wide variety of possibilities, which sets the stage for Pat Hutchins' book. The story that follows will certainly be a richer experience if the children have already begun to exercise their imaginations about what the wind might blow away.

CONNECTING BOOKS AND FINGERPLAYS

Look for other connections between books and fingerplays, even similarities of rhythm and language. This classic fingerplay, for example, is a perfect companion to Mary Ann Hoberman's *A House is a House for Me* (1978):

Here is a nest for the robin;	cup both hands together
Here is a hive for the bee;	put fists together
Here is a hole for the bunny;	form circle with both hands
And here is a house for me.	fingertips together over head

With very little trouble, the text can even be made to match the language in Hoberman's book, as follows (use the same hand motions):

A nest is a house for a robin;
A hive is a house for a bee;
A hole is a house for a bunny;
But a house is a house for me.

Create your own movements to go with the rest of the book, or simply invite children to repeat the "house is a house for me" refrain, which occurs throughout in the book. By adding audience participation and movement, the book can be read cover to cover in a group storytime, whereas if simply read aloud, there really isn't enough action to sustain the entire book through a storytime session.

FINGERPLAYS AND FLANNELBOARDS

Louise Binder Scott recognized the value of connecting active verse with the immediacy of the flannelboard in her book *Rhymes for Fingers and Flannelboards* (1960). The flannelboard articulates the drama of the verse and reinforces the basic sequences. It offers visual reminders for both text and movement and connects the rhyme with concrete, familiar objects. The flannelboard is a particularly useful medium for teaching counting rhymes. Identical figures—whether they are bees, frogs, hats, or flowers—are easily added or subtracted from the frame. If the children have the opportunity to manipulate the figures themselves (perhaps while the adult recites the rhyme), they will process the content of the verse more rapidly.

Directions for constructing a flannelboard and patterns for flannelboard pieces (for fingerplays) can be found in Scott (1960) as well as in Judy Sierra and Robert Kaminski's *Multicultural Folktales: Stories to Tell Young Children* (1991) and Liz and Dick Wilmes' *Felt Board Fun* (1984).

FINGER PUPPETS

A number of fingerplay sources recommend the use of finger puppets to dramatize and enliven the verse. This natural introduction to puppetry avoids some of the pitfalls of beginning with hand puppets. It also enables everyone to participate in the puppet play. A simple story line is already in place. The characters can be made to enter or exit by bending the fingers down or putting the hand behind the back.

All sorts of finger puppets can be used. The quickest finger puppet is created by simply painting a face directly on the finger. A simple "wig" can be created by gluing bits of yarn over a thimble. Band-aids can be transformed into finger puppets by drawing faces on them. Another approach is to use colored modeling clay, which is molded around the finger. Four- and five-year-olds enjoy shaping their own finger puppets and changing their features.

For a storytime situation, the most practical option is to have paper finger puppets cut out beforehand. (This can take a lot of time, but makes a good project for volunteers.) Finger puppets are not only reminders of the storytime, but are also nice "prizes" for the children to take home. When sent home along with a copy of the fingerplay, there is a good chance that children will get their parents to try the rhyme with them. Oldfield (1982) offers simple patterns for cut-out paper puppets that correspond to the fingerplays in her book. Other patterns can be copied from Hunt and Renfro (1982), Ross (1971), Hutchings (1973), and Wilt (1977).

Finally, there is Lynda Roberts' ingenious finger puppet mitt, a glove with velcro strips sewn onto the fingertips. The finger puppets, made of felt or other cloth, attach to the velcro and can be mixed and matched as desired. Her *Mitt Magic* (1985) gives directions for creating the mitt and a number of characters suitable for fingerplays. Ready-made mitts and character sets are also available. (See listing for the Monkey Mitt in the Supplemental Bibliography, p. 123.)

EXTENDING ACTIVE VERSE TO DRAMA

We have already seen how fingerplays can be expanded into action rhymes. Strictly speaking, this is not truly drama because the action is parallel rather than interactive. The more interactive forms need to be introduced slowly. Mary Jackson Ellis offers this game to gently introduce preschoolers to drama in her book *Finger Play Approach to Dramatization* (1960, 7):

> Miss Muffet sits on the piano bench, chair, or stool (children decide). The group repeats the rhyme. When the spider's name is mentioned, he comes out from behind the piano, desk, or cupboard (choice of the children), and sits beside Miss Muffet, who immediately runs away. Audience is delighted and will beg for another turn (with new characters).

> Little Miss Muffet
> Sat on a tuffet,
> Eating some curds and whey;
> Along came a spider,
> And sat down beside her,
> And frightened Miss Muffet away.

This activity is an outstanding dramatic game for several reasons. First of all, the whole group is involved at all times, even when the role may be that of the "chorus." Second, the roles of the leading characters are simple and clear, and the actors need not have any fear of failure. Third, as the parenthetical comments indicate, the children are given choices about staging, which, though elementary, are an integral part of the drama. Finally, the verse will bear many repetitions in this form because the suspense of waiting to be chosen as Miss Muffet or the spider maintains interest. With so many repetitions, one can be sure that all of the children will have learned the verse well before the end of the game.

As we have seen in Chapter 2, fingerplays can be used as a stepwise movement toward drama. The first step is to make the fingerplay interactive, usually with pairs of children. "Here's a cup" provides one example of this process. In her early childhood workshops, Bev Bos offers this fingerplay as a model:

Here is a bunny	hold up two bent fingers
with ears so funny.	wiggle fingers
Here is his hole	
in the ground.	make circle with thumb and four fingers of other hand
When a noise he hears,	
He pricks up his ears,	straighten two fingers in "V" shape
And jumps in his hole	
in the ground.	jump fingers into hole on other hand

To expand this into an interactive action rhyme, the children divide into pairs. One child assumes the part of the bunny by putting his or her hands up to the ears and wagging them back and forth. The other child makes a circle with his or her arms, indicating the "hole in the ground." When it's time to jump, the bunny hops once, then "dives" into the empty space in the circle. Be sure to have the children immediately switch roles and repeat the rhyme, since the part of the bunny is much more fun.

Many subtraction rhymes can be easily converted into dramatic games. Choose five children to be the frogs and recite the following rhyme:

Five little froggies	children crouch in a row, like frogs
sat on the shore,	
One went for a swim,	first frog leaps, swims off
then there were four.	
Four little froggies	
looked out to sea,	
One went swimming,	second frog leaps and swims off
and then there were three.	

Three little froggies said,
"What can we do?"   **children repeat**
One jumped in the water,   **third frog leaps and swims off**
then there were two.

Two little froggies
sat in the sun,
One swam off,   **fourth frog leaps and swims off**
and then there was one.

One little froggie said,
"This is no fun!"   **last frog repeats**
He dived in the water,   **fifth frog leaps and swims off**
and then there were none.

If this is done in a larger group, repeat until all the children have had a turn. Encourage those who are not participating as "frogs" at the moment to recite the verse along with you. After the first or second time through, most of the children will join in.

FINGERPLAYS AND ACTION RHYMES IN PICTURE BOOKS

While most collections of fingerplays and action rhymes are designed for adult presentation, some of the best-known rhymes have been adapted into picture books. These books often include easy-to-follow pictorial directions for movements and colorful illustrations that augment and enliven the story line. A bibliography of active verse in picture books can be found at the end of this chapter.

It is important to share these books with children because they deepen the experience of active rhymes with visual and artistic dimensions. They are also useful as memory aids when children are learning new verses. These picture books link oral, written, visual, and kinesthetic language forms. They also provide a means of balancing differences in learning styles that many young children are beginning to exhibit. Visual learners, in particular, benefit from the additional cues offered by picture books. In addition to his other contributions to the fingerplay literature, Marc Brown has created a series of attractive toy books ("Play Pops," 1989), which include not only pictorial diagrams for the movements but cleverly engineered pop-ups that will delight toddlers and preschoolers.

Collections of active verse in picture book format—such as those by Marc Brown and Sarah Hayes—are especially convenient, as they contain several rhymes and offer excellent pictorial directions for hand movements. They are also useful for getting more parent involvement and follow-through at home.

WRITING AND ADAPTING FINGERPLAYS

It may not always be possible to find a suitable fingerplay for a particular purpose. In such an event, writing your own verse might be the best choice. Carol Ann Piggins suggests several guidelines for writing effective fingerplays (Piggins 1981). To these, I have added a few other ideas for writing good fingerplays:

Simplicity. The completed fingerplay should roll easily off the tongue and be easy to remember. Avoid complicated language. Keep the movements simple and clear. Try them in the mirror; abbreviate them if they appear too complex.

Brevity. Think economically. Try to make a complete statement in as few words as possible. The lines should be short; six to eight words is ideal, and the fewer lines, the better. For the youngest children, aim for four lines or less; for preschool ages and above, up to eight lines.

Focus. Keep the fingerplay narrowly focused on one or two concepts. The more ideas you attempt to include in a single verse, the more likely they will be obscured.

Relevance. Choose familiar things in the child's world as subjects. Make the verse close to home. "Customize" it for your particular child, school, or library.

Action. Choose active verbs that describe or lend themselves to movement, such as hopping, running, climbing, crawling, jumping, twirling, dancing, galloping, and so forth.

Metaphor. This is the poetic "glue" that binds the concept to the child's experience. It is one thing to literally describe an object, event, or process; it is quite another to give children the opportunity to be these things or to see them imaginatively reflected in other familiar experiences. Starting at about the age of three, children respond well to simple metaphors. An abundance of nonliteral speech is part of the language-rich environment we are striving to create.

Meter and Rhyme. Remember that rhythm and sound are features that make verses easy to remember and fun to say. Review the section on "Evaluating Fingerplays" in Chapter 2 (p. 13.)

Repetition. A repeated key word or phrase not only makes a fingerplay easier to remember, but it also helps tie the verse together and reinforces the concepts that are being taught.

Sequence. Tell a story or describe a process as an orderly sequence of steps or events. Even if the verse is to be an action rhyme, some ordering principle should inform the text. For example, the action rhyme, "Head and shoulders, knees and toes" has no "story line," but it follows the structure of the body, beginning at the top and moving down. This sequential structuring not only makes for a better verse, but benefits the cognitive development of children who are just learning to put things around them in an abstract order.

Closure. Craft the closing line so that it has a satisfying "ring." Complete the thought, end the story, provide an "answer" to the "question" raised in the opening lines.

PRINCIPLES OF WRITING FINGERPLAYS APPLIED

Here is an example, which was conceived for a library preschool storytime that featured Barbara Berger's *Grandfather Twilight* (1984) and Mirra Ginsburg's *Where Does the Sun Go at Night?* (1981). The storytime dealt with the rising and setting of the sun and grew as a response to the natural question of preschoolers: "What happens to the sun at night?" The mytho-poetic answer offered in the imaginative stories above is much closer to the child's experience and in a sense more "accurate" than an adult, scientific explanation, which is too abstract to be understood by preschoolers and irrelevant to their world. In keeping with this understanding, I created a fingerplay to complement these picture books. The purpose of the fingerplay was to emphasize the analogy of sunset and sunrise to sleeping and waking.

I am the sun,	hold arms in circle over head
shining hot and bright,	
When I go to sleep,	rest head on hands; "go to sleep"
day turns into night.	
When I wake up,	stretch and yawn
I stretch and yawn	
And turn the darkness	hold arms in circle, as in beginning
into dawn.	

This fingerplay uses a simple metaphor to illustrate a single concept, relates it to the child's own experience (going to sleep and waking up), has easily imitated movements, incorporates meter and rhyme as memory aids, and follows a logical sequence with a satisfying ending. It has two parallel statements of cause and effect, repeating the words "When I . . ." and "turns into . . ." and mirrors the cycle of sunrise-sunset-sunrise by closing with the same movement as the opening. It is easily mastered by three- to five-year-olds in two or three trials.

USING EXISTING FINGERPLAYS OR ACTION RHYMES AS PATTERNS

One method of creating new active verses is to adapt the structure (including meter and rhyme scheme) of an existing verse to a new theme or concept. An example of this can be found in Kathy Overholser's *Let Your Fingers Do the Talking* (1979), where she uses the pattern of Vachel Lindsay's "The Turtle" to create a new fingerplay about Thanksgiving. Here is Lindsay's original (as traditionally performed):

There was a little turtle,	make circle with thumb and index finger
He lived in a box.	form box with both hands
He swam in a puddle,	point in circles on palm
He climbed on rocks.	climb with fingers on palm
He snapped at a mosquito,	snap with fingers and thumb
He snapped at a flea,	repeat
He snapped at a minnow,	repeat
He snapped at me.	snap toward self
He caught the mosquito,	grab air with fist
He caught the flea,	repeat
He caught the minnow,	repeat
But he didn't catch me.	point to self and shake head "no"

Now here's Overholser's patterned fingerplay (notice the change in rhyme scheme in the second and third verses):

Once there was a Pilgrim	no movement for first stanza
Who tried every way	
To catch a turkey	
For Thanksgiving Day.	
He said, "caught you" to the turkey	same movements as in "The Turtle"
He said, "caught you" to the hen	for remainder of the rhyme
He said, "caught you" to the pumpkin	
He said, "caught you" to me!	

Well, he caught that turkey
And he caught that hen
He even got the pumpkin,
But he didn't catch me!

Admittedly, the "cloned" poem lacks the music of the original, but it has value as a teaching tool. Children who know the first rhyme will recognize it in the second. Here's another example with the same rhythm, rhyme scheme, and structure, but with entirely different movements:

There was a little boy	
Who lived next door.	
When I was five years old,	**show five fingers**
He was only four.	**show four fingers**
He took my toy red race car.	**grab air**
He took my yellow ball.	**repeat**
He took my cats-eye marbles.	
He even took my doll.	
He gave me back my race car.	**hold out palm**
He gave me back my ball.	**repeat**
He gave me back my marbles.	
But he won't give back the doll.	**clutch hands to chest**

As variations or patterned fingerplays are learned, children will begin to experiment on their own. The technique of using existing verses as patterns for new poems is effective with primary grade children to get them started writing poetry. (See pp. 95–97 for how to introduce this.)

REFERENCES

Berger, Barbara. *Grandfather Twilight*. New York: Philomel Books, 1984.

Carle, Eric. *The Very Hungry Caterpillar*. Cleveland: Collins / World, [1976].

Catterwell, Thelma. *Aldita and the Forest*. 1st American ed. Boston: Houghton Mifflin, 1989, 1988.

Cullum, Carolyn N. *The Storytime Sourcebook*. New York: Neal-Schuman Publishers, Inc., 1990.

Ellis, Mary Jackson. *Finger Play Approach to Dramatization*. Minneapolis: T.S. Denison, 1960.

Ets, Marie Hall. *Gilberto and the Wind*. New York: Viking Press, [1963].

Ginsburg, Mirra. *Where Does the Sun Go at Night?* New York: Greenwillow Books, 1981.

Hoberman, Mary Ann. *A House is a House for Me.* New York: Viking Press, 1978.

Hunt, Tamara, and Nancy Renfro. *Puppetry in Early Childhood Education.* Austin, TX: Nancy Renfro Studios, 1982.

Hutchings, Margaret. *Making and Using Finger Puppets.* New York: Taplinger Publishing Co., 1973.

Hutchins, Pat. *The Wind Blew.* New York: Macmillan, [1974].

MacDonald, Margaret Read. *Booksharing: One Hundred One Programs to Use with Preschoolers.* Hamden, CT: Shoe String Press (Library Professional Publications), 1985.

Oldfield, Margaret. *Finger Puppets and Finger Plays.* Minneapolis: Creative Storytime, 1982.

Overholser, Kathy. *Let Your Fingers Do the Talking.* Minneapolis: T.S. Denison, 1979.

Piggins, Carol Ann. *Early Years,* March 1981.

Roberts, Lynda. *Mitt Magic: Finger Plays for Finger Puppets.* Mt. Rainier, MD: Gryphon House, 1985.

Ross, Laura. *Finger Puppets: Easy to Make, Fun to Use.* New York: Lothrop, Lee and Shepard, 1971.

Scott, Louise Binder. *Rhymes for Fingers and Flannelboards.* St. Louis: Webster, 1960.

Sierra, Judy, and Robert Kaminski. *Multicultural Folktales: Stories to Tell Young Children.* Phoenix, AZ: The Oryx Press, 1991.

Wilmes, Liz, and Dick Wilmes. *Felt Board Fun.* Elgin, IL: Building Blocks; Mt. Rainier, MD: Distributed by Gryphon House, 1984.

Wilt, Joy. *Puppets With Pizazz: 52 Finger and Hand Puppets Children Can Make and Use.* Waco, TX: Creative Resources, 1977.

FINGERPLAYS AND ACTION RHYMES IN PICTURE BOOKS

Brown, Marc Tolon. *Can You Jump Like a Frog?* (and other titles in the "Play Pops" series). New York: Dutton, 1989.

———. *Finger Rhymes.* New York: Dutton, 1980.

———. *Hand Rhymes.* New York: Dutton, 1985.

Cope, Wendy. *Twiddling Your Thumbs: Hand Rhymes.* Boston: Faber & Faber, 1988.

DeMuth, Vivienne. *Ten Little Fingers, Ten Little Toes: Nursery Games and Finger Plays for the Very Young.* New York: Gingerbread House, 1979.

Griego, Margot C. *Tortillitas Para Mama, and Other Nursery Rhymes / Spanish and English.* New York: Henry Holt, 1981.

Hawkins, Colin, and Jacqui Hawkins. *Incy Wincy Spider.* New York: Viking Kestrel, 1985.

———. *Round the Garden.* New York: Viking Kestrel, 1985.

———. *The Elephant.* New York: Viking Kestrel, 1985.

———. *This Little Pig.* New York: Viking Kestrel, 1985.

Hayes, Sarah. *Clap Your Hands: Finger Rhymes.* Boston, New York: Lothrop, 1988.

———. *Nine Ducks Nine.* New York: Lothrop, Lee & Shepard, 1990.

———. *Stamp Your Feet: Action Rhymes.* Boston, New York: Lothrop, 1988.

Hellard, Susan. *This Little Piggy.* New York: Putnam, 1989.

Kemp, Moira. *Hey Diddle Diddle.* New York: Dutton, 1991.

———. *Hickory Dickory Dock.* New York: Dutton, 1991.

———. *I'm a Little Teapot.* Toronto: Kids Can Press, 1987.

———. *Knock at the Door.* Los Angeles: Price/Sloan/Stern, 1987.

———. *Pat-a-Cake, Pat-a-Cake.* Toronto: Kids Can Press, 1987.

———. *Round and Round the Garden.* Toronto: Kids Can Press, 1987.

———. *This Little Piggy.* New York: Dutton, 1991.

Knight, Joan. *Tickle-Toe Rhymes.* New York: Orchard Books, 1989.

Koontz, Robin. *This Old Man: The Counting Song.* New York: Dodd, Mead, 1988.

Lamont, Priscilla. *Ring-a-Round-a-Rosy: Nursery Rhymes, Action Rhymes and Lullabies.* Boston: Little, Brown, 1990.

Leydenfrost, Robert. *Ten Little Elephants.* Garden City, NJ: Doubleday, 1975.

McNally, Darcie, adapt. *In a Cabin in a Wood.* New York: Dutton, 1991.

Ormerod, Jan. *Rhymes Around the Day.* New York: Lothrop, Lee & Shepard, 1983.

Peek, Merle. *The Balancing Act: A Counting Song.* New York: Clarion, 1987.

Ra, Carol F. *Trot, Trot, to Boston: Play Rhymes for Baby*. New York: Lothrop, 1987.

Rosen, Michael. *We're Going on a Bear Hunt*. New York: McElderry Books, 1989.

Silverman, Maida. *Baby's First Finger Rhymes*. New York: Putnam, 1987/Grosset & Dunlap, 1987.

Sivulich, Sandra. *I'm Going on a Bear Hunt*. New York: Dutton, 1973.

Stobbs, William. *This Little Piggy*. London: Bodley Head, 1981.

Westcott, Nadine Bernard. *Peanut Butter and Jelly: A Play Rhyme*. New York: Dutton, 1987.

Wilkin, Eloise Burns. *Rock-a-Bye, Baby: Nursery Songs and Cradle Games*. New York: Random House, 1981.

Wilkin, Esther. *Play with Me*. New York: Golden Press, 1988.

Williams, Jenny. *Here's a Ball for Baby: Finger Rhymes for Young Children*. New York: Dial Books for Young Readers, 1987.

Williams, Sarah. *Round and Round the Garden: Play Rhymes for Young Children*. Oxford, New York: Oxford University Press, 1983.

Wood, Audrey, and Don Wood. *Piggies*. New York: Harcourt Brace Jovanovich, 1991.

Yamaguchi, Marianne. *Finger Plays*. New York: Holt, Rinehart & Winston, 1970.

CHAPTER 7

Active Verse for Older Children

All too often, fingerplays and action rhymes are abandoned as children enter the primary grades. This is unfortunate because by the age of six or seven, fine motor control is developed to a high degree and larger attention spans and memories make possible the performance of some of the more interesting and sophisticated active verses.

Perhaps teachers assume that the children will find active verses immature. This assumption will be vindicated if they are not properly introduced. Six- to eight-year-olds are increasingly concerned about the opinions of their peers and will often look around at others before deciding whether or how to participate.

There are ways of using peer attitudes to involve children in active verse; some of these techniques will be introduced later in this chapter. Individual teachers will have to pick and choose from the activities suggested below, but they have all been successfully field tested with primary grade children.

DEVELOPMENTAL CHARACTERISTICS
SIX-YEAR-OLDS

After the relative stability of the fifth year, sixes enter a period of unrest and disequilibrium. For many children, the transition to "real school" is difficult, not because they are not eager to learn and have new experiences, but because they may lack the energy and determination to stick to the things they start. Sixes prefer a flow of activity to the mastery of individual tasks. They may need help focusing and find beginnings much easier than endings.

For sixes, all things come in extremes. Emotional responses are hot or cold. The child "loves" or "hates" things; lukewarm responses are much more rare. Imaginative play is very important at this age, as children become more interested in trying out adult roles. This play is most often social and frequently in pairs. There is still little awareness of the larger group as a whole, but this awareness begins to develop now and continues through the eighth year, where it blossoms.

Language skills now extend into reading, where great pride is taken in the ability to decode and read alone. There is not yet much concern for exactitude in reading; sixes will add or exchange words in a written text to conform to their own sense of balance. They seem to prefer things in self-complementing pairs: sun and moon, night and day, boy and girl. They may interchange pronouns to suit this sense of balance.

The relationship between home and school is important to sixes, though they may not volunteer much information at home as to the events of the school day. They enjoy bringing items for show-and-tell and returning with artwork produced in the classroom. Frequent parent-teacher communication is needed to help sixes adjust to the rigors of all-day school.

SEVEN-YEAR-OLDS

Sevens often appear reflective or even withdrawn. It is an assimilating age in which children become avid observers and listeners. They are processing a great deal of material internally, so it is important to give them plenty of time to reflect after activity. Sevens may be very self-critical, often correcting themselves verbally. They are also quite sensitive to the criticism and praise of adults, especially their teacher. A personal relationship with the teacher becomes important, sometimes all important; many seven-year-olds develop crushes on their teachers. They need plenty of verbal reminders. Even when they know what should happen next, they may ask, "Is it time for . . . ?" They appear to be testing their own sense of time and order with that of adults.

Sevens are also becoming more sensitive to the attitudes of their peers. While they are very concerned with fairness in actions, the intentions of others begin to assume an importance unknown in previous years.

Children are generally more persistent now. Their tolerance for repetition is far greater than it was a year ago. They may repeat a task or performance many times to gain mastery. The scattered play of sixes gives way to more focused interests and an intensity of purpose that can appear stubborn.

Sevens are gaining a time orientation that they were not cognitively equipped for until this year. They become more interested in time and may ask for watches to keep track of time themselves. They are also gaining competency in reading, though they may read mechanically, rushing through the words with little inflection, eager to get on to the next page or the next book. Sevens also love riddles and tongue twisters and delight in repeating them to adults as well as their peers. They are highly motivated to practice language skills and often prefer oral to written arithmetic.

EIGHT-YEAR-OLDS

There is a psychological recapitulation to the expansiveness of the four-year-old during this energetic and exploratory year. Eights have seemingly boundless energy, spending most of their day in "high gear." They may find classroom "seat work" confining, even intolerable, and must be frequently admonished to stop talking.

Their insatiable curiosity comes with new conceptual powers to evaluate and depersonalize. The animistic thinking that dominated earlier concepts of the world gives way to genuine causal reasoning. Physical forces can now be understood as inanimate and impersonal. Some eights may even become averse to metaphoric and anthropomorphic language, because it isn't "true." They are beginning to process information through "concrete operations," as Piaget termed it.

Eights are less dependent on their teacher and more sensitive to peer attitudes. They generally do not like to play alone. Dyads ("two-somes") are still the most common social structures, but eights may frequently change their pairings, forming and dissolving alliances. Near the end of the eighth year, the experiments in friendship often lead children into lasting partnerships ("buddies"), which will dominate in the upper elementary grades. For the first time, however, children have both the ability and interest in working together as a group. They take pride in their class and enjoy fully interactive group games.

This is a golden year for organized dramatic play. Eights are interested in characters and are willing to memorize lines and rehearse for a dramatic performance. They are able to allow others to stand in the lime-light, but also feel strongly about everyone getting a turn. Many eight-year-olds begin to report on the events of the school day for the first time. They love to recreate performances for their parents and siblings and insist on doing the whole performance whether anyone cares to listen or not.

ACTIVE VERSE FOR PRIMARY GRADES
JUMP ROPE AND COUNTING-OUT RHYMES

Primary-age children will be learning these rhymes on the playground anyway; why not adopt and make use of them in the classroom? Jump rope rhymes serve several functions in play. They help synchronize mind and body, making it easier to keep jumping over a longer period of time. They are also used to keep track of how many jumps each player has made (the further one gets in the rhyme, the more jumps completed). Jumping rope is good aerobic exercise and develops motor skills, coordination, and rhythm. Physical education teachers who use jump ropes can enhance the activity by learning jump rope rhymes, either from books or from the children themselves. Some good printed sources are Cole (1989), Mitchell (1979), Hastings (1990), and Corbett (1989). Some of these rhymes are vaguely "naughty," which will add to children's enjoyment. This jump rope rhyme (remembered from my childhood) illustrates the point:

> Peel a banana upside down,
> Stick it in the toilet, flush it down.
> Flush it down where the alligators go;
> Watch the banana tree grow, grow, grow:
> One, two, three, four, five . . . (until jump is missed)

The emerging sense of fairness and turn-taking is organized through counting-out rhymes, which are impersonal methods of determining who will be *it* in a game. By the age of eight, most children have learned a handful of these through oral traditions on the playground. There are a number of excellent written sources for counting-out rhymes, including Delamar (1983), Oakley (1989), Bolton (1969), Corbett (1989), and Cole and Calmenson (1990).

CLAPPING RHYMES

Another type of playground folklore with instructional value is the clapping rhyme. Clapping rhymes are played in pairs, with partners facing one another. They involve alternating clapping patterns, which are often intricate and require much concentration and practice. The basic patterns found in most clapping rhymes are

(1) Clap your own hands together.

(2a) Clap right hand against partner's left hand (straight across).

(2b) Clap left hand against partner's right hand.

(3) Clap both hands against partner's hands (straight across).

(4a) Clap right hand against partner's right hand (crossed pattern).

(4b) Clap left hand against partner's left hand.

(5) Clap hands on thighs (right hand on right thigh, left on left).

(6) Clap hands on thighs in cross pattern (right hand on left thigh, etc.).

(7) Cross hands on chest.

This clapping rhyme, sung to a melody well known to school-age children (for notation, see Wirth 1983, 14), is of moderate complexity. (Numbers over the words refer to the patterns listed above). Many variations of it can be found on the playground; here is a version I learned from my daughter:

<pre>
1-   3- 1 -5   -1   -3-1-5 -
When Billy Boy was one,
1- 3-   1   -5 -1   -3 -1-5 -1
He learned to suck his thumb;
4a-1   -4b -1   -4a-1   -4b -1
Thumb-sucker, thumb-sucker,
3 - 1- 3 -1- 3   7   - 5 -
Half - past one Cross -down,

1 -   5 -1   -3   -1 -5-1-3 -
When Billy Boy was two,
1- 5   - 1 -3 -1   -5-1 -3-1
He learned to tie his shoe;
Shoe-tyer, shoe-tyer . . . etc.

When Billy Boy was three,
He learned to climb a tree;
Tree-climber, tree-climber . . . etc.

When Billy Boy was four,
He learned to shut the door;
Door-shutter, door-shutter . . . etc.

When Billy Boy was five,
He learned to shuck and jive;
Shuck and jiver, shuck and jiver . . . etc.

When Billy Boy was six,
He learned to pick up sticks;
Stick picker-upper, stick picker-upper . . . etc.
</pre>

When Billy Boy was seven,
He learned to pray to Heaven
Heaven-prayer, Heaven-prayer . . . etc.

When Billy Boy was eight,
He learned to close the gate;
Gate-closer, gate-closer . . . etc.

When Billy Boy was nine,
He learned to climb a vine;
Vine-climber, vine-climber . . . etc.

When Billy Boy was ten,
He learned to chase the hen,
Hen-chaser, hen-chaser . . . etc.

Encourage children to invent their own variations, both for the clapping pattern and the words (e.g., "When Billy Boy was three, he learned to skin his knee . . ."). As an activity, have them work in pairs and develop their own routines; each pair then performs for the whole class. A game that children enjoy playing already thereby becomes an exercise in cooperative problem solving, communication skills, and physical coordination.

SUBSTITUTION SONGS AND RHYMES

"Substitution rhymes" are verses that are recited or sung in full the first time through, but gradually altered with subsequent repetitions. Many of these are learned at summer camps. Here is an example:

(sung to the tune of "The Battle Hymn of the Republic")

Little Peter Rabbit . . .	**make rabbit ears with hands**
. . . had a fly	**make fingers fly away**
. . . upon his ear,	**point to ear**

Little Peter Rabbit had a fly upon his ear,
Little Peter Rabbit had a fly upon his ear,

And he flicked it . . .	**flick ear**
. . . 'til it flew away.	**make fingers fly**

88

The first time through, all of the words are sung together with the movements. On the second verse, leave out the word "rabbit" and do only the "rabbit ear" motion when that word comes up. On the next pass, leave out "rabbit" and "fly" in the song, doing only the motions that stand for them. In the last verse, leave out all of the key words: "rabbit," "fly," and "ear." It takes some practice to maintain the rhythm of the song, especially at a brisk tempo. Children enjoy mastering this song and trying to outdo each other. It is also very satisfying for them to watch adults struggle with the performance of substitution rhymes, as they are equally (or perhaps even more) challenging to grown-ups.

"The Three Cornered Hat" (sung to the traditional tune) is another challenging substitution rhyme, which adds the difficulty of changing the order in which the substituted words appear:

My hat,	place hands over head
it has three . . .	show three fingers
. . . corners	make triangle with fingers
Three corners has my hat;	continue motions with words
And had it not three corners,	
It would not be my hat.	

The first time through, sing all of the words and do all of the movements. The second time through, do not sing the word "corners" (just do the movement). The third time through, eliminate "corners" and "three." Finally, be silent on "corners," "hat," and "three." The constant changing of the order in which the key words appear keeps everyone on their toes, and gradually increasing the tempo makes it even more challenging. The song can also be learned and performed in German, as follows:

> Mein Hut, der hat drei Ecken,
> Drei Ecken hat mein Hut,
> Und hat er nicht drei Ecken
> Es ware nicht mein Hut.

A SINGING GAME VARIATION

One way to use these rhymes and songs is to have everyone stand facing in one direction and to appoint a leader (usually the winner of the last game). The leader chooses which words are to be substituted and controls the tempo of the song. As it is performed, the leader attempts to "catch" people making mistakes. As in "Simon

Says," the group is narrowed down until only a single person remains. This person becomes the new leader.

EXTENDED ACTION RHYMES

Certain action rhymes are useful with kindergartners and primary grade children as introductions to drama, or simply as group games. The call and response chant "We're going on a bear hunt" is an engaging audience-participation storytelling game that can be done with small or large groups without rehearsal. (It must be memorized by the storyteller or teacher, however.) Many children learn this at summer camp and will enjoy repeating it during the school year.

The leader sets the pace for the chant by alternately slapping the thighs and clapping the hands. (For kindergarten, it is better to slap thighs only, since many fives and sixes are unable to keep up the alternating pattern while they repeat words at the same time.) Every line is echoed by the group. Without much explicit instruction, the children will make every attempt to emulate the volume, rhythm, and inflection of each line, so be sure to play with these elements.

Leader	Group
We're going on a bear hunt!	
	We're going on a bear hunt!
O.K.	
	O.K.
Let's go.	
	Let's go.
Walking along.	
	Walking along.
Oh, look!	
	Oh, look!
I see a tree.	
	I see a tree.
Can't go over it.	
	Can't go over it.
Can't go under it.	
	Can't go under it.
Have to climb up it.	
	Have to climb up it.

mime climbing motions with hands

90

Now to climb down it.

Now to climb down it.

resume slapping thighs, clapping hands

Walking along.

Walking along.

Oh, look!

Oh, look!

I see grass.

I see grass.

Can't go over it.

Can't go over it.

Can't go under it.

Can't go under it.

Have to go through it.

Have to go through it.

swish palms together, then resume slapping thighs, clapping hands

Walking along.

Walking along.

Oh, look!

Oh, look!

I see water.

I see water.

Can't go over it.

Can't go over it.

Can't go under it.

Can't go under it.

Have to swim through it.

Have to swim through it.

mime swimming movements; resume slapping thighs, clapping hands

Walking along.

Oh, look!

I see mud.

Can't go over it.

Can't go under it.

Have to walk through it.

Walking along.

Oh, look!

I see mud.

Can't go over it.

Can't go under it.

Have to walk through it.

open and close hands alternately, make slurping sounds; resume slapping thighs and clapping

Walking along.

Oh, look!

I see a cave.

Let's stop.

Walking along.

Oh, look!

I see a cave.

Let's stop.

stop clapping

Let's look inside.

I can't see.

Get your flashlight.

Doesn't work.

Let's look inside.

I can't see.

Get your flashlight.

Doesn't work.

Uh-oh.

Uh-oh.

I feel something.

I feel something.

It's big and furry!

It's big and furry!

It has a wet nose.

It has a wet nose.

I think it's a bear.

I think it's a bear.

It IS a bear!

It IS a bear!

Run for your life!

Run for your life!

resume alternate slapping thighs and clapping, but in rapid tempo; retrace steps through mud, water, grass, and tree (or whatever obstacles you have chosen)

stop clapping

Whew!

Whew!

We're safe.

We're safe.

Want to hunt tigers now?

Want to hunt tigers now?

Maybe tomorrow.

Maybe tomorrow.

To create variations, ask children to supply the "obstacles," which can be mountains, rivers, freeways, or whatever suggests itself to their fertile imaginations. After this chant has been learned, install children as chant leaders, and allow them to control the tempo of the chant.

This is an excellent game to sharpen listening skills, as children must carefully follow the tempo, inflection, volume, and rhythm of the words. It is also a good game to insert in a storytime for some active participation.

The Subject Index lists rhymes in Arabic, French, German, Hindi, Italian, Japanese, Russian, Spanish, Tagalog, Turkish, and Yiddish. These rhymes provide an enjoyable introduction to other languages. Like folktales, their very existence confirms a commonality of human experience: while the sound of the language may differ, virtually all cultures have fingerplay nursery rhymes and counting-out rhymes. This German counting-out rhyme teaches the cardinal numbers to twelve in German:

Eins, zwei, Polizei,	(one, two, policeman)
Drei, vier, Officier,	(three, four, officer)
Funf, sechs, alte Hex,	(five, six, old witch)
Sieben, acht, gute Nacht,	(seven, eight, good night)
Neun, zehn, Capitan,	(nine, ten, Captain)
Elf, zwolf, junge Wolf,	(eleven, twelve, young wolf)
Drinn' steckt eine Maus,	(in pops a mouse)
Die muss 'naus.	(out goes you!)

There are a number of sources for fingerplays and action rhymes in other languages. (See the Supplemental Bibliography for a list.) One such publication in picture book format is Griego's *Tortillitas Para Mama* (1981), which is ideal for use with children in the primary grades. Not only are there Spanish fingerplays with English translations, but pictures that present a great deal of cultural information about daily life in Mexico.

CHILDREN AS FOLKLORISTS: CLASS PROJECT

One exercise that can teach a number of skills simultaneously is to have the children collect their own folk rhymes from the playground and create an illustrated book as a class project. These can include fingerplays, action songs, counting and counting-out rhymes, jump rope songs and rhymes, clapping rhymes, and so forth. Have each child collect and perform a rhyme for the class. When cast in the role of "folklorists," many children who might otherwise reject fingerplays as "babyish" can relate to them from the safety of the "observer's" viewpoint. Third graders can begin to transcribe the rhymes themselves; younger children will need to have the teacher do this for them. When the rhymes have been transcribed, they can be compared with one another and classified. Questions to raise include, "What is the function of the rhyme?" "At what age is it learned?" "How do kids learn it, from adults or other children?" Children not only learn about oral traditions and folklore, but also gain writing and reasoning skills through the transcription process and by examining variations and making choices about which material to include. Illustrating the rhymes also makes a great art project. Alvin Schwartz's easy reader, *I Saw You in the Bathtub, and Other Folk Rhymes* (1989), is a good model for a project of this kind.

WRITING FINGERPLAYS WITH CHILDREN

Another activity that can be used to get around negative attitudes about fingerplays is having children write their own verses "for younger kids." It is helpful to use a familiar pattern, such as a "subtraction rhyme." (See discussion on p. 79.) Here is a typical subtraction rhyme; it is performed by holding up all five fingers at the beginning and then bending them down one at a time:

> Five little chickadees peeping at the door,
> One flew away, then there were four.
> Four little chickadees sitting on a tree,
> One flew away, then there were three.
> Three little chickadees looking at you.
> One flew away, then there were two.
> Two little chickadees sitting in the sun,
> One flew away, and then there was one.
> One little chickadee left all alone,
> One flew away, and then there were none.

There are many fingerplays that follow this pattern, which could be abstracted as follows:

> Five little . . . (rhymes with "four")
> One . . . , then there were four.
> Four little . . . (rhymes with "three")
> One . . . , then there were three . . .

Allow the children to deduce this formula by offering several examples. Once the framework is understood, they will be ready to create their own subtraction rhymes using the same pattern. Setting the rhymes is the next step. By good fortune, the first five cardinal numbers are easy to rhyme. Have students make lists of possible rhymes for each couplet:

four	three	two	one, none
more	me	chew	done
store	see	few	fun
tore	bee	clue	sun
chore	flea	stew	won
poor	key	new	bun

The longer the lists they make, the better. Then they are ready to choose subjects for the rhymes. Animals work well, but just about any topics are possible. Here's an example of a clever substitution rhyme written by a third grader:

Five little eggs	show five fingers
at the corner store,	
One rolled off the shelf,	roll hands
then there were four.	show four fingers
Four little eggs	
came home with me,	
The grocery bag ripped,	cup hands, then "dump" contents of empty palms
then there were three.	show three fingers
Three little eggs	
all white and new,	
One broke open,	make fist, extend fingers suddenly
then there were two.	show two fingers
Two little eggs boiled	
'til they were done,	
I gave one to my friend,	hold hands out, palms up, offer one hand
then there was one.	show one finger
One little egg	make circle with thumb and index finger
balancing on my head,	carefully place "egg" on head
If that one falls off,	roll eyes up
they'll all be dead.	

Notice how the rhyme has been altered for the last two lines, lending a marvelous comical twist to the verse. It is also worth noting how well-ordered this poem is; there is good storytelling from the beginning to the end. A coherent "history" of the five eggs is presented, from their origin at the "corner store" (obviously, an urban child) to the precarious state of the last remaining egg, left balancing on the head. The verse ends with dramatic tension (will the egg fall?) and a bit of personification (the eggs have "died"), which contributes to the sophisticated humor of the poem.

Other patterns can be discovered and adapted. There are many pedagogical advantages to this approach. First, it is a method that brings immediate success, overcoming the children's discouragement of not knowing where to begin. Second, it is often possible to use an established pattern of movement to tell many different stories, a discovery that can serve to convey the richness of movement as metaphor. Third, it teaches children about structure, meter, and rhyme scheme in poetry as they work with these elements to create their own verses. The activity could be followed up by inviting younger children into the classroom to teach them the new fingerplays.

REFERENCES

Bolton, Henry Carrington. *The Counting-Out Rhymes of Children: Their Antiquity, Origin, and Wide Distribution.* New York: D. Appleton & Co., 1888; Detroit: Singing Tree Press, Book Tower, 1969.

Cole, Joanna. *Anna Banana: 101 Jump-Rope Rhymes.* New York: Morrow Junior Books, 1989.

Cole, Joanna, and Stephanie Calmenson. *Miss Mary Mack, and Other Children's Street Rhymes.* New York: Morrow Junior Books, 1990.

Corbett, Pie, ed. *The Playtime Treasury: A Collection of Playground Rhymes, Games, and Action Songs.* New York: Doubleday, 1989.

Delamar, Gloria T. *Children's Counting-Out Rhymes, Fingerplays, Jump-Rope, and Bounceball Chants and Other Rhythms.* Jefferson, NC: McFarland, 1983.

Griego, Margot C. *Tortillitas Para Mama, and Other Nursery Rhymes / Spanish and English.* New York: Henry Holt, 1981.

Hastings Jr., Scott E., ed. *Miss Mary Mac All Dressed in Black: Tongue Twisters, Jump Rope Rhymes, and Other Children's Lore from New England.* Little Rock, AR: August House, 1990.

Mitchell, Cynthia. *Halloweena Hecatee, and Other Rhymes to Skip To.* 1st ed. New York: Crowell, 1979.

Oakley, Ruth. *Chanting Games.* New York: Marshall Cavendish, 1989.

Sandoval, Ruben. *Games, Games, Games = Juegos, Juegos, Juegos: Chicano Children at Play: Games and Rhymes.* Garden City, NY: Doubleday, 1977.

Schwartz, Alvin. *I Saw You in the Bathtub, and Other Folk Rhymes.* New York: Harper & Row, 1989.

Wirth, Marian, and Verna Stassevitch. *Musical Games, Fingerplays and Rhythmic Activities for Early Childhood.* West Nyack, NY: Parker, 1983, p.14.

BOOKS ON CHILD DEVELOPMENT, AGES SIX THROUGH EIGHT

Ames, Louise Bates, and Frances L. Ilg. *Your Eight-Year-Old: Lively and Outgoing.* New York: Delacorte Press, 1989.

———. *Your Seven-Year-Old: Life in a Minor Key.* New York: Delacorte Press, 1985.

———. *Your Six-Year-Old: Defiant But Loving.* New York: Delacorte Press, 1979.

Chess, Stella. *Know Your Child: An Authoritative Guide for Today's Parents.* New York: Basic Books, 1987.

Gesell, Arnold, et al. *The Child from Five to Ten.* Rev. ed. New York: Harper & Row, 1977.

The Growing Years: A Guide to Your Child's Emotional Development from Birth to Adolescence. The New York Hospital-Cornell Medical Center, Department of Psychiatry. New York: Atheneum, 1988, 1987.

Healy, Jane M. *Your Child's Growing Mind: A Parent's Guide to Learning from Birth to Adolescence* 1st ed. Garden City, NY: Doubleday, 1987.

CHAPTER 8

Active Verse for E.S.L. and Special Needs Children

Fingerplays and action rhymes can teach children with special needs in a variety of ways. In this chapter, we will discuss applications in teaching English as a Second Language, speech and language improvement, work with mentally retarded and emotionally disturbed children, the hearing impaired, and children with physical disabilities. The intent is to show the value of active verse in teaching children with special needs and to provide representative examples of activities appropriate to these needs. Teachers and parents can take these examples as models to guide them in their own creative uses of active verse in the special needs curriculum. Most of the material from previous chapters can be applied directly, keeping in mind that children with special needs are often developmentally immature and must be met at their *observed developmental stage*. The primary differences in using active verses with these populations are that (1) additional criteria for their selection may be required; and (2) certain adaptations may be necessary to meet special needs.

ENGLISH AS A SECOND LANGUAGE (E.S.L.)
BENEFITS OF ACTIVE VERSE IN TEACHING E.S.L.

Active verse can be a powerful teaching tool for E.S.L. As anyone who has learned a foreign language knows, the learner relies heavily on physical cues to establish and relate meanings. Gestures and facial expressions constitute a nonverbal parallel text that gives the learner reference points. This is why carrying on a telephone conversation is such a challenge for foreign speakers. The physical analog built into the fingerplay punctuates all of the main ideas of the text, providing natural reinforcement for the basic meaning of each line. There is no one-to-one correspon-

99

dence of word and gesture, but a holistic sense of the language is conveyed, which may help E.S.L. students grasp wholes, not just parts.

Physical movement aids E.S.L. students in other ways as well. The activity helps to get the language into the body. This additional "anchor" can speed the learning process considerably. In the teaching of E.S.L., the Chinese proverb quite literally holds true: "I hear and I forget; I see and I remember; I do and I understand."

Because the physical movements are fun to do, positive attitudes are nurtured. The value of this can hardly be overstated. A wide range of studies have shown that a child's attitude may have more impact on the learning process than any other single factor. It is far easier to get children to repeat a game than a drill, and fingerplays can supply many of the benefits of both.

From the point of view of text alone, there are good arguments for using metered verse with E.S.L. students. Its rhythmic quality aids both fluency and pronunciation. It has been observed by some E.S.L. teachers that children are often able to sing or chant sounds and words which otherwise present them with difficulties. Rhymes provide not only enjoyable sounds, but memory aids and "markers" as well. Repetition is built into many fingerplays and action rhymes, and verse is much more amenable to repetition than straight prose.

Fingerplays can teach pronunciation, vocabulary, verb conjugation, and grammatical structure. The next section will provide some direction in choosing active verse that will meet the teacher's learning objectives for each of these areas.

SELECTION

All of the criteria for good poetry should be applied to verses selected for use in teaching E.S.L. There are, however, a number of additional considerations that should be taken into account. First, one must beware of unconventional sentence structures, such as are often found in Mother Goose rhymes. Verb order is frequently reversed (e.g., "Here am I, little Jumping Joan . . .") and archaic conjugations may cause confusion to non-native speakers (e.g., "Tom, Tom, the piper's son / Stole a pig, and away he run"). It is best to avoid these constructions in favor of simple and grammatically correct English.

It is important to analyze the grammatical structure of the fingerplays to be used, so that they can be progressively arranged. A good beginning rhyme may contain only present-tense verbs or none at all, as in this action song for naming body parts:

(sung to the tune of "There's a Tavern in the Town")

Head and shoulders, knees and toes,   **point to each body part as named**
    knees and toes.

Head and shoulders, knees and toes,
    knees and toes.
Eyes and ears and mouth and nose,
Eyes and ears and mouth and nose,   **sing very softly**
Eyes and ears and mouth and nose,   **sing this line loudly**
Head and shoulders, knees and toes,
    knees and toes.

This verse consists simply of eight nouns, with no other word or part of speech but the conjunction "and." The eight body parts are quickly learned using this action song. No explanation or translation is necessary because the vocabulary words are defined by pointing to each body part as it is named. The vehicle of music makes it easy to memorize, and the frequent repetitions within the verse offer plenty of reinforcement. (The repetition of the middle section is the author's own variation. This has been done so that the facial features are repeated as well as the other body parts. By singing the repeated line softly and then loudly, the interest and energy of the whole action song is maintained.)

FINGERPLAYS FOR PRONUNCIATION

E.S.L. teachers are already well aware of sounds in the English language that present special problems for their students. Spanish-speaking children, for example, have difficulties with a number of sounds that are not present in their native tongue, such as the "a" in "at" or "fan." Rather than presenting children with mechanical drills, which will require a great deal of extrinsic motivation, a well-chosen fingerplay can be highly effective. The following action rhyme provides practice in producing the short "a" sound in "map":

Clap your hands, clap your hands,   **actions follow text**
Clap them just like me.

Flap your arms, flap your arms,
Flap them just like me.

Tap your knees, tap your knees,
Tap them just like me.

Clap your hands, clap your hands.
Now rest them quietly.

Adaptations may be necessary for pedagogical reasons. The rhyme above was altered to focus on and repeat the "a" sound, and the last line, which originally read

"Now let them quiet be," has been grammatically restructured so that it does not inadvertently teach an improper construction.

Several other English language sounds that present difficulty for Spanish-speaking children follow, with rhymes that will help in their mastery. These have been tested with Spanish-speaking children in the Fresno, California, area (*Language*, 1966):

1. "J" as in "John"; "i" as in "fish":

Jack be nimble,	hold index finger up with one hand for "candlestick;" "walk" with
Jack be quick,	index and middle finger of other hand toward candlestick
Jack jump over	jump fingers over candlestick
the candlestick.	

2. "Th" as in "this":

This is the mother,	show thumb
This is the father,	show index finger
This is the brother tall;	show middle finger
This is the sister,	show ring finger
This is the baby,	show pinky
Oh, how we love them all.	put hand to heart, then extend with palm up

3. "Z" as in "zap"; "u" as in "up":

Fuzzy wuzzy was a bear	cup hands to ears
Fuzzy wuzzy had no hair	place hands on head
If fuzzy wuzzy had no hair,	
He wasn't very fuzzy, was he?	shake head "no"

4. "X" as in "mix"; "a" as in "at":

Six little ducks that I once knew,	show six fingers (1)
Fat ones,	show thumb (2)
skinny ones,	show pinky (3)
fair ones, too.	show other fingers (4)

But the one little duck   show index finger   (5)
With the feather on his back,   place hand against back and wave fingers   (6)
He led the others with his
"quack, quack, quack."   put palms together and clap hands, hinged at
                                           the thumbs   (7)

Quack, quack, quack,
Quack, quack, quack,
He led the others with his
"quack, quack, quack."

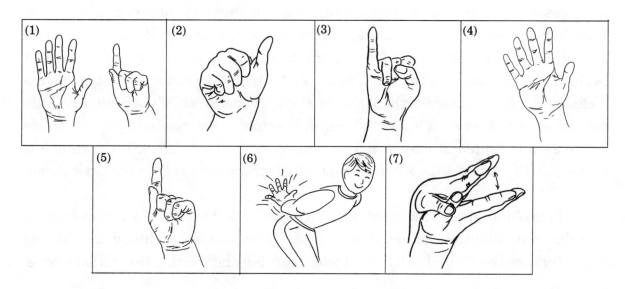

5. "Sh" as in "shot":

Shake, shake, knock, knock,   alternately shake fist and pound on palm through rhyme
Shake, shake, knock, knock,
Play the tambourine.

Shake, shake, knock, knock,
Shake, shake, knock, knock,
Play the tambourine.

ACTIVE VERSE IN SPEECH AND LANGUAGE THERAPY

Fingerplays can also be helpful in working with children who have speech or language impairments, including poor articulation; stuttering and language delays, such as lack of speech; low (passive and active) vocabulary; and immature sentence structure.

Articulation problems may be the result of hearing loss, or cognitive delays or disorders affecting the speech-producing mechanism. Recognition of a potential articulation problem should be guided by an understanding of normal speech development. Although children vary in the rate at which they master the basic consonant sounds of the language, the following guidelines represent fairly reliable averages. By the age of three-and-a-half, most will have control over *b, p, n, w,* and *h*. At four-and-a-half, they will have mastered *d, t, g, k, y,* and *ng*. By five-and-a-half, articulation of the troublesome *f* is efficient. At six-and-a-half, they will master *v, th* (as in "the"), *sh,* and *l*. By the age of seven-and-a-half, the production of consonants includes the fully mature articulation of *s, z, r, th* (as in "thin"), *wh, ch,* and *j*. Be concerned and observant, but not alarmed, if a child is not mastering these sounds at the ages indicated; it may or may not indicate a speech defect. If the child has persistent difficulties, a diagnosis by a qualified speech-language pathologist should be sought.

To help children with articulation difficulties, look for fingerplays with compelling rhythmic qualities that emphasize the problem sounds. A child who is having difficulty with the *f* sound will benefit from learning and reciting this action rhyme:

Fee, fie, fo, fum,	count fingers, starting with pinky
See my finger,	make a fist; extend index finger
See my thumb.	point to thumb; then open up hand
Fee, fie, fo, fum,	count fingers again, then make fist with index finger and thumb extended
Finger's gone	bend index finger down
So is thumb.	bend thumb down

The consonant changes from *s* to *f* to *th* are not easy, but the strong rhythm of the verse and the high appeal of the words from the fairy tale ("fee, fie, fo, fum") will propel the rhyme through many repetitions. Have the children try it in a giant's voice, then in a silly high voice. Whisper or shout the verse; try it fast and slow. When they do it again in their natural voice, it is likely to be much better. Here's a rhyme that makes extensive use of the *k* sound:

Big clocks make a sound like	swing arms slowly and rhythmically
Tick, tock, tick, tock.	

Small clocks make a sound like	speak at higher pitch, swing arms faster
Tick, tock, tick, tock.	
Tiny clocks make a sound like	speak at very high pitch, swing arms faster
Tick, tock, tick, tock,	
Tick, tock, tick, tock.	

Fingerplays which reiterate problematic sounds offer something that drills cannot: intrinsically motivated practice. The teacher or speech and language therapist has ulterior motives for the selection of particular rhymes, but should resist a didactic approach to their use and avoid extrinsic rewards for their performance beyond gentle encouragement. A genuine display of enthusiasm for the fingerplay is the best means of stimulating the child's intrinsic motivation. This, in turn, is more likely to lead the child to success.

STUTTERING

Children who stutter rarely do so when they sing, chant, or recite. Strongly rhythmic speech seems to carry them through trouble spots. A child who has extreme difficulty saying a short phrase without stuttering may turn around and sing "Twinkle, Twinkle, Little Star" with perfect articulation. Fingerplays and action rhymes can be used to give children who stutter more experiences of fluent speech. These successes are vital to improving their self-esteem (which can be very low) and in helping them to realize that they can speak without stuttering. Children who stutter usually have one or two leading consonants that give them particular difficulties; a common problem consonant is the leading *t*. Choose a verse with a strong sing-song rhythm, or better yet, an action song. Here's an action song with lots of leading *t*'s:

Teddy bear, teddy bear,	stand; actions follow text
Turn around;	
Teddy bear, teddy bear,	
Touch the ground.	
Teddy bear, teddy bear,	
Show your shoe;	
Teddy bear, teddy bear,	
That will do.	sit down

LANGUAGE IMPAIRMENTS

The language-impaired child may or may not have a learning disability. While children with language impairments are often assumed to be delayed learners, the possible reasons for the impairment are diverse, including hearing loss or poor auditory discrimination, underdeveloped sequencing ability, language-impoverished environment, and cognitive delays (Liebergott et al. 1978). If the causes for the language impairment are mostly environmental, a period of immersion in a language-rich environment, coupled with developmentally appropriate language arts activities, will improve the deficiency. Persistence and encouragement are vital. If the child has low self-esteem—often the case with language impairment—a new foundation of confidence must be built through stepwise increments of success. Fingerplays and action rhymes, graduated to suit the child's current abilities, can provide these successes. Active verse is also well suited for

- Expansion of attention span
- Improvement of listening skills
- Learning to follow directions
- Bridging conceptual gaps
- Increasing comprehension
- Learning more complex grammatical structures
- Vocabulary enrichment

The fingerplay activities in the foregoing chapters can be used with language-impaired children once their developmental capabilities have been assessed. If a child appears to be arrested at a sensory-motor stage of cognition, then active verses appropriate for use with toddlers should be selected. It is extremely important to avoid frustration, so work up to more complex rhymes gradually.

Active verses should be chosen to meet the instructional objectives set as a result of observation. For example, a child whose language-impairment derives in part from poor sequencing ability can be aided by rhymes that tell a simple story, such as "The Eensy Weensy Spider":

The eensy weensy spider   thumb to forefinger of each hand for "spider climb"   (1)
Climbed up the water spout.

Down came the rain   flutter fingers down for rain   (2)
And washed the spider out.   sweep hands down and to sides   (3)

Out came the sun   arms make circle over head   (4)
And dried up all the rain;

And the eensy weensy spider   imitate spider climb again   (5)
Climbed up the spout again.

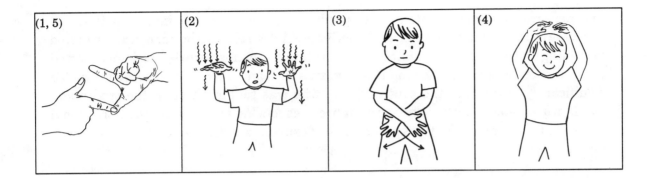

The plot of this fingerplay consists of a series of four events, connected in a logical sequence:

1. spider climbs
2. rain thwarts spider
3. sun thwarts rain
4. spider climbs again

Visual representations of the rhyme, such as felt figures (e.g., spider, spout, rain, and sun) on a flannelboard, or Colin Hawkins' picture book, *Incy Wincy Spider* (1985), will help to reinforce the sequence visually as well. By connecting the spoken word to actions and a visual sequence that is repeated (and always in the same order), we help strengthen the child's conceptual ability to follow, remember, and generate sequences of words and ideas.

CHILDREN WITH LEARNING DISABILITIES

Some of the characteristics of learning disabilities are impulsiveness, distractibility, short attention span, inability to follow directions, hyper- or hypoactivity (listlessness), physical awkwardness, and perseveration (repeating an action over and over again). While normal children may exhibit any of these characteristics, children with learning disabilities have persistent difficulties with several of these behaviors (Hayden et al. 1978). They are likely to have speech and motor difficulties and fewer social skills than average. They are also very likely to have low self-esteem.

By beginning with simple fingerplays and repeating them often, children with learning disabilities are given successes that build upon one another. The link between intellectual, social, and perceptual-motor skills can be used to teach the learning disabled using holistic methods, including physical movement. Gearheart (1973, 44) cites a number of studies that suggest the value of using active games to teach children with learning disabilities:

Another group of investigations has produced evidence which indicates that the privilege of participating in games will motivate children to learn better concepts related to reading and language. Humphrey, in several studies of this nature, has demonstrated that children taught various language concepts with an "active game method" learned significantly more than the control group who was taught through the traditional medium of language workbooks.... Humphrey has concluded that the high motivational state elicited in game situations produces the desired results in language skill improvement.

MENTALLY RETARDED AND EMOTIONALLY DISTURBED CHILDREN

One of the challenges of teaching mentally retarded or emotionally disturbed children is that activities must be short, engaging, and constantly shifting, so as not to tire them. Enjoyable and stimulating activities of five minutes or less are not always easy to find, especially those that meet the teacher's learning objectives for speech and language. Fingerplays are brief and engaging; they afford the possibility of novelty within a structure and familiar form.

Fingerplays and action rhymes serve other special needs of these children, too. They provide immediate results, inspire intrinsic motivation, and offer opportunities for structured parallel play. This is especially important for children whose social skills are limited and who may become noncooperative, aggressive, or otherwise out of control in unstructured play with their peers.

Fingerplays are also good transition activities (see p. 50), as they help capture the attention of children who have difficulty disengaging from their immediate activity. The daily use of "ritual" fingerplays for transition times helps children regulate their own activity to mesh with the school schedule and the needs of the group. Such rituals also provide a sense of comfort and stability, establishing a strong emotional "safety net" over which novel and challenging activities can be attempted.

A four-year demonstration project at the University of Iowa showed significant gains for trainable and educable mentally handicapped children when language activities—including fingerplays—were integrated into all curriculum areas (*Classroom Approach to Language Development for Mentally Retarded Children: Trainable and Primary Level,* 1973). An emphasis on verbal communication lays the foundation for other types of learning and builds a relationship of trust between child and teacher or care-giver.

FINGERPLAYS, SIGN LANGUAGE, AND THE HEARING IMPAIRED

Every active verse has two parallel texts: the spoken word and the accompanying silent text of gesture. Although there is no standardized "syntax" for fingerplay movements, there are obvious conventions that appear again and again (such as the use of the "V" sign for a rabbit). As hearing children begin to learn these conventions, their interest in and understanding of how movement conveys meaning can be naturally directed toward learning a standard sign language. Highly recommended for this purpose are the Handtalk books by Remy Charlip (1974, 1987) and George Ancona (1989), which are written for children and illustrated with color photographs.

If hearing impaired children are mainstreamed in the classroom, this interest has immediate practical significance. Fingerplays and action rhymes can serve as a bridge to learning signed English. There are even a number of fingerplays that incorporate sign language into the movements. These are listed in the Subject Index under the heading of "Sign Language."

CHILDREN WITH PHYSICAL DISABILITIES

Fingerplays are satisfying games for children with physical disabilities, although some adaptations may be required to compensate for their physical limitations. The major factors to consider are

- Active limbs
- Range of motion
- Coordination
- Flexibility
- Strength

A great many fingerplays can be used as is. Other fingerplays and action rhymes must be re-choreographed for the child who is wheelchair-bound or wears a prosthetic device. Here is an action rhyme that has been adapted so it can be performed in a wheelchair and with one hand only (the original fingerplay can be found in Chapter 9):

I saw a little rabbit	make "V" sign for rabbit
go hop, hop, hop.	bounce hand up and down
I saw his ears	
go flop, flop, flop.	wiggle fingers for ears

I saw his nose

  go wink, wink, wink.   **move nose up and down**

I saw his eyes

  go blink, blink, blink.   **blink three times**

I said, "Little rabbit,

  won't you stay?"   **beckon with index finger**

He looked at me

  and he hopped away.   **make "V" sign and hop it away**

The familiar action rhyme, "I'm a Little Teapot," can be performed in a variety of ways, depending upon the range of motion possible for the child. If both arms can be held up and the child can bend at the waist, simply perform the rhyme as written in a sitting position. If only one hand is available or if bending at the waist is difficult, it can be performed as a fingerplay, as follows:

I'm a little teapot,

Short and stout;   **hold out fist**

Here is my handle,   **extend thumb**

Here is my spout.   **extend index finger for spout**

When I get all steamed up,

Hear me shout,

Just tip me over   **tip hand forward to pour**

And pour me out.

Similar modifications can be made for other action rhymes. If the child is mainstreamed, it is important to have alternative versions ready when action rhymes are taught and to present them in a straightforward way, neither overlooking nor mitigating the differences of the child with a disability. The teacher is not only instructing the child to make the best use of his or her own capabilities, but modeling respectful attitudes for the other children in the classroom.

REFERENCES

Ancona, George. *Handtalk Zoo.* New York: Four Winds Press, 1989.

Charlip, Remy. *Handtalk: An ABC of Finger Spelling and Sign Language.* New York: Parents' Magazine Press, 1974.

———. *Handtalk Birthday: A Number and Story Book in Sign Language.* New York: Four Winds Press, 1987.

Classroom Approach to Language Development for Mentally Retarded Children: Trainable and Primary Level. Speech and Hearing Staff of State Services for Crippled Children. Health Services and Mental Health Administration (DHEW), Rockville, MD. Maternal and Child Health Service. Iowa City, IA: University of Iowa, 1973.

Farnham-Diggory, Sylvia. *Learning Disabilities: A Psychological Perspective.* Cambridge, MA: Harvard University Press, 1978.

Gearheart, B.R. *Learning Disabilities: Educational Strategies.* St. Louis: C.V. Mosby Co., 1973.

Hawkins, Colin, and Jacqui Hawkins. *Incy Wincy Spider.* New York: Viking Kestrel, 1985.

Hayden, Alice H., et al. *Mainstreaming Preschoolers: Children with Learning Disabilities.* Washington, DC: U.S. Government Printing Office, 1978.

Keiran, Shari Stokes, et al. *Mainstreaming Preschoolers: Children with Orthopedic Handicaps.* Washington, DC: U.S. Government Printing Office, 1978.

Language. Fresno City Unified School District, Calif. Washington, DC: Office of Education (DHEW), Bureau of Elementary and Secondary Education, 1966.

Liebergott, Jacqueline, et al. *Mainstreaming Preschoolers: Children with Speech and Language Impairments.* Washington, DC: U.S. Government Printing Office, 1978.

Moran, Joan M., and Leonard H. Kalakian. *Movement Experiences for the Mentally Retarded or Emotionally Disturbed Child.* Minneapolis: Burgess Publishing Co., 1977.

CHAPTER 9

A Core Repertoire of Active Verse

Teachers and librarians who use active verses will develop a unique repertoire of material that suits the particular needs and interests of their group. There are some rhymes the children will ask for again and again, and these will gradually form a body of local folklore that helps define the group. While it is impossible to predict which verses will have staying power with any given group, I have identified a number of fingerplay "classics" that every teacher should know. These are time-tested verses with broad appeal and are often shared through oral traditions among teachers, care-givers, and librarians.

A useful way to keep track of favorite fingerplays is to maintain a small flip file. Three-by-five cards are an ideal size because they provide enough room for the text, but can be kept in a pocket or purse for quick reference. A ring binder on either corner will hold the stack together, and white tape serves well for index tabs.

A "core" repertoire of easy fingerplays can be maintained by frequent repetition. Even when children have moved on to much more complex fingerplays and action rhymes, they will continue to enjoy these "old favorites."

The following verses will help to form a core repertoire. These fingerplays and action rhymes have been selected on the basis of quality, usefulness as "daily" or "ritual" verses, and frequency of occurrence in the sources indexed in this book. They are also those most likely to be encountered in some kind of oral tradition. Though they should be memorized, keeping them in your flip file will remind you of them and help refresh your memory at a moment's notice. This is particularly helpful in situations where a spontaneous fingerplay would be desirable.

THE APPLE TREE

Away up high in the apple tree,   begin standing, hold hands up
Two little apples smiled at me.   point to self, smile

So I shook that tree
As hard as I could,   pretend to shake tree
Down came the apples,   hand flutter down
Ummmm, were they good!   rub tummy

AUTUMN LEAVES

begin in standing position

Little leaves fall gently down,   raise hands over head, then flutter fingers down
Red and yellow,
orange and brown;
Whirling, whirling,
round and round,   add rotating motions
Quietly, without a sound;
Falling softly to the ground,   slowly lower body to floor
Down and down and down and down.

THE BEEHIVE

Here is a beehive;   cup hands together
Where are the bees?
Hidden away where nobody sees.   peek inside cupped hands
Now they come creeping out of the hive—
One, two, three, four, five!   show thumb and fingers, one by one
Buzz-z-z-z-z-z-z-z-z-z!   make fingers fly away

CAN YOU HOP LIKE A RABBIT?

begin in standing position

Can you hop like a rabbit?   put hands to ears and hop
Can you jump like a frog?   crouch down and jump
Can you fly like a bird?   wave arms
Can you run like a dog?   run in place while "dog paddling"
Can you walk like a duck?   place hands on hips and waddle

Can you swim like a fish?   make waves with hands
And be still, like a good child—   fold hands, stand still
As still as this?

COBBLER, COBBLER

Cobbler, cobbler, mend my shoe.   pound one fist on the other hand
Have it done by half past two;   show two fingers
Stitch it up, stitch it down,   mime sewing motions; hold "needle" by thumb
Make the very best shoes in town.   and index finger; "stitch" on other hand

THE EENSY WEENSY SPIDER

The eensy weensy spider   thumb to forefinger of each hand for "spider climb"
Climbed up the water spout.
Down came the rain   flutter fingers down for rain
And washed the spider out.   sweep hands down and to sides
Out came the sun   arms make circle over head
And dried up all the rain;
And the eensy weensy spider   imitate spider climb again
Climbed up the spout again.

FIVE LITTLE MONKEYS

Five little monkeys   hold up five fingers
jumping on the bed,   move fingers up and down
One fell off   show one finger
and broke his head.   hold head in hands
Mama called the doctor   pretend to hold phone
and the doctor said:
"No more monkeys
jumping on the bed!"   put one hand to hip and shake index finger sternly

Repeat with four, three, two, and one little monkey.

FIVE LITTLE PUMPKINS

Five little pumpkins	
sitting on a gate.	hold up five fingers
The first one said,	hold up one finger
"It's late, it's late!"	point to wrist
The second one said,	hold up two fingers
"There are witches in the air."	point to air
The third one said,	hold up three fingers
"I don't care."	shake head three times
The fourth one said,	hold up four fingers
"Let's run, let's run."	"run" with two fingers
The fifth one said,	hold up five fingers
"It's Halloween fun!"	cup hand to mouth and shout
"Oooooooooo" went the wind,	wave hands, wiggle fingers
And OUT went the light,	clap loudly on "OUT"
And five little pumpkins	show five fingers
Rolled out of sight.	roll hands

FIVE LITTLE SOLDIERS

Five little soldiers,	show five fingers
standing in a row.	
Three stood straight,	show thumb, index, and middle fingers
And two stood so.	ring finger and pinky bent
Along marched the captain,	march with two fingers of other hand
And what do you think?	
Up jumped the soldiers,	
Quick as a wink!	straighten "lazy" fingers

GRANDMA'S GLASSES

Here are Grandma's glasses.	thumbs and index fingers make circles around eyes
Here is Grandma's hat.	put fingertips together over head
This is the way	
she folds her hands	fold hands
And lays them in her lap.	put hands in lap

HEAD AND SHOULDERS, KNEES AND TOES

(sung to the tune of "There's a Tavern in the Town")

	performed standing
Head and shoulders, knees and toes,	point to each body part as named; when rhyme
knees and toes;	is familiar, try leaving out selected words and
Head and shoulders, knees and toes,	silently pointing to omitted body part
knees and toes.	
Eyes and ears and mouth and nose,	
Head and shoulders, knees and toes,	
knees and toes.	

HERE IS A BUNNY

Here is a bunny	hold up two bent fingers
with ears so funny.	wiggle fingers
Here is his hole	
in the ground.	make circle with thumb and four fingers of other hand
When a noise he hears,	straighten two fingers in "V" shape
He pricks up his ears,	
And jumps in his hole	
in the ground.	jump fingers into hole on other hand

HERE'S A CUP

Here's a cup,	make fist of one hand
and here's a cup,	make fist of other hand
And here's a pot of tea.	extend thumb of one hand
Pour a cup,	pouring motions
Pour a cup,	
And have a cup with me!	pretend to drink

HICKORY, DICKORY, DOCK

Hickory, dickory, dock,   bend arm at elbow, palm out, move arm back and
                                     forth, like a pendulum   (1)

The mouse ran up the clock,   run fingers up arm   (2)
The clock struck one,   clap hands loudly   (3)
The mouse ran down,   run fingers back down arm   (4)
Hickory, dickory, dock.   wave arm back and forth   (5)

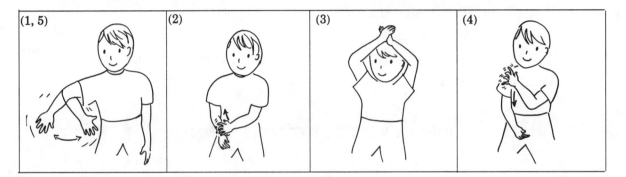

HOUSES

Here is a nest for the robin;   cup both hands together
Here is a hive for the bee;   put fists together
Here is a hole for the bunny;   form circle with both hands
And here is a house for me.   fingertips together over head

I CAUGHT A HARE ALIVE

One, two, three, four, five,   count on fingers of one hand
Once I caught a hare alive.   snap fist closed
Six, seven, eight, nine, ten,   count on fingers of other hand
Then I let it go again.   hold both hands open

I'M A LITTLE TEAPOT

performed standing

I'm a little teapot,
Short and stout.
Here is my handle,   **put one hand on hip**
Here is my spout.   **stretch out other arm for spout**

When I get all steamed up,
Hear me shout;
Just tip me over   **bend body toward extended arm**
And pour me out.

JOHNNY POUNDS WITH ONE HAMMER

performed standing

Johnny pounds with one hammer,   **pound with one fist in rhythm**
one hammer, one hammer.
Johnny pounds with one hammer,
all day long.

Johnny pounds with two hammers,   **pound with both fists**
two hammers, two hammers.
Johnny pounds with two hammers,
all day long.

Johnny pounds with three hammers . . .   **pound both fists, stomp one foot**

Johnny pounds with four hammers . . .   **pound both fists, stomp both feet**

Johnny pounds with five hammers . . .   **pound fists, stomp feet, nod head**

Johnny is so tired,   **continue pounding in slow motion**
so tired, so tired.
Johnny is so tired,
all day long.

Johnny goes to sleep now,   stop hammering, drop head, close eyes
to sleep now, to sleep now,
Johnny goes to sleep now,
all night long.

substitute child's name for "Johnny" if desired

LITTLE RABBIT

I saw a little rabbit   performed standing
go hop, hop, hop.   hop three times
I saw his ears
go flop, flop, flop.   put hands to ears and flop three times
I saw his nose
go wink, wink, wink.   move nose up and down
I saw his eyes
go blink, blink, blink.   blink three times
I said, "Little rabbit,
won't you stay?"   beckon with index finger
He looked at me
and he hopped away.   hop

TEN LITTLE FINGERS

I have ten little fingers,   hold all ten fingers up
And they all belong to me.   point to self
I can make them do things,
Would you like to see?

I can shut them up tight;   make fists
I can open them wide;   extend fingers
I can put them together;   clasp hands
And I can make them all hide.   hands behind back

I can put them up high;	reach hands over head
I can put them down low;	touch floor
I can fold them together,	clasp hands, lace fingers
And hold them just so.	place hands in lap

THIS LITTLE PIGGY

This little piggy went to market,	point to thumb
This little piggy stayed home,	point to index finger
This little piggy had roast beef,	point to middle finger
This little piggy had none,	point to ring finger
This little piggy cried,	point to little finger
"Wee, wee, wee," all the way home.	wiggle little finger, put behind back

THE TURTLE

There was a little turtle,	make circle with thumb and index fingers
He lived in a box.	form box with both hands
He swam in a puddle,	point in circles on palm
He climbed on rocks.	climb with fingers on palm
He snapped at a mosquito,	snap with fingers and thumb
He snapped at a flea,	repeat
He snapped at a minnow,	repeat
He snapped at me.	snap toward self
He caught the mosquito,	grab air with fist
He caught the flea,	repeat
He caught the minnow,	repeat
But he didn't catch me.	point to self and shake head "no"

(poem by Vachel Lindsay)

WHERE IS THUMBKIN?

(sung to the tune of "Frere Jacques")

Where is Thumbkin,	start with both hands behind back
Where is Thumbkin?	

Here I am,	bring out one hand, **show thumb**
Here I am.	bring out other hand, **show thumb**
"How are you today, sir?"	wiggle one thumb up **and down**
"Very well, I thank you!"	wiggle other thumb **in response**
Run away,	put one hand **behind back**
Run away.	put other hand **behind back**
Where is Pointer? . . .	**repeat sequence with index finger**
Where is Tall One? . . .	**repeat with middle finger**
Where is Ring Boy (/Girl)? . . .	**repeat with ring finger**
Where is Pinky? . . .	**repeat with pinky**

THE WHEELS ON THE BUS

The wheels on the bus go	
round and round,	**trace circles with index fingers**
Round and round, round and round;	
The wheels on the bus go	
round and round,	
All through the town.	
The people on the bus	
go up and down . . .	**bounce up and down**
The money on the bus goes	
clink, clank, clunk . . .	**mime putting coins into coin box**
The driver on the bus says,	
"Move on back . . . "	**point with index finger**
The children on the bus say,	
"Yak, yak, yak . . . "	**imitate mouth talking with hand**

The mothers on the bus say,
"Sh, sh, sh . . . "   **put finger to lips for "Sh" sounds**

The wipers on the bus go
swish, swish, swish . . .   **palms face out and "wipe" back and forth**

The horn on the bus goes
honk, honk, honk . . .   **use palm to honk imaginary horn**

The wheels on the bus go
round and round . . .   **repeat first verse**

(If it's too hard for the children to say "swish, swish, swish," substitute "wipe, wipe, wipe" or just enjoy stumbling over the words together!)

CHAPTER 10

Supplemental Bibliography

Since active verse is verbal and physical, and auditory and visual, it lends itself to a variety of presentation media. Records, tapes, and videos are very useful, especially for the adult who is just starting out and does not have a "live" teacher at hand. They are also fun for children as sing- and play-along activities. This list also offers a number of specialized sources for active verse in other languages.

FILMSTRIPS, FILMS, AND VIDEOS

Bower, "Bugs." *Rainy Day Finger-Play & Fun Songs*. [videocassette] N. Miami Beach, FL; Middlesex, NJ; IJE Inc.; New Age Video, 1988.

Brown, Marc. *Hand Rhymes*. [filmstrip (162 fr.) + cassette (21 min.) + teacher's guide] Random House/Miller-Brody, 1986.

———. *Marc Brown Does Hand Rhymes*. [videocassette (20 min.) + videogram] Newbery Award Records, Inc.; Hightstown, NJ: Random House Video, 1989.

———. *Play Rhymes*. [filmstrip (120 fr.) + cassette (11 min.) + guide] Westminster, MD.: Random House School Division, 1988.

———. *Play Rhymes*. [videocassette (11 min.)] Newbery Award Records, Inc.; Hightstown, NJ: Random House Video, 1989.

Clever, Mary. *Songs and Fingerplays for Little Ones, a Teaching Aid*. [videocassette (22 min.)] Clever Productions (P.O. Box 6038, Salinas, CA 93912-6038), 1988.

Hands Grow Up. [16 mm film (6 min.)] Chicago: Encyclopedia Britannica Educational Films, 1969.

Put the Kettle On. [16 mm film (11 min.)] Palisades Educational Films, 1976.

Put Your Hands on Top of Your Head. [16 mm film (4 min.)] Sutherland Learning Associates, 1973.

Rain, Rain, Go Away. [16 mm film (11 min.)] Palisades Educational Films, 1976.

Sharon, Lois and Bram's Elephant Show: Live in Your Living Room. [videocassette (30 min.)] Scarborough, Ont.: A & M Video, 1989.

Some Like It Cold. [16 mm (11 min.)] Palisades Educational Films, 1976.

FINGER PUPPET SETS

Monkey Mitt: Colored Seals; Monkey Mitt: Halloween; Monkey Mitt: Meet the Shapes; Monkey Mitt: Vowels. [finger puppet sets contain 1 mitt and 5 puppet characters] The Puppet Source [distributor]: Van Nuys, CA: Langtry Publications, 1980.

FOREIGN LANGUAGES

Ada, Alma Flor. *Asserr-in, Asserr-an: Folklore Infantil*. Donars Publications, 1979.

Bentzien, Karlheinz. *Ene Mene Tintefass, Rate, Rate, was is das?* Freiburg: Herder, 1978.

Bolton, Henry Carrington. *The Counting-Out Rhymes of Children: Their Antiquity, Origin, and Wide Distribution*. New York: D. Appleton and Co., 1888; Detroit: Singing Tree Press, Book Tower, 1969.

Charles, Ann P. *Fingerplays for Early Childhood in Cree and English*. La Rouge, Sask.: Holland-Dalby, 1988.

Chen, Shu-an. *Shou Chi Yao*. (2 v.) Hong Kong: Hsin Ya Erh T'ung, 1979.

Cseke, Miklos, Mariann Csekene Koszter, and Miklos Dolnik. *Jo Jatek: Az Ujj, A Kez, A Kar*. Budapest: Mora, 1984.

Griego, Margot C. *Tortillitas Para Mama, and Other Nursery Rhymes /Spanish and English*. New York: Henry Holt, 1981.

Jimenez, Emma Holguin, and Conchita Morales Puncel. *Para Chiquitines: Cancioncitas, Versitos y Juegos Meniques*. Glendale, CA: Bowmar Publishing Co., 1969.

Lehman, Patrician Jedrek. *At Babci's Knee: A Collection of Rhymes, Verses, Finger Plays, Games, etc.* [cassette + book] Manlius, NY: Talent-Ed, 1985.

Medina, Arturo. *Pinto Marana: Juegos Populares Infantiles.* (2 v.) Valladolid, Spain: Editorial Minon, 1987.

Meinerts, Eva. *Das ist der Daumen: Fingerspiele und Lieder fur die Kleinsten.* Munich: C. Bertelsmann, 1969.

Rimas y Cancioncitas Para Ninos. Houston, TX: Houston Public Library, 1984.

Sandoval, Ruben. *Games, Games, Games = Juegos, Juegos, Juegos: Chicano Children at Play: Games and Rhymes.* Garden City, NY: Doubleday, 1977.

Scott, Anne Leolani. *The Laughing Baby: Remembering Nursery Rhymes and Reasons.* South Hadley, MA: Gergin & Garvey, 1987.

Shou Chih Yu Hsi. Hong Kong: Hsin Feng Wen Hua Shih Yeh Kung Ssu, 1981.

Si Hinlalaki: Pag Kasama, Laging Okey. Quezon City, Philippines: Children's Communication Center, 1983.

Viggos Visor: Visor och Lekar for Sma Barn. Stockholm: Bonniers Junior Forlag, 1988.

Writers Program, New Mexico Staff. *The Spanish-American Song and Game Book.* AMS Press, Reprint of 1942 Edition.

PERIODICALS

Building Blocks Newspaper. Building Blocks, 38W567 Brindlewood; Elgin, IL 60123.

Kidstuff: A Treasury of Early Childhood Materials. Guidelines Press, 1307 S. Killian Drive; Lake Park, FL 33403.

RECORDS AND CASSETTES

Beall, Pamela Conn. *Wee Sing.* [cassette + songbook] Los Angeles: Price/Stern/Sloan, 1988.

Biscoe, Patsy. *Happy Birthday!* [record] Christchurch, New Zealand: Music World Ltd., 1978.

Brown, Marc Tolon. *Hand Rhymes; and Play Rhymes* [2 cassettes + 2 books + teacher's guide] Random House / Miller-Brody Productions, 1988.

Carfra, Pat. *Songs for Sleepyheads and Out-of-Beds!* [cassette] Victoria, B.C.; Scarborough, Ont.: LL Records; A & M Records, 1984.

Finger Play Songs and Games (v1 & v2) [record + teacher's manual] Great Neck, NY: Classroom Materials, 1969.

Gallina, Jill. *Hand Jivin.'* [record or cassette] Freeport, NY: Educational Activities, 1980.

Glazer, Tom. *Let's Sing Fingerplays.* [cassette] Mount Vernon, NY: CMS Records, Inc., 1970, 1979.

Hallum, Rosemary. *Fingerplay Fun!* [record or cassette] Freeport, NY: Educational Activities, 1979.

———. *Fingerplays and Footplays.* [cassette] Freeport, NY: Educational Activities, 1987.

Hammett, Carol. *Preschool Action Time Activities and Fingerplays.* [record] Long Branch, NJ: Kimbo Educational, 1988.

Lande, Kay. *Busy Fingers.* [record] Staten Island, NY: Kaneil Music Co., 1979.

Lehman, Patricia J., and Alicja Padzik. *At Babci's Knee.* [cassette] Manlius, NY: Talent-Ed, 1985.

Lyons Group. *The Backyard Show.* [cassette + book] Allen, TX: Lyons Group, 1988.

Matsushita, Marjorie. *Finger Games.* [record] Freeport, NY: Educational Activities, 1965.

McGrath, Bob. *The Baby Record.* [record] South Plainfield, NJ: Passport Records, marketed by Jem Records, 1984.

Michaels, Jenny. *Music for 2's & 3's: A Special Activity and Gamesong Album for the Very Young.* [cassette (44 min.)] Mount Vernon, NY: CMS Records, 1982.

Para Chiquitines. [record] Glendale, CA: Bowmar Publishing Co., 1969.

Pierce, June, comp. *The Romper Room Book of Finger Plays and Action Rhymes.* [record + book] New York: Golden Record, 1979.

Playtime Favorites. [record] [NJ]: Peter Pan, 1981.

Sing a Song of Action. [2 records + teacher's guide] Long Branch, NJ: Kimbo Educational; Mills Music [publisher], 1979.

Stafford, Anita F. *Funny Tunes.* [6 cassettes + teacher's guide + reproducible packet] Denton, TX: Human Technology Institute, 1985.

———. *Nature Tunes.* [6 cassettes + teacher's guide + reproducible packet] Denton, TX: Human Technology Institute, 1985.

Stallman, Lou. *Finger Games—Circle Games.* [record] Stallman Records, 1977.

Stewart, Georgiana Liccione. *Finger Play & Developmental Hand Exercises,* v1 & v2. [record or cassette] Long Branch, NJ: Kimbo Educational, 1977.

Weimer, Tonja Evetts. *Fingerplays & Action Chants: Animals,* v1. [cassette] Pittsburgh, PA: Pierce Evetts, 1986.

———. *Fingerplays & Action Chants: Family and Friends,* v2. [cassette] Pittsburgh, PA: Pierce Evetts, 1986.

Williams, Sarah. *Round and Round the Garden.* [cassette] New York: Oxford University Press, [1984].

PART 2

SUBJECT AND FIRST LINE INDEXES TO FINGERPLAYS AND ACTION RHYMES

HOW TO USE INDEXES

SUBJECT HEADINGS

Active verses have been indexed under about 600 subject headings and 550 cross-references. There are a large number of subdivided headings, such as "BIRDS—OWLS" or "COMMUNITY HELPERS—DOCTORS." This method of indexing was preferred where the more general category is a typical theme or curricular unit, or where it would be impossible to predict which specific categories (i.e., which species of birds, among all possible) might have verses about them. Please note that in all cases where subjects are subdivided, a cross-reference has been added from the more specific term to the more general.

USING THE SUBJECT INDEX

Sources for the rhymes are identified by a code, as shown in the following examples:

code for book   page number

Yo-La:18*

asterisk (*) indicates musical notation

pound sign (#) identifies verse as action rhyme

Fl-Ri9:48# D.S.L.

D.S.L. indicates Standard "Deaf Sign Language"

Each source code has two parts, a code for the book and the page number (if available). The author-title code comes first, followed by a colon (:) and the page number on which the verse can be found. As noted in the examples above, action rhymes are marked with a pound sign (#) for quick identification, and rhymes accompanied by a musical score are followed by an asterisk (*). Generally speaking, it is best to identify as many alternatives as possible and note their sources.

When codes have been noted, turn to the Key to the Sources Indexed on pages 250–52 to find full bibliographic information, including author, title, and imprint.

FIRST LINE VARIANTS

Every attempt has been made to gather all minor variants of an active verse under a single first line. In cases where the first few words of the variant are significantly different, a *See* reference, rather than a separate listing, has been provided. For example, "The Eensy Weensy Spider" is sometimes spelled "The Incy, Wincy Spider" or even "The Inky, Pinky 'Pider," but is essentially the same fingerplay. My method of assigning a dominant version was simply to count the number of occurrences of each version and to choose the most frequent as dominant.

In cases where different active verses had the same first lines (such as "Clap your hands"), I added a few more words of each verse to distinguish the two.

SUBJECT INDEX

SUBJECT INDEX

ACTIVITIES—PLAYING (continued)

This is the way these girls and boys
Fl-Ri9:92

Two cozy homes stand upon a hill
Ca-Li:23

What shall we do when we all go out?
Sh-Sh:20*#

ACTIVITIES—PLAYING BALL

Throw it, catch it
Ka-Fa:11#

ACTIVITIES—PRETENDING

I can be an airplane flying in the air
Sc-RhL:43#

I have ten fingers with which I like to play
Ca-Li:34

I like to pretend that I am a rose
Fl-Ri9:73
Pe-Fi:20
Sc-Rh:128

I'm a bear—hear me growl!
Fl-Ri9:73#

In a corner of the city is a high stone wall
Vo-Ac:20#

Let's pretend we're having fun
Wi-Ci:117
Wi-Ev:37

Oh, let's pretend! Yes, let's pretend
Ca-Li:60#

ACTIVITIES—RUNNING

Esther passed her sister. Was her sister running faster?
Do-Mo:95#

ACTIVITIES—SAWING

The carpenter's hammer goes rap, rap, rap
Fl-Ri9:43

"Pound, pound, pound," says the little hammer
Fl-Ri9:39#
Gr-Le:89

ACTIVITIES—SEWING

Mummy has scissors, snip, snip, snip
Ka-Le:18
Ma-Ga:37

Scissors, scissors, cut a dress
Ja-Fi:35

There was a tailor had a mouse
Gl-Ey:70*

This is mother's needle
El-FP:38
Pe-Fi:28

Under a toadstool, there sat a wee elf
Sc-Rh:99

Wind the bobbin up
Ma-Ga:122*

Wind, wind, wind the bobbin
Gr-Le:78

ACTIVITIES—SLEDDING

Here's a great big hill
Fl-Ri9:7
Gr-Le:23
Le-Fi:112
Wi-Ci:46

Snow piled up will make a hill, make a hill, make a hill
Cr-Fi:29

ACTIVITIES—SPINNING

Help me wind my ball of wool
Ma-Ga:32*#

ACTIVITIES—STRETCHING

Bend and stretch, reach for the stars
Fl-Ri9:7#
Wi-Ev:17#

Flop your arms, flop your feet
Mo-Pr:146#

Hands on hips; now turn around
Sc-RhL:43#

How tall am I?
Ka-Le:8#

I can make myself get smaller, smaller, smaller
Mo-Pr:148#

I can reach high, I can reach low
Pe-Fi:27#

I'm very, very tall
Cr-Fi:3

If you can stand on the tip of your toes
Sc-RhL:37#

Make yourself tall, raise your hands in the air
Sc-RhL:49#

Please stand on tiptoes
Sc-RhL:33#

Raise your arms away up high
Cr-Fi:108#

Reach for the ceiling
Fl-Ri9:78#
Ta-Ju:78#
Wi-Ev:12#

Stand up straight, now turn around
Ga-Bu2:9

Stretch, stretch away up high
Cr-Fi:9#
Fl-Ri9:86#
Sc-Rh:111#
Sc-RhL:47#

Stretch up high
Cr-Fi:3#

Tap your head and tap your shoe
Sc-RhL:39#

Touch your shoulders. Touch your knees
Ka-Le:8#, 10#

Under the spreading chest-nut-tree
De-Ch:57#

Up I stretch on tippy toe
Ma-Ga:142*#

ACTIVITIES—SWEEPING

With my little broom I sweep, sweep, sweep
Ka-Le:10
Ma-Ga:33*#
Tw-Rh

ACTIVITIES—SWIMMING

Five little ducks swimming in the lake
Ol-Fi

Five little fishes were swimming near the shore
Fl-Ri9:30

I can dive. I can swim.
Ka-Fa:15#

Junior the Frog jumped into the pond
Do-Mo:9#

ACTIVITIES—SWINGING

Hold on tightly as we go
Gr-Le:77

ACTIVITIES—WALKING

Can you walk on tip-toe
Ha-St:7#
Ma-Ga:139#
Or-Rh#
Tw-Rh#

Can you walk on two legs, two legs, two legs?
Ma-Ga:143*#

First he walks upon his toes
Ma-Ga:146*#

Five little ladies going for a walk
Ma-Ga:134

Here are little Jim and Jane going for a walk
De-Ch:32

Let's go walking in the snow
Fl-Ri9:101#
Wi-Ev:134

A little boy went walking one lovely summer day
De-Ch:9
Fl-Ri9:53
Le-Fi:59
Mo-Pr:150
Po-Fi:30*
Wi-Ci:113

A little girl went walking
Wi-Ev:187

Long legs, long legs, slowly stalking
Ma-Ga:144*#

Mommy and Daddy take big steps
Ga-Bu2:22

Mr. Duck went out to walk
Cr-Fi:62
De-Ch:23
Fl-Ri9:59
Pe-Fi:23
Sc-Rh:33
Wi-Ev:65

One morning the little Indian boy woke up
Ma-Ga:162#

Pennsylvania Pete had a pair of handy feet
Do-Mo:67#

Slowly, slowly walks my Granddad
Ma-Ga:172*#

Taking a walk was so much fun
El-Fi:17
El-Fi:19#

A tall thin man walking along
Ma-Ga:168*#

Walk very slowly, hands by your sides
Sc-RhL:31#

ACTIVITIES—WASHING

Dirty hands are such a fright
Cr-Fi:5

I brush my teeth sparkling clean—up and down, up and down
Ga-Bu2:20

AMPHIBIANS—TURTLES

I have two little turtles
Vo-Ac:22

Myrtle was a turtle with a polka-dotted shell
Do-Mo:44#

One baby turtle alone and new
Ro-Mi:17

One little turtle feeling so blue
Pe-Fi:31
Sc-Rh:94

One little turtle lived in a shell
Sc-RhL:176

There was a little turtle
Br-Fi:4
Fl-Ri9:58
Gl-Ey:76*
Gr-Le:33
Ha-Cl:24
Ka-Le:30
Le-Fi:67
Ta-Ju:81

This is my turtle
Fl-Ri9:65
Gr-Le:32
Ka-Le:30
Le-Fi:48
Pe-SP:93
Wi-Ev:84

The turtle just floats in water this deep
Co-Zo:45

ANATOMY *See:* **Body parts**

ANGELS

Chatter with the angels soon in the morning
Wi-Mu:28*#

Three little angels all dressed in white
Gl-Do:100*

ANGER *See:* Emotions—Anger

ANIMAL HABITATS

The fish lives in the brook
De-Ch:28
Gr-Le:81
Pe-Fi:28

How does a caterpillar go?
Ma-Ga:44*

Ten little fishes swim to and fro
De-Ch:29

ANIMAL SOUNDS

"Bow-wow," says the dog
Fl-Fi:24
Sh-Sh:49

Cats purr. Lions roar.
Ka-Le:7

The cows on the farm go, moo-oo, moo-oo
Cr-Fi:46

Detras de dona Pata
Fl-Ri9:82

The dog says bow wow
Ra-Tr

Dolly Duck has lost her quack
Do-Mo:34

I had a bird and the bird pleased me
Gl-Ey:10*

I had a little rooster and the rooster pleased me
Gl-Do:44*

I'm a bear—hear me growl!
Fl-Ri9:73#

I'm a cat—hear me Me-ow!
Ol-Fi

In a puddle sat a duck
Do-Mo:11

Odie Coyote, with ev-e-ry note, he
Do-Mo:46

One little mouse, squeakety, squeak!
Sc-RhL:163#
Sc-RhL:56

The pig goes oink, oink
Co-Zo:36#

When a mouse wants to speak
Ga-Bu2:60

With a "Cock-a-doodle-do, cock-a-doodle-do,"
Ga-Bu2:64

ANIMALS *See also:* **Amphibians; Fishes; Insects; Mammals; Marine Life; Reptiles; Spiders**

Around and around the merry-go-round the animals chase and glide
Vo-Ac:8#

At the zoo we saw a bear
Ro-Mi:20

Be one puppy trying to catch her tail
Sc-RhL:60#

"Bow-wow," says the dog
Fl-Fi:24
Sh-Sh:49

Can you hop like a rabbit?
Fl-Ri9:2#
Wi-Ev:186#

The circus is coming, the circus is coming!
Sc-RhL:140#

The cows on the farm go, moo-oo, moo-oo
Cr-Fi:46

Detras de dona Pata
Fl-Ri9:82

Five little bugs came out to play
Sc-RhL:59

Frogs jump. Caterpillars hump.
Fl-Ri9:51#

Here goes a turtle up the hill
Ra-Tr

Here is a nest for the robin [Mr. Bluebird]
Cr-Fi:31
De-Ch:35
Fl-Ri9:44
Le-Fi:74
Pe-SP:100
Sc-Rh:86
Wi-Ev:80

Here is a piggie, fat and round
Sc-RhL:165

Here is an ostrich straight and tall
Sc-RhL:189#

Here is hungry Piggie Snout
Fl-Ri9:67
Sc-Rh:27

Here is the ostrich straight and tall
Le-Fi:68
Ma-Ga:101
Wi-Ro:13

Hop like a bunny, run like a dog
Le-Fi:63

How does a caterpillar go?
Ma-Ga:44*

I can be an airplane flying in the air
Sc-RhL:43#

I had a bird and the bird pleased me
Gl-Ey:10*

I had a little rooster and the rooster pleased me
Gl-Do:44*

I have ten fingers; I have ten toes
Sc-RhL:29

I have ten fingers with which I like to play
Ca-Li:34

I heard a bee go buzzing by
El-FP:36

I saw one hungry little mouse
Sc-RhL:177

I see one kitten
Fl-Fi:10

I see three—one, two, three
Fl-Ri9:47
Sc-Rh:51

I'm a bear—hear me growl!
Fl-Ri9:73#

If I were a dog
Cr-Fi:46

If I were a little bird, high up in the sky
Ma-Ga:153*#

In the farmyard at the end of the day
Fl-Ri9:24

Into their hives the busy bees crawl
Sc-Rh:120

Let's see the monkeys climbing up a tree
Ma-Ga:102

A little brown rabbit one summer day
Sc-RhL:124

One big rhinoceros yawns politely with no fuss
Sc-RhL:137

One dog, two cats
Sc-RhL:167

One fat frog, sitting on a log
De-Ch:51

One little mouse, squeakety, squeak!
Sc-RhL:163#
Sc-RhL:56

One little rhinoceros
Sc-Rh:16

One, one. A farm is lots of fun
Sc-RhL:58

One, one; the zoo is lots of fun!
Sc-Rh:17
Sc-RhL:58
Wi-Ev:76

One, two, kittens that mew
Mo-Th:67

ANIMALS—CATS (continued)

Here is the little puppy
  Ca-Li:37
I am a cat, orange and white
  Ka-Fa:18#
I am the witch's cat
  Gr-Le:96
I have a cat
  Wi-Mu:182
I have a dog
  El-FP:50
I have a little kitten
  Cr-Fi:42
I have a little kitty
  El-FP:9
  Pe-Fi:27
I know a little pussy
  Ma-Ga:94*
I love little pussy, her coat is so warm
  Mo-Th:69
I saw two cats, two, two, two
  Sc-RhL:174
I'm just a lonely little kitten
  Fl-Ri9:58
In a Dapper Chapeau and a matching cravat
  Do-Mo:29#
A kitten is fast asleep under the chair
  Cr-Fi:42
A kitten is hiding under a chair
  Gr-Le:32
A kitten stretches and makes herself long
  Sc-RhL:49#
Kitty, kitty, kitty, kitty
  Gr-Le:42
A little mouse hid in a hole
  Le-Fi:66
A little mouse went creeping, creeping, creeping into the house
  Mo-Pr:145
Little Robin Redbreast sat upon a tree
  De-Ch:41
"Misery, misery!" moaned the rat
  Do-Mo:30#
A mouse chased a pussy cat
  Do-Mo:23

A mouse heard a pussy cat moaning one day
  Do-Mo:19
Mr. Kelly got a cat
  Do-Mo:27
Mr. O'Malley lives back in the alley
  Do-Mo:18#
Mrs. Kitty, nice and fat
  Fl-Ri9:62
  Po-Fi:58*
Mrs. O'Malley, you old alley cat!
  Do-Mo:18#
My cat has blue eyes and the softest of paws
  Mc-Fi:9
Old Lady Brady has twenty-four cats
  Do-Mo:123
One kitten with a furry tail
  Sc-Rh:30
One little cat and two little cats
  Cr-Fi:42
One little kitten, one
  Sc-Rh:32
One little kitten, two little kittens
  Sc-RhL:54
One little, two little, three little kittens
  Fl-Ri9:56
One, two, three, four; these little pussy cats came to my door
  Cr-Fi:91
  Ma-Ga:152
Pretty little pussy cat
  Ma-Ga:158*
Pussy cat, pussy cat, where have you been?
  Mo-Th:21
Soft kitty, warm kitty
  Fl-Ri9:82
  Wi-Ev:60, 71
Softly, softly creeps the pussy cat
  Cr-Fi:42
Someone call the cat!
  Do-Mo:22#
Tabitha Cat has a bell on her hat
  Do-Mo:22
There once were two cats of Kilkenny
  Ca-Li:29

There were five little kittens
  Pu-ABC:16
This is a pussy, sleek and gray
  Cr-Fi:42
This is my book; it will open wide
  Br-Ha:5
This little kitten said, "I smell a mouse."
  De-Ch:53
  Sc-Rh:33
This little pussy drinks her milk
  Cr-Fi:42
Three fat kittens were playing in the sun
  Sc-RhL:173#
Three mice went into a hole to spin
  Mo-Th:68
Two little kittens found a ball of yarn
  El-FP:46
Two little puppy dogs lying in a heap
  De-Ch:34
When all of my cats are asleep in the sun
  Sc-RhL:175

ANIMALS—CHIPMUNKS

The chipmunk, so cute, darts over a pole
  Co-Zo:15#
Five furry chipmunks we simply adore
  Sc-RhL:182
A little striped chipmunk
  Sc-Rh:96

ANIMALS—COWS

The cow bows her head and gives a big moo
  Co-Zo:16#
Cow, cow, her tail goes swish
  Pu-ABC:12
Did you feed my cow?
  Fl-Ri9:18
Here is the barn so big, don't you see?
  Fl-Ri9:16
  Wi-Ev:65
This cow has a nose that is soft as silk
  Sc-RhL:163
This little cow eats grass
  Ca-Li:23
  Cr-Fi:43
  De-Ch:46

Fl-Ri9:92
  Gr-Le:38
  La-Ri:22
  Ma-Ga:15
  Ma-Re:14
  Mo-Th:17
  Pa-Gi:66
  Ra-Tr
  Sc-La:100
  Sc-Rh:103
This mooly cow switched her tail all day
  De-Ch:47
This old cow will give no milk!
  Do-Mo:15#
"Well now," said Alice the Cow
  Do-Mo:15

ANIMALS—COYOTES

Odie Coyote, with ev-e-ry note, he
  Do-Mo:46

ANIMALS—DEER

The doe with white spots
  Co-Zo:17
A handsome deer
  Do-Mo:12#

ANIMALS—DOGS

Call the puppy
  Fl-Ri9:74
  Wi-Ev:71
The dog barks bow wow
  Co-Zo:18#
Five little puppies gnawed on a bone
  Sc-RhL:53
Five little puppies in the yard
  Ga-Bu2:58
Five little puppies were playing in the sun
  Ka-Le:40
  Sc-Rh:36
Five little puppy dogs
  Fl-Ri9:74
Fleagle the Beagle
  Do-Mo:32
Here is a roof on top of a house
  Sc-RhL:162
Here is the little puppy
  Ca-Li:37
I had a little poodle
  Fl-Ri9:45
I have a dog
  El-FP:50
I have a little puppy, he loves to romp with me
  Ka-Fa:18

ANIMALS—HORSES (continued)

Oh, the horse stood around with his foot on the ground
Gl-Do:37*#

Old Ned has two ears that go flop, flop, flop
De-Ch:33

One little pony so full of fun
Sc-RhL:169#

The pony is small but strong as can be
Co-Zo:36#

Ride a cock horse to Banbury Cross
Ma-Ga:16
Ma-Re:20
Mo-Ca:16
Mo-Th:77
Sc-La:70
Sh-Sh:33
Tw-Rh
Yo-La:24*

Ride with me on the merry-go-round
Fl-Ri9:79
Sc-Rh:15
Wi-Ev:195

Shoe a little horse
Ma-Ga:20
Ra-Tr
Sc-La:94
Sh-Sh:82

Shoe the colt
Yo-La:28

Shoe the pony, shoe
Mo-Th:32

Ten galloping horses galloping through the town
Ha-Cl:10
Ma-Ga:132

Ten little ponies in a meadow green
Fl-Ri9:91

This is the way the ladies ride
Ca-Li:47
Fo-Sa:100
Ma-Re:21
Mo-Th:81
Po-Da:61
Sh-Sh:15
We-Fi2:15
Yo-La:26*

This is the way they ride in the city
Ma-Re:21

Trot, trot to Boston, trot trot to Linn
Mo-Th:78
Sc-La:76
Yo-La:28

Trot, trot, trot
Ma-Ga:17*
Sc-La:71*

ANIMALS—KANGAROOS

The brown kangaroo is very funny
Cr-Fi:79

If you should meet outside a zoo
Do-Mo:49#

Jump, jump, jump goes the big kangaroo
Fl-Ri9:5
Le-Fi:71
Mc-Fi:41

Jump-jump! Kangaroo Brown
Ma-Ga:105*#

The kangaroo's jump is bigger than mine
Co-Zo:26#

One hoppity-loppity kangaroo
Sc-RhL:143#

Said the king kangaroo, "What can I do?"
Cr-Fi:79

ANIMALS—KOALA BEARS

The koala hangs by claws on the tree
Co-Zo:26

ANIMALS—LAMBS

The lambs, all woolly
Co-Zo:27

One little lamb put on records
Kn-Ti

This is the meadow where all the long day
De-Ch:7
Po-Fi:14*
Sc-RhL:164
Wi-Ev:65

ANIMALS—LEOPARDS

The leopard cat's eyes have very good sight
Co-Zo:28#

ANIMALS—LIONS

Lily's a lady, a lioness lady
Do-Mo:36

The lions in the cave
Co-Zo:28#

ANIMALS—LLAMAS

Five strong llamas travel in a bevy
Mc-Fi:38

The llama looks down
Co-Zo:29

ANIMALS—MICE

Aunt Matilda baked a cake
Do-Mo:85

Creep, little mouse, creep, creep, creep
Ka-Le:38

Creep, little mousie, come along to me
Ma-Ga:152

Creep mouse, creep mouse, all around town
Wi-Pl

Dormy, dormy, dor-mouse, sleeps in his little house
Mo-Th:35

Five little mice came out to play
Fl-Ri9:30
Ma-Ga:131
We-Fi1:19

Five little mice looked for something to eat
Sc-RhL:169

Five little mice on the pantry floor
Br-Fi:16
De-Ch:8
Po-Fi:42*
Ro-Mi:39
Sc-Rh:89

Five little mice ran around the house
Sc-RhL:177

Five little mice ran out to the farm
Sc-RhL:169#

Five little mice went out to play
Ka-Le:38
Sc-RhL:53

Five little mice were hungry as could be
Cr-Fi:47

Here's a little mousie peeking through a hole
Ha-Cl:13

Hickory, dickory, dock
Be-We:13*
Ca-Li:21
Cr-Fi:95
De-Ch:39
Gl-Ey:32*
Gl-Mu:61*
Gr-Le:31
Ha-St:15
Ka-Fa:19

Ke-Hi
La-Ri:40
Mo-Pr:152
Mo-Th:22
Pe-SP:94
Po-Da:29
Sh-Sh:94
Wi-Ro:26
Yo-La:8*

I think I'll build a little house
Fl-Fi:34

I'm glad I'm not a mouse or bat!
Do-Mo:19

In a Dapper Chapeau and a matching cravat
Do-Mo:29#

In a tiny little hole
Ga-Bu2:61

A little mouse came out to take a peek
Sc-Rh:39

A little mouse hid in a hole
Le-Fi:66

A little mouse went creeping, creeping, creeping into the house
Mo-Pr:145

A mouse chased a pussy cat
Do-Mo:23

A mouse heard a pussy cat moaning one day
Do-Mo:19

The mouse in the box runs right up to me
Co-Zo:31

A mouse lived in a little hole
Ha-Cl:14
Ko-Da:31
Ma-Ga:152

Mousie comes a-creeping, creeping
Wi-Ro:15

Mrs. Kitty, nice and fat
Fl-Ri9:62
Po-Fi:58*

Now I'll tell you a story, and this story is new
Ma-Ga:164

On Lavender Avenue Leander lives
Do-Mo:118#

Once there lived a quiet mouse
Co-Ee:18

ANIMALS—SQUIRRELS (continued)

These are the brown leaves fluttering down
Fl-Ri9:83
Wi-Ci:21

This is the squirrel that lives in a tree
Sc-Rh:89
Sc-RhL:183

This little squirrel said, "Let's run and play."
De-Ch:52
Gr-Le:35

Two little squirrels were scampering through the wood
Sc-RhL:55

Whirlee, twirlee, look at the squirrel
Ka-Fa:11

Whisky, frisky, hoppity hop
Br-Fi:25
De-Ch:24
Fl-Ri9:83
Ka-Le:34
Ma-Ga:90
Pe-SP:101

ANIMALS—TIGERS

Don't shake hands with tigers, 'cause
Do-Mo:36

One little tiger had a tantrum
Kn-Ti

This little tiger is very wild
Cr-Fi:77

The tiger wants meat to put in his jaws
Co-Zo:44

Walk, walk, softly—slow—This is the way the tigers go
Sc-RhL:137#

ANIMALS—WALLABIES

Raleigh the Wallaby
Do-Mo:49#

ANIMALS—WEASELS

All around the cobbler's bench
Be-We:41*
Gl-Ey:64*
Ma-Re:68
Sc-La:86
Sh-Sh:47*

ANIMALS—WOLVES

The wolf gives a howl that's scary to hear
Co-Zo:46#

ANIMALS—WORMS

The earthworm can crawl like this—very slow
Co-Zo:20

Inchworm, inchworm moves so slow
Le-Fi:61

Ooey, Gooey was a worm
Wi-Mu:184

A tiny, tiny worm
Ma-Ga:41

Under a stone where the earth was firm
Ma-Ga:149

Wiggly, wiggly, wiggly worm
Ka-Le:41

ANIMALS—YAKS

The yak has long hair under it I'll hide
Co-Zo:47#

ANIMALS—ZEBRAS

The zebra's a horse with stripes black and white
Co-Zo:47#

ANTEATERS *See:* Animals—Anteaters

ANTELOPES *See:* Animals—Antelopes

ANTS *See:* Insects—Ants

APPLES *See:* Food—Apples

APRIL FOOL'S DAY *See:* Holidays—April Fool's Day

ARABIC *See:* Foreign Languages—Arabic

ARMS *See:* Body Parts—Arms

ART

Hands are blue. Hands are green
Ka-Fa:13

Here's a piece of modelling clay
Co-Tw:19

"I am going to work," said Mister Thumb
Sc-RhL:24

ARTISTS *See:* Community Helpers—Artists

ASTRONAUTS *See:* Community Helpers—Astronauts

ASTRONOMY *See:* Earth; Moon; Solar System; Space; Stars; Sun

AUSTRALIA *See:* Countries—Australia

AUTOMOBILES

Auto, auto may I have a ride?
Fl-Ri9:4
Gr-Le:24

Click-clack, click-clack
Cr-Fi:85

Everybody out the door! All aboard for Singapore!
Do-Mo:64#

Here comes a policeman riding on a bicycle
Ma-Ga:71*

Here is a car, shiny and bright
Cr-Fi:86

I had a little engine
Ma-Ga:70*

Let's drive our auto down the street
Gr-Le:25

Let's ride the bumps
Fl-Ri9:79

Open the car door
Fl-Ri9:40

This is our family car
Wi-Ev:190

This old car is out of gas!
Do-Mo:80#

Uncle Henry bought a car
Do-Mo:98#

"Vroom!" says the engine
Cr-Fi:86

The windshield wipers on our car are busy in the rain
Gr-Le:24

AUTUMN *See:* Seasons—Autumn

AVIATION *See:* Airplanes

BABIES

Baby's eyes, Baby's nose
Ja-Fi:1

Baby's fingers, baby's nose
Sc-RhL:28

Five fingers on this hand
Fl-Ri9:26
Gr-Le:11
Ka-Le:13
Ma-Re:15
Pe-SP:94
Sc-La:107
Wi-Ev:41

Five little babies say, "Goodnight."
Ro-Mi:42
Sc-Rh:79

Here are the lady's knives and forks
Be-We:11
De-Ch:3
Fl-Ri9:62
Fo-Sa:103
Le-Fi:81

Ma-Ga:36
Mo-Th:54
Pe-Fi:18
Pe-SP:100
Sc-Rh:80
Sh-Sh:72
We-Fi2:11
Wi-Mu:155
Yo-La:11

Here is Baby's tousled head
Cr-Fi:108
Sc-Rh:79

Here's a ball for baby
Cr-Fi:18
De-Ch:10
Fl-Ri9:1
La-Ri:18
Le-Fi:86
Ma-Ga:51
Ma-Re:18
Mo-Th:53
Sc-La:114
Wi-He
Wi-Ro:39
Ya-Fi

I see one kitten
Fl-Fi:10

I started my life
Cr-Fi:11

If a baby blew a bubble
Do-Mo:114

John Brown's baby had a cold upon its chest
Ta-Ju:100*
Yo-La:22*

Laughing Baby Johnny knows
Ja-Fi:5

Little baby in the cradle
Ka-Fa:15

Little fingers, little toes
Ka-Fa:14

Mommy rocks the baby and tells him not to wiggle
Ga-Bu2:15

One little baby rocking in a tree
Br-Ha:6
La-Ri:26
Ro-Mi:41

Our little baby has ten toes
El-FP:29

Rock-a-bye baby, on the treetop
De-Ch:1
Gr-Le:52
Mo-Th:36
Wi-Pl

BEDTIME *(continued)*

There were ten in the bed
Gl-Do:96*
Po-Da:68
Sc-RhL:33#
Sh-Sh:88*

They call me Little Sleepy Head
Cr-Fi:7

This is baby ready for a nap
Ra-Tr
Wi-Ci:110

This is little sleepy head
Ga-Bu2:19

This little boy is just going to bed
Cr-Fi:7
De-Ch:31
Fl-Ri9:35
Le-Fi:42
Pa-Gi:16
Pe-Fi:11
Sc-Rh:80

This little fellow is ready for bed
Gr-Le:101

This little girl is ready for bed
Pe-Fi:21

Two little hands go clap, clap, clap
De-Ch:65#
Wi-Ci:11#
Wi-Ev:12#

We are baby robins in a nest
Sc-RhL:46#

When cold winds blow
Fl-Ri9:103
Wi-Ci:46
Wi-Ev:130

When the hands on the clock show it is time for bed
El-Fi:21
El-Fi:23#

BEES *See:* **Insects—Bees**

BEETLES *See:* **Insects—Beetles**

BEHAVIOR

Five little children went to school
Co-Tw:28

Oliver Brown was sent to bed
Do-Mo:118

One little tiger had a tantrum
Kn-Ti

Pollyanna ate a banana
Do-Mo:91#

Pollyanna hid in a box
Do-Mo:103#

Sometimes my hands are naughty
Cr-Fi:107

BEHAVIOR—FIGHTING

There once were two cats of Kilkenny
Ca-Li:29

Two bad boys one cold stormy night
Fl-Fi:38

Two little monkeys fighting in bed
Br-Ha:9
Cr-Fi:77

BEHAVIOR—LISTENING

I try to listen and obey
Cr-Fi:13

Only one can talk at a time
Ka-Le:46

There was an old owl who lived in an oak
Cr-Fi:95

BEHAVIOR—MANNERS

I have to learn to be polite
Cr-Fi:4

I watch my table manners
Cr-Fi:13

Let's play the Please and Thank you game!
Vo-Ac:18#

My hands say thank you
Fl-Ri9:64#

Never go to lunch with a dinosaur
Wi-Ev:127

Pitty Pat and Tippy Toe
Mc-Fi:22

Some special words we need to know
Cr-Fi:4

Someone is knocking, one, two, three
Sc-Rh:86

Three little pigs and a little pig more
Ma-Ga:80

BEHAVIOR—OBEDIENCE

Five little ducks went out to play
Fl-Ri9:75
Ka-Le:29
Sc-RhL:166

I try to listen and obey
Cr-Fi:13

I wish I were an octopus
Fl-Fi:25#

Merrie, Merrie, pick some berries
Do-Mo:89

Said the big mother duck to the little baby duck, "Be careful what you eat!"
Ka-Le:42

Soy chiquita, soy bonita
Gr-To

This is the way these girls and boys
Fl-Ri9:92

Two lips to smile the whole day through
Fl-Ri9:97

BELLS *See:* **Musical Instruments—Bells**

BELONGINGS

Here are the lady's knives and forks
Be-We:11
Co-Ee:29
De-Ch:3
Fl-Ri9:62
Fo-Sa:103
Le-Fi:81
Ma-Ga:36
Mo-Th:54
Pe-Fi:18
Pe-SP:100
Sc-Rh:80
Sh-Sh:72
We-Fi2:11
Wi-Mu:155
Yo-La:11

I have a ball, it is big and round
El-FP:60

A purse is a very nice thing to be
Sc-RhL:24

This is my book; it will open wide
Br-Ha:5

BENDING *See:* **Activities—Stretching**

BICYCLES

Here comes a policeman riding on a bicycle
Ma-Ga:71*

I rode my bike down Downer's hill
Do-Mo:99

Listen! Listen! Close your eyes!
Do-Mo:113

My bicycle is shiny and new
Cr-Fi:87

My little tricycle has wheels so fine
Cr-Fi:85

My tricycle has three big wheels
Ga-Bu2:45

One wheel, two wheels on the ground
Fl-Ri9:63
Sc-Rh:130

Two wheels, three wheels on the ground
Wi-Ev:29

BIRDS

The animals that can fly are birds
Cr-Fi:41

As I was walking down a lane I saw an apple tree
Mc-Fi:47

A birdie had a dirty beak
Do-Mo:34

Birdies flying to and fro
De-Ch:5

Chai aar (Bird comes)
Sc-La:49

Climbing up the apple tree
Do-Mo:59#

Dos pajaritos muy sentados
Fl-Ri9:19

Five baby birds in a nest in a tree
Cr-Fi:30

Five little birds sitting in the sun
Cr-Fi:41

Five little birds without any home
Cr-Fi:90
Fl-Ri9:27

Five little Jinny birds, hopping by my door
Ro-Mi:25

Fly, fly, fly away
Ov-Le:38

Go to sleep now, little bird
El-Fi:15
El-Fi:16#

Here are two tall telegraph poles
Cr-Fi:31
De-Ch:26

Here is a tall, straight tree
Pe-Fi:13

BIRDS—DUCKS (continued)

Dolly Duck has lost her quack
Do-Mo:34

Dos patitos se encontraron
Sc-RhL:146

The duck swims along, her babies behind
Co-Zo:19

Five little ducks swimming in the lake
Ol-Fi

Five little ducks that I once knew
Br-Ha:22
Co-Ee:10*
Fl-Ri9:75
Ka-Le:29
Wi-Ci:83
Wi-Ev:69

Five little ducks went in for a swim
Gr-Le:36
Sc-RhL:168

Five little ducks went out to play
Fl-Ri9:75
Ka-Le:29
Sc-RhL:166

Five little ducks went swimming one day
Gl-Ey:26*
Ma-Ga:136*
Ro-Mi:30
We-Fi1:29

Five yellow ducklings, dash, dash, dash!
Sc-RhL:165#

Have you seen the little ducks
Ma-Ga:81*#
Po-Da:50#

I'm a duck—I quack, quack, quack
Le-Fi:65

If I could have a windmill
Sh-Sh:62#

In a puddle sat a duck
Do-Mo:11

The mallard swims fast
Co-Zo:29#

Mr. Duck went out to walk
Cr-Fi:62
De-Ch:23
Fl-Ri9:59
Pe-Fi:23
Sc-Rh:33
Wi-Ev:65

Nine ducks nine walked out in a line
Ha-Ni

Now I'm up. Now I'm down
Cr-Fi:14#

"Quack, quack," goes his bill
Pu-ABC:12#

Said the big mother duck to the little baby duck, "Be careful what you eat!"
Ka-Le:42

Six little ducks without a shoe
De-Ch:66#

Ten fat ducks came waddling down the lane
Sc-RhL:161#

Ten fuzzy ducklings
Sc-Rh:27

Ten little ducklings
Sc-Rh:27

There's a little white duck sitting in the water
Gl-Ey:46*

Two ducks met
Sc-RhL:146

Two little ducks that I once knew
Gr-Le:71

Waddle, waddle, waddle duck
De-Ch:62#

BIRDS—EAGLES

The eagle stands proud
Co-Zo:19

BIRDS—FLAMINGOS

Be like the flamingo
Le-Fi:68#

Ringo Flamingo, a bird with a flare
Do-Mo:52#

BIRDS—GEESE

The Canadian geese flying in a V
Co-Zo:14

The goose moves his beak to make a big hiss
Co-Zo:24

Here's a string of wild geese
Mo-Th:55

Mr. Gander and Mrs. Goose
Sc-Rh:28

One little gosling hatched today
Sc-RhL:166#

One little gosling, yellow and new
Sc-Rh:28

BIRDS—GROUSES

A mother grouse and her four young chicks were eating all they could
Mc-Fi:46

BIRDS—MAGPIES

I saw eight magpies in a tree
Ba-On

BIRDS—OSTRICHES

The ostrich can whirl
Co-Zo:32#

BIRDS—OWLS

Here's a wide-eyed owl
Cr-Fi:60

A little boy went into a barn
De-Ch:31

One little owl played violin
Kn-Ti

The owl on the branch has eyes big and bright
Co-Zo:33

An owl sat alone on the branch of a tree
Ca-Li:37
Cr-Fi:60
De-Ch:57
Fl-Ri9:71
Pe-St:96
Sc-Rh:101

A sad old owl sat in a tree
El-FP:14

Said Mr. Owl sitting in the tree
Cr-Fi:4There was a big owl who lived up in a tree
Pu-ABC:17

There was an old owl who lived in an oak
Cr-Fi:95

This little owl has great, round eyes
Sc-RhL:70#

The wise old owl
Fl-Fi:11

BIRDS—PARAKEETS

The parakeet walks along a straight line
Co-Zo:33#

BIRDS—PARROTS

The parrot will say "Hello, what's your name?"
Co-Zo:34

You can hear the jingle-jangle of the parrots in the jungle
Mc-Fi:38

BIRDS—PEACOCKS

The peacock struts by, his plumes in array
Co-Zo:34#

BIRDS—PELICANS

The pelican's pouch is filled to the brim
Co-Zo:35#

BIRDS—PENGUINS

One royal penguin
Ca-Li:24

The penguin scratches himself in the sun
Co-Zo:35#

A penguin, when he goes somewhere
Do-Mo:45#

The penguins are marching, one by one
Mc-Fi:37#

Three little penguins dressed in white and black
Sc-RhL:102#

BIRDS—PIGEONS

My pigeon house I open wide
Cr-Fi:31#
Ma-Ga:157*#

Ten little pigeons sat in a line
Cr-Fi:30

There were two little pigeons
Fl-Fi:33

Three little pigeons sitting on a fence
Sc-Rh:34

BIRDS—ROBINS

Five little robins in a sycamore tree
Sc-Rh:95

Five little robins lived in a tree
Cr-Fi:30
Fl-Ri9:32
Ro-Mi:27

Little Robin Redbreast sat upon a rail
Ca-Li:45#
De-Ch:40#
Gr-Le:37#
Ka-Fa:20#
Pe-SP:104
Sc-Rh:103#

Little Robin Redbreast sat upon a tree
De-Ch:41

BLACKBIRDS *See:* Birds—
Blackbirds
BLOCKS *See:* Toys—Blocks
BOARS *See:* Animals—Boars
BOATS
*Five little sailors putting
out to sea*
Sc-Rh:23
Sc-RhL:154
*Here is the sea, the wavy
sea*
Ma-Ga:112
*I go to the seashore every
day*
Fl-Fi:21
*I love to row in my big
blue boat*
Ma-Ga:111*#
*Michael, row the boat
ashore*
Gl-Do:74*
*Mommy's arms are a
little boat*
Wi-Pl
Row, row, row your boat
Gr-Le:26#
Ha-St:13#
La-Ri:9#
Ma-Ga:116*#
Po-Da:45#
Sh-Sh:83*#
Wi-Mu:56*#
Wi-Ro:19#
Some boats are big
Wi-Ev:190
*Ten little tug boats out in
the bay*
Mc-Fi:15
*Ten little tugboats are
out on the sea*
Sc-RhL:193
*This is the boat, the
golden boat*
Ma-Ga:114
*This is the way, all the
long day*
Gr-Le:26
*Two little boats are on
the sea*
Ma-Ga:115*#
BODY PARTS
*Baby's fingers, baby's
nose*
Sc-RhL:28
Beat, beat with your feet
Wi-Ev:208
*Clap, clap, clap your
hands, clap your hands
together*
Ka-Le:1#

*Clap your hands, clap
your hands*
Gr-Le:10#
Ka-Le:6#
Ta-Ju:74#
Wi-Ro:45#
*Clap your hands, touch
your toes*
Be-We:45*#
*Come follow, follow,
follow*
Gr-Le:9
*Fee, Fi, Fo, Fum,
Measure my arm,
measure my nose*
Mo-Pr:147#
Five fingers on this hand
Fl-Ri9:26
Gr-Le:11
Ka-Le:13
Ma-Re:15
Pe-SP:94
Sc-La:107
Wi-Ev:41
*Grandmother Thee Thee
That*
Sc-Rh:81
Hand on myself
Cr-Fi:9#
*Head and shoulders
baby, 1-2-3*
Sh-Rh:18*#
*Head and shoulders,
knees and toes*
Be-We:46*#
Fl-Ri9:39#
Fo-Sa:46#
Gl-Do:30*#
Le-Fi:16#
Ma-Ga:125#
Ma-Re:48#
Mo-Pr:145#
Po-Da:63#
Pu-ABC:14#
Sc-RhL:36#
Sh-Sh:12#
Ta-Wi:13#
Wi-Ev:17#
Here are my ears
Fl-Ri9:41
Ma-Re:48
*Here are my eyes, my
hair, my nose*
Ka-Le:1
*Here are my fingers and
here is my nose*
Sc-RhL:33#
Here we go Looby Loo
Fo-Sa:18*#
Gl-Do:33*#
Ko-Da:20*#
Mo-Pr:164#

*I have five fingers on
each hand*
Cr-Fi:92
Fl-Ri9:21
Ka-Le:13
Mc-Fi:9
*I have ten little fingers
and ten little toes*
Cr-Fi:92
De-Ch:65#
Ka-Le:12
Pa-Gi:29
*I have two eyes to see
with*
Fl-Ri9:46#
Ka-Le:4#
I point to myself
Gl-Do:50*#
*I'm all full of hinges and
everything bends*
Ka-Le:5
*If a bird you want to
hear*
Ka-Le:4
Little fingers, little toes
Ka-Fa:14
*Match the fingers on
your hands*
Sc-RhL:31#
Musun-de (Make a fist)
Sc-La:54
My eyes can see
Fl-Fi:48
Ta-Ju:79
My hands can clap
Ka-Le:13
*My hands upon my head
I place*
Co-Ee:52*
Cr-Fi:3#
De-Ch:38#
Fl-Ri9:59#
Gr-Le:12#
Ka-Le:44#
Le-Fi:25#
Ma-Re:49#
Wi-Mu:158#
Wi-Ro:27#
*My neck has hinges that
move it so*
Sc-RhL:46#
Oliver Twist, twist, twist
Sh-Rh:15#
On my face I have a nose
Pe-Fi:17
*One, one. One head rests
on a pillow in a bed*
Sc-Rh:50

*Our heads, our shoul-
ders, our knees, our
toes*
Ka-Le:7#
*Our little baby has ten
toes*
El-FP:29
A pair of ears to listen
Vo-Ac:11#
*A pair of eyes here on my
face*
Sc-RhL:57#
*Put my hand on my self,
self!*
Wi-Mu:18*
Put your finger in the air
Gl-Ey:66*#
Ta-Ju:108*
*Robot, robot, do as I
command!*
Le-Fi:85#
See my eyes
Cr-Fi:14#
Shake your head
Ka-Fa:9#
*She waded in the water
and she got her feet all
wet*
Gl-Do:93*#
*Stand up straight, now
turn around*
Ga-Bu2:9
*Ten little fingers, ten
little toes*
Ka-Le:1
*Tete, epaules, genoux et
pieds*
Sh-Sh:12#
*To draw a person in the
air*
Cr-Fi:10
*Touch your left knee,
then your right*
Sc-RhL:36#
*Touch your nose; touch
your chin*
Fl-Ri9:96#
Ka-Le:1#, 6#
Ma-Re:14#
Sc-Rh:113#
*Touch your shoulders.
Touch your knees*
Ka-Le:8#, 10#
*Two lips to smile the
whole day through*
Fl-Ri9:97
*Two little hands go clap,
clap, clap*
De-Ch:65#
Wi-Ci:11#
Wi-Ev:12#

BODY PARTS—FINGERS *(continued)*

Mr. Thumb is strong and small
  Sc-RhL:25

Mr. Thumbkin Left and Mr. Thumbkin Right
  Sc-Rh:115

My fingers are so sleepy
  Br-Fi:30
  Gr-Le:43
  Ka-Le:45
  Ka-Le:5

Oh! where are the merry, merry Little Men
  Po-Fi:10*

One—a stick
  Ka-Le:13

One finger is short and fat!
  Vo-Ac:12

One finger, one thumb
  Gl-Do:83*#
  Gl-Mu:64*#

One finger, two fingers
  Sc-RhL:27

One little finger wiggles in the sun
  Sc-RhL:26

One, two, three, four, five in a row
  Cr-Fi:91
  Fl-Ri9:11
  Sc-Rh:53

One, two, three, four, five in a row, are fingers on the right you know
  Sc-RhL:25

Open, shut them
  Co-Ee:12*
  Cr-Fi:8
  De-Ch:29
  Fl-Ri9:70
  Gr-Le:79
  Ka-Le:5
  Le-Fi:20
  Ma-Re:18
  Mo-Pr:145
  Pe-Fi:12
  Pe-SP:95
  Sc-Rh:110

Pal'chik-malchik (Little boy-finger)
  Sc-La:108

Rickety, tickety, look at me
  Be-We:31

See my fingers walking, walking
  Ma-Ga:121

Si pregunta alguien
  Fl-Ri9:74

Son mi dedos
  Fl-Ri9:17

Tan, tan
  Fl-Ri9:87

Ten little finger men
  Sc-Rh:111

Ten little finger soldiers standing in a row, up the hill—down the hill, marching they will go
  Fl-Ri9:89
  Wi-Ci:106

Ten little gentlemen standing in a row
  Ma-Ga:125

Ten little men standing in a row
  Gr-Le:70

Ten little men standing straight
  Wi-Ro:16

Ten little soldiers stand up straight
  Ka-Le:24
  Ma-Ga:127

They do so, so, so
  Gr-Le:4

This is little Tommy Thumb
  De-Ch:49
  Gr-Le:4

This is the man that broke the barn
  Mo-Th:18

This is the way my fingers stand
  Fl-Ri9:9
  Gr-Le:3

This is Thomasina Thumb
  Co-Tw:26

This one's old, this one's young
  De-Ch:49

Thumb bold
  Mo-Th:18

Thumb man says he'll dance
  Cr-Fi:2
  Gr-Le:8
  Le-Fi:17

Thumbkin, Pointer, Middleman big
  Gr-Le:3

Tommy Thumb, Tommy Thumb
  Ma-Ga:169*
  Wi-Ro:35

Two fat gentlemen met in a lane
  Co-Ee:48
  Ha-Cl:8
  Ma-Ga:126
  Po-Da:42
  Wi-Ro:22

Upon each hand a little band
  De-Ch:50

Wake up, little fingers, the morning has come
  Fl-Ri9:101
  Sc-Rh:109

What can your fingers do for you?
  Sc-RhL:28

Where is thumbkin? Where is thumbkin?
  Be-We:17*
  Br-Fi:10
  Cr-Fi:2
  De-Ch:25
  Fl-Ri9:104
  Gl-Ey:88*
  Gl-Mu:66*
  Gr-Le:6
  Ka-Le:9
  Le-Fi:28
  Pe-SP:106*
  Sc-La:110*
  Sh-Sh:19*
  We-Fi2:33
  Yo-La:18*

Wiggle, wiggle, fingers
  Fl-Ri9:105

BODY PARTS—HANDS

Abranlas, cierrenlas
  Fl-Ri9:1

Clap, clap, clap! One, two, three
  Ka-Le:14

Clap, clap, clap your hands, As slowly as you can
  Be-We:12
  Br-Fi:23
  Ma-Re:68

Clap, clap hands, one, two, three
  Wi-Ro:10

Clap with me, one, two, three
  Le-Fi:26

Clap your hands 1, 2, 3
  Ma-Re:18

Con esta mano derecha
  Fl-Ri9:2

Con las manos
  Sc-Rh:44
  Sc-RhL:149

Dirty hands are such a fright
  Cr-Fi:5

Dos manos tengo para trabajar
  Fl-Ri9:60

Hands can lift a box or chair
  Ka-Le:9#

Hands on shoulders, hands on knees
  Fl-Ri9:10#
  Gr-Le:13#
  Ka-Fa:17#
  Ka-Le:6#
  Le-Fi:23#
  Ma-Re:49#
  Mo-Pr:147#
  Pe-Fi:12#
  Pe-SP:93#
  Ta-Ju:76

I can knock with my two hands
  Ma-Ga:119*

I can wiggle my fingers just like this
  Ga-Bu2:10

I have two hands, a left and a right
  Ga-Bu2:12

I squeeze a lemon just like this
  Mc-Fi:18

Let your hands so loudly clap, clap, clap
  Ma-Ga:123#
  Ma-Re:69#

My hand scoops things up
  Sc-RhL:30

My hands are such good helpers
  Ka-Le:13
  Pe-Fi:30

Now my hands are on my head
  De-Ch:32

Open your fingers
  Sc-RhL:37#

Right hand, left hand, put them on my head
  De-Ch:15
  Fl-Ri9:80

Roll, roll, roll your hands
  Fl-Ri9:34#
  Le-Fi:24#
  Ma-Re:68#
  Pe-Fi:19
  Sc-Rh:110#

COMMUNITY HELPERS— DENTISTS (continued)

If I were Mr. Dentist
Ka-Le:26

When I try to count my teeth
Sc-RhL:157

COMMUNITY HELPERS— DOCTORS

I'd like to be a doctor
Ka-Le:27

My father said, "It's doctor day."
Wi-Ev:159

COMMUNITY HELPERS— FARMERS

The farmer plants the seeds
Fl-Ri9:24#

First the farmer plows the ground
Fl-Ri9:24#

First the farmer sows his seeds
De-Ch:62#

Five little farmers woke up with the sun
De-Ch:22
Fl-Ri9:29
Wi-Ev:168

Old Farmer Giles, he went seven miles
Ma-Re:20
Mo-Th:44

When a farmer's day is done
Ka-Le:25

COMMUNITY HELPERS— FIREFIGHTERS

Clang, clang goes the fire truck
Cr-Fi:81

Do you know the fireman, the fireman, the fireman?
Ka-Le:23

The fire station's empty
Wi-Ev:177

Firman the Fireman! I need you!
Do-Mo:73#

Five little firemen sit very still
Fl-Ri9:29
Ka-Le:21
Ro-Mi:45
Sc-Rh:25

Five little firemen standing in a row
Ka-Le:23

Four busy firefighters could not retire
Sc-RhL:157

I'd like to be a fireman with a ladder and a hose
Ka-Le:22

I'm a little fireman, waterproofed from head to toe
Ka-Le:22

Ten brave firemen sleeping in a row
Cr-Fi:81#
De-Ch:60#
Pa-Gi:37

Ten little firemen sleeping in a row
Co-Ee:6
Gr-Le:53
Ka-Le:21
Le-Fi:79

This is a fire engine
El-FP:73

COMMUNITY HELPERS— GROCERS

If I were a grocery man
Pe-Fi:14

COMMUNITY HELPERS— LIBRARIANS

The librarian helps the visitors find
Wi-Ev:155

COMMUNITY HELPERS—MAIL CARRIERS

The police officer stands so tall and straight
Wi-Ev:155

Rat-a-tat-tat, rat-a-tat-tat
Ka-Le:27

This is the way the postman comes walking down the street
El-Fi:37
El-Fi:39#

COMMUNITY HELPERS—MILK DELIVERERS

Five little milkmen got up with the sun
El-Fi:11#
El-Fi:9
Pe-Fi:9

COMMUNITY HELPERS— MOUNTIES

A mother grouse and her four young chicks were eating all they could
Mc-Fi:46

COMMUNITY HELPERS—ORGAN GRINDERS

The organ man, the organ man
De-Ch:60#

COMMUNITY HELPERS—PILOTS

I hear the jet tearing through the sky
Ka-Fa:12

COMMUNITY HELPERS—POLICE OFFICERS

Five police officers standing by a door
Ro-Mi:46

Five strong policemen standing by a store
Ka-Le:23
Sc-Rh:25

Here comes a policeman riding on a bicycle
Ma-Ga:71*

I'm the policeman, yes I am
Ka-Le:24

Mr. Policeman wears a silver badge
Cr-Fi:81

The police officer stands so tall and straight
Wi-Ev:155

Police officers are helpers
Le-Fi:79

The policeman walks with heavy tread
Ka-Le:24#
Ma-Ga:161#

Standing on the corner in his uniform of blue
Vo-Ac:23

The traffic policeman holds up his hand
Cr-Fi:81

We are brave police officers standing in a row
Pa-Gi:62#

COMMUNITY HELPERS—POSTMEN *See:* Community Helpers—Mail Carriers

COMMUNITY HELPERS—SAILORS

Five little sailors putting out to sea
Sc-Rh:23
Sc-RhL:154

Have you ever, ever, ever in your long-legged life
Co-Pl:53#
Gl-Do:72*#

Old Davy Jones had one little sailor
Mo-Th:60

A sailor went to sea, sea, sea
Wi-Mu:58*#

Ten jolly sailor boys dressed in blue
Cr-Fi:84

Ten little sailors standing in a row
Sc-Rh:23

COMMUNITY HELPERS— SHEPHERDS

Little Boy Blue, come blow your horn
Cr-Fi:96
De-Ch:41
Sc-Rh:106

COMMUNITY HELPERS— SHOEMAKERS

Cobbler, cobbler, mend my shoe
Ba-On
Co-Pl:93#
Fl-Ri9:15
Fo-Sa:100
Gl-Ey:69*
Gr-Le:18
Ma-Ga:174*
Mo-Th:100
Sh-Sh:46
Tw-Rh
Wi-Mu:28*
Wi-Ro:28

The cobbler, the cobbler, makes my shoes
De-Ch:30

Crooked heels and scuffy toes
Wi-Ci:15

I am a cobbler
Fl-Ri9:44
Ha-Cl:7

There's a cobbler down our street
Ma-Ga:161#

COMMUNITY HELPERS— STREET VENDORS

The man with the cart has a little red bell
Fl-Fi:30

COMMUNITY HELPERS—WINDOW WIPERS

Up goes the ladder to the side of the wall
Sc-RhL:151

COMMUNITY HELPERS— WOODCUTTERS

¡Aserrín!
Sc-Rh:43

Chip-chop, chip-chop, Chipper, Chopper Joe
Ma-Ga:173*#

La da ju (We push the big saw)
Sc-La:89

**CONCEPTS—OPEN AND
SHUT** *(continued)*
 De-Ch:20
 Gl-Ey:72*
 Gl-Mu:60*
 Gr-Le:3
 Ka-Le:2
 Le-Fi:18
 Pa-Gi:58
 Pe-SP:102
 Sh-Sh:18
 Ta-Wi:100
 Wi-Ev:12
 Wi-Ro:18
*I shut the door and
 locked it tight*
 Gr-Le:81
Open, shut them
 Co-Ee:12*
 Cr-Fi:8
 De-Ch:29
 Fl-Ri9:70
 Gr-Le:79
 Ka-Le:5
 Le-Fi:20
 Ma-Re:18
 Mo-Pr:145
 Pe-Fi:12
 Pe-SP:95
 Sc-Rh:110
*This is EAST, and this
 is WEST*
 Cr-Fi:7
CONCEPTS—PAIRS
A pair of ears to listen
 Vo-Ac:11#
CONCEPTS—QUANTITY
A few is not so many
 Do-Mo:122
**CONCEPTS—RIGHT AND
LEFT**
Bow, bow, bow Belinda
 Gl-Do:8*#
*The clock ticks, the clock
 tocks*
 Sc-RhL:42#
*Close my eyes, shut them
 tight*
 Cr-Fi:91
*Five finger people, left
 and right*
 Sc-RhL:23
Here we go Looby Loo
 Fo-Sa:18*#
 Gl-Do:33*#
 Ko-Da:20*#
 Mo-Pr:164#
*I can raise my right
 hand*
 Sc-RhL:34#

*I have two hands, a left
 and a right*
 Ga-Bu2:12
*Left to the window, right
 to the door*
 Le-Fi:15
*Mittens for the snow
 time*
 Sc-RhL:99
*Mr. Thumbkin Left and
 Mr. Thumbkin Right*
 Sc-Rh:115
Point to the right of me
 Gr-Le:11
 Sc-La:114
*Pointing left, the waxing
 moon*
 De-Ch:21
*Right hand, left hand,
 put them on my head*
 De-Ch:15
 Fl-Ri9:80
Stand on right foot
 Cr-Fi:8#
*Ten fat turkeys standing
 in a row*
 De-Ch:75
*Ten little Indian boys
 standing in a row*
 Gr-Le:90
 Ma-Ga:126
*This is high, and this is
 low*
 De-Ch:25
*This is my right foot;
 this is my left*
 Le-Fi:27#
*This is my right hand, I
 raise it up high*
 Be-We:32
 Co-Ee:27
 Cr-Fi:8
 De-Ch:36
 Fl-Ri9:91
 Gr-Le:9
 Le-Fi:14
 Mo-Pr:147
 Pe-Fi:13
 Pe-SP:97
*Touch your left knee,
 then your right*
 Sc-RhL:36#
*Two hands have I to
 hold in sight*
 De-Ch:20
*Two little hands, so
 clean and bright*
 Le-Fi:27
*Up to the ceiling, down
 to the floor*
 Co-Ee:26

*Watch me jump, watch
 me hop*
 Ka-Fa:9#
*You put your right foot
 in*
 Co-Pl:44#
 Gl-Do:35*#
**CONCEPTS—SAME AND DIF-
FERENT**
*Match the fingers on
 your hands*
 Sc-RhL:31#
CONCEPTS—SHAPES
*A basketball is round
 and hard*
 Cr-Fi:91
*Close my eyes, shut them
 tight*
 Cr-Fi:91
*Draw a circle, draw a
 circle*
 Fl-Ri9:19
 Sc-Rh:113
 Wi-Ev:46
*Draw a square, draw a
 square*
 Wi-Ev:46
*Draw a triangle, draw a
 triangle*
 Wi-Ev:46
Earth is round
 De-Ch:57#
*Here is a big, round
 doughnut*
 Sc-RhL:34#
*Here is a doughnut, big
 and fat*
 Pa-Gi:46
Here's a ball of yarn
 Pu-ABC:21
*Jack Frost paid me a
 visit*
 Sc-Rh:121
*Mysterious boxes under
 the tree*
 Sc-RhL:91#
*One straight finger
 makes a line*
 Cr-Fi:90
*Wheels, wheels, wheels
 go around, around*
 Sc-RhL:191
CONCEPTS—SIZE
Baby's shoes
 Wi-Ro:24
A great big ball
 Co-Ee:23
 Gr-Le:64
*Here I have a new
 balloon*
 Sc-Rh:132

*Here is a giant who is
 tall, tall, tall*
 Sc-Rh:98#
How tall am I?
 Ka-Le:8#
*I can make myself get
 smaller, smaller,
 smaller*
 Mo-Pr:148#
I can stand away up tall
 Cr-Fi:4#
I'm a great, tall pine tree
 Sc-RhL:34#
*I'm rather short—not tall
 at all*
 Do-Mo:70#
I'm stretching very tall
 Be-We:38*#
I'm very, very tall
 Cr-Fi:3
*Make yourself as tall as
 a house*
 Sc-RhL:32
*Sometimes I am very,
 very small*
 Ka-Le:11#
*There once was a man
 who was tall, tall, tall*
 Ca-Li:54#
*There was a great big
 stilt man*
 Gr-Le:50
This is a little balloon
 Pa-Gi:84
*This is narrow. This is
 wide.*
 Le-Fi:21#
*We are brave police
 officers standing in a
 row*
 Pa-Gi:62#
**CONCEPTS—SPATIAL RELA-
TIONSHIPS**
Hands up, hands down
 Ka-Fa:18
*Over and over and over
 and over*
 Ka-Fa:8
*Over and under, in front
 of, beside*
 Do-Mo:114#
CONCEPTS—SPEED
*The earthworm can
 crawl like this—very
 slow*
 Co-Zo:20
*I can make myself get
 smaller, smaller,
 smaller*
 Mo-Pr:148#

Inchworm, inchworm moves so slow
Le-Fi:61
Roll your hands, roll your hands
De-Ch:32
Slowly, slowly, very slowly
Ma-Ga:13
Sc-La:96
The snail is so slow, the snail is so slow
Gr-Le:37
CONCEPTS—TIME
DING! DONG! Tell me, did the school bell ring?
Do-Mo:100
CONCEPTS—UP AND DOWN
Heels and toes
Sc-RhL:32#
Here we go up, up, up
Fl-Ri9:42#
Gr-Le:76#
Ra-Tr
I'm a funny little puppet clown
Fl-Ri9:48#
Sc-Rh:132#
Sc-RhL:47#
Jack-in-the-box jumps up to see
Pu-ABC:15
Left to the window, right to the door
Le-Fi:15
The noble Duke of York
De-Ch:2
Fo-Sa:37*
Gr-Le:53
Pe-SP:109*
Sc-La:82
Wi-Mu:185*
Yo-La:6*
Now I'm up. Now I'm down
Cr-Fi:14#
Point to the right of me
Gr-Le:11
Sc-La:114
Roly poly, roly poly, up, up, up
Ma-Ga:121
The seesaw goes up
Gr-Le:78
Tall shop in the town
Ma-Ga:66*#
Po-Da:51#
Wi-Ro:33#
There was a funny little man
Cr-Fi:18
De-Ch:23

Fl-Ri9:35
Sc-Rh:112
This is EAST, and this is WEST
Cr-Fi:7
This is high, and this is low
De-Ch:25
This is narrow. This is wide.
Le-Fi:21#
Up a step, and up a step, and up a step and up
Gr-Le:79
Up and down, and up and down
Fl-Ri9:88
Up the steps we will go
Gr-Le:78
Up to the ceiling, down to the floor
Co-Ee:26
Up, up, very slowly
Sc-RhL:50#
CONGO *See:* **Countries—Congo**
CONSTRUCTION *See:* **Activities—Building**
COOKIES *See:* **Food—Baked Goods**
COOKING *See:* **Activities—Cooking**
COUNTING OUT RHYMES
Bee, bee bumblebee
Gr-Le:73
Eeny, meeny, miney, mo
Ba-On
Gr-Le:73
One potato, two potato
De-Ch:49
Fo-Sa:198
Oa-Ch:15
One silk, two silk, three silk, zan
Gr-Le:74
One, two, three, four, five, six, seven
Ba-On
One, two, three, four, five, six, seven, all good children go to Devon
Gr-Le:71
One, two, three, four, Mary at the cottage door
Gr-Le:74
COUNTING RHYMES *See also:* **Concepts—Number Concepts; Subtraction Rhymes**
Ant, ant, under a plant
Sc-RhL:189

The ants go marching one by one
Gl-Do:3*
Baby, baby, little as can be
Sc-Rh:46
Sc-RhL:150
Be one puppy trying to catch her tail
Sc-RhL:60#
Bee, bee bumblebee
Gr-Le:73
Bimbo, bimbo, piccolino
Sc-Rh:46
Sc-RhL:149
"The bunnies now must go to bed"
De-Ch:46
The clouds are dark and in our town
Sc-RhL:100
Cluck, cluck, cluck, cluck, good morning, Mrs. Hen
Ka-Le:31
"Come my bunnies, it's time for bed."
Cr-Fi:70
Fl-Ri9:94
Coming downstairs, well, what do we see?
Sc-RhL:93
Dive, little goldfish one
Sc-RhL:57
Eins, zwei, Polizei
Sc-Rh:47
Sc-RhL:150
The first girl / boy said, "It's a very dark sky."
Sc-RhL:75
The first hat is mine. I wear it for fun.
Sc-RhL:156
The first little frog stubbed her toe
Sc-RhL:180*#
The first little ghost floated by the store
Sc-RhL:71
The first little kite that was sailing by
Sc-RhL:114#
The first little pig danced a merry, merry jig
De-Ch:52
The first little pig squeals and squeals
Sc-RhL:164#

The first little rabbit went hop, hop, hop
Sc-RhL:120#
The first one is little and quite fat
Sc-RhL:23
The first umbrella is red
Sc-RhL:111
The first yellow pumpkin said, "Oh, my!"
Sc-RhL:81
Five baby birds in a nest in a tree
Cr-Fi:30
Five big turkeys sitting on the gate
Ro-Mi:67
Five birthday candles; wish there were more
Ca-Li:25
Five bright stars on a Christmas Night
Ro-Mi:71
Sc-Rh:65
Five busy honey bees were resting in the sun
Sc-RhL:183
Five Christmas stockings were hanging in a row
Sc-RhL:92
Five flying saucer men were sitting on the stars
Sc-RhL:195
Five green goblins danced on Halloween
Sc-RhL:73
Five little ants in an ant hill
Gr-Le:63
Five little astronauts ready for outer space
Ka-Le:25
Five little bears were sitting on the ground
Sc-RhL:144#
Five little birds sitting in the sun
Cr-Fi:41
Five little boys with five dirty faces
Fl-Fi:46
Five little bugs came out to play
Sc-RhL:59
Five little bunnies are such dears!
Sc-RhL:182
Five little busy bees on a day so sunny
Sc-Rh:97

COUNTING RHYMES (continued)

Five little candles on a birthday cake
Co-Tw:10

Five little children on Thanksgiving Day
Ro-Mi:66

Five little cubby bears tumbling on the ground
Le-Fi:64

Five little ducks swimming in the lake
Ol-Fi

Five little ducks went in for a swim
Gr-Le:36
Sc-RhL:168

Five little elves met one autumn day
Sc-RhL:196

Five little farmers woke up with the sun
De-Ch:22
Fl-Ri9:29
Wi-Ev:168

Five little firemen sit very still
Fl-Ri9:29
Ka-Le:21
Ro-Mi:45
Sc-Rh:25

Five little firemen standing in a row
Ka-Le:23

Five little froggies sitting on a lily pad
Cr-Fi:44

Five little froggies standing in a row
We-Fi1:15

Five little kites flying high in the sky
Ro-Mi:55

Five little kittens on a summer day
Ka-Le:39

Five little ladies going for a walk
Ma-Ga:134

Five little leaves in the autumn breeze
Ro-Mi:61

Five little mice looked for something to eat
Sc-RhL:169

Five little mice ran out to the farm
Sc-RhL:169#

Five little mice were hungry as could be
Cr-Fi:47

Five little pigs were eating corn
Sc-RhL:52

Five little Pilgrims on Thanksgiving Day
De-Ch:76
Sc-Rh:62

Five little Pixies decided to have tea
Sc-RhL:194

Five little polliwogs swam near the shore
Sc-RhL:179

Five little ponies all dapple gray
Fl-Ri9:31

Five little pussy cats
Sc-Rh:31

Five little reindeer standing in a row
De-Ch:81

Five little sailors putting out to sea
Sc-Rh:23
Sc-RhL:154

Five little snowmen, happy and gay
El-Fi:41
El-Fi:42#
Fl-Ri9:32
Ol-Fi
Pe-Fi:25

Five little squirrels sitting in a tree
Cr-Fi:43
De-Ch:47
Fl-Ri9:83
Gr-Le:63
Ka-Le:34
Ma-Ga:91
Pe-SP:101
Ro-Mi:15
Sc-Rh:88
Sc-RhL:182

Five little tadpoles went for a swim
Sc-RhL:179

Five little valentines were having a race
Fl-Ri9:100
Wi-Ci:68

Five merry bells at Christmas time
De-Ch:81

Five oranges growing on a tree
Wi-Ev:96

Five strong llamas travel in a bevy
Mc-Fi:38

Five yellow pumpkins side by side
Sc-RhL:80

Flowers tall, flowers small
Pe-Fi:9
Sc-Rh:127

Four big jack o'lanterns made a funny sight
Sc-RhL:73

Four busy firefighters could not retire
Sc-RhL:157

Four little raindrops sat upon a cloud
Sc-RhL:108

Four scarlet berries
Ma-Ga:96

Four young frogs were swimming in a pond
Sc-RhL:179

Fred had a fishbowl
Sc-Rh:53
Wi-Ev:71

Go to rest while I count one: One
Sc-RhL:48

A great big ball
Gr-Le:64

Here is a big, round, bouncy ball
Fl-Ri9:93
Sc-Rh:131

Here is a round, sweet lollipop
Sc-RhL:35#

Here is a tall, straight tree
Pe-Fi:13

Here is my little garden bed
Sc-RhL:122

Here is the beehive, where are the bees?
Be-We:11
Br-Ha:14
Ca-Li:19
Cr-Fi:36
Cr-Fi:46
De-Ch:50
Fl-Ri9:6
Ha-Cl:12
Ka-Le:41
Le-Fi:55
Ma-Ga:43
Ma-Re:19
Ov-Le:32
Pe-Fi:13
Po-Fi:54*
Ro-Mi:23

Wi-Ci:113
Wi-Ro:34

Here's a ball, and here's a ball
Cr-Fi:91
De-Ch:12
Fl-Ri9:42
Le-Fi:87
Pe-Fi:21
Sc-Rh:131
We-Fi2:19
Wi-Ci:51
Wi-Ev:46, 182

How many eggs can your basket hold?
Cr-Fi:72

How many people live at your house?
Ha-Cl:29

I can count. Want to see?
Cr-Fi:92

I have five fingers on each hand
Cr-Fi:92
Fl-Ri9:21
Ka-Le:13
Mc-Fi:9

I have two hands, a left and a right
Ga-Bu2:12

I like one friendly puppy because
Sc-RhL:170*

I put on my raincoat
Sc-RhL:110

I saw a little lady bug flying in the air
Ro-Mi:36

I saw eight magpies in a tree
Ba-On

I saw one hungry little mouse
Sc-RhL:177

I saw two cats, two, two, two
Sc-RhL:174

I see three - one, two, three
Fl-Ri9:47
Sc-Rh:51

If you can stand on the tip of your toes
Sc-RhL:37#

In my little garden with a lovely view
Sc-RhL:113

"It is time for my piggies to go to bed"
Ro-Mi:47
Sc-Rh:34

GAMES—TICKLING RHYMES (continued)

Sc-La:100
Sc-Rh:103

This little piggy went to market
Br-Fi:8
Cr-Fi:45
De-Ch:45
Fl-Ri9:92
Fo-Sa:100
Gl-Ey:80*
Gl-Mu:62*
Gr-Le:32
Ha-Th
He-Th
Ke-Th
Ko-Da:28
La-Ri:10
Le-Fi:32
Ma-Ga:13
Mo-Ca:12
Mo-Th:15
Oa-Ch:7
Po-Da:48
Ra-Tr
Sc-La:93
Sh-Sh:45
St-Th
Tw-Rh
We-Fi1:13
Wi-Ev:65
Wi-He
Wi-Mu:186
Wi-Pl
Wi-Ro:36
Yo-La:21

Tickly, tickly, in your hand
Mo-Th:26

Toc, toc, toc, petit pouce, leve-toi!
Sc-La:98

Tut pen' (Here's a stump)
Sc-La:95

Une poule sur un mur
Sc-La:102

"Who's that tickling my back?" said the wall.
Sc-La:96
Th-Ca

GAMES—TOE COUNTING RHYMES

Bye, baby bunting
De-Ch:55
Gl-Do:12*
Gl-Mu:68*

The first little pig danced a merry, merry jig
De-Ch:52

Harry Whistle
Oa-Ch:7

"Let us go to the wood," said this pig
Mo-Th:17

Little pig, Pillimore
Or-Rh

One little beaver worked hard as can be
Kn-Ti

One little bunny grew carrots
Kn-Ti

One little grizzly grew grumpy
Kn-Ti

One little hippo brought a blanket
Kn-Ti

One little kid took a limo
Kn-Ti

One little lamb put on records
Kn-Ti

One little monkey laughed loudly
Kn-Ti

One little owl played violin
Kn-Ti

One little panda read music
Kn-Ti

One little piggy wore leggings
Kn-Ti

One little possum ate a parsnip
Kn-Ti

One little skunk smelled of violets
Kn-Ti

One little tiger had a tantrum
Kn-Ti

See-saw, Margery Daw, the hen flew over the malt house
Mo-Th:16

This bunny's ears are tall and pink
De-Ch:54

This is mother; this is father
De-Ch:48
Gr-Le:41
Ka-Le:17
We-Fi2:13

This little bear has a soft fur suit
De-Ch:48

This little cow eats grass
Ca-Li:23
Cr-Fi:43
De-Ch:46
Fl-Ri9:92
Gr-Le:38
La-Ri:22
Ma-Ga:15
Ma-Re:14
Mo-Th:17
Pa-Gi:66
Ra-Tr
Sc-La:100
Sc-Rh:103

This little froggy broke his toe
De-Ch:46

This little kitten said, "I smell a mouse."
De-Ch:53
Sc-Rh:33

This little pig had a rub-a-dub
Co-Pl:102
Sh-Sh:45

This little piggy went to market
Br-Fi:8
Cr-Fi:45
De-Ch:45
Fl-Ri9:92
Fo-Sa:100
Gl-Ey:80*
Gl-Mu:62*
Gr-Le:32
Ha-Th
He-Th
Ke-Th
Ko-Da:28
La-Ri:10
Le-Fi:32
Ma-Ga:13
Mo-Ca:12
Mo-Th:15
Oa-Ch:7
Po-Da:48
Ra-Tr
Sc-La:93
Sh-Sh:45
St-Th
Tw-Rh
We-Fi1:13
Wi-Ev:65
Wi-He
Wi-Mu:186
Wi-Pl
Wi-Ro:36
Yo-La:21

This little puppy broke his toe
Ka-Le:40

This little puppy said, "Let's go out to play"
De-Ch:46

This mooly cow switched her tail all day
De-Ch:47

This one's old, This one's young
De-Ch:49

This pig got into the barn
Mo-Th:16

Wee Wiggie, Poke Piggie
Ma-Re:14
Mo-Th:17

Whose little pigs are these, these, these?
Mo-Th:16

GARDENING *See:* **Activities—Gardening**

GARDENS

Come see my small garden, how sweetly they grow
De-Ch:12

Five little peas in a pea-pod pressed
Ma-Ga:43
Po-Da:32
Sh-Sh:73
Th-Ca

Flowers in the garden
El-FP:64

Here is my little garden bed
Sc-RhL:122

I dig the ground and plant the seeds
Pe-SP:103

I have a special piece of land
Wi-Ev:88

I work in my garden
Ja-Fi:45

In my little garden with a lovely view
Sc-RhL:113

Old Tom Tomato, like a red ball
Ma-Ga:45

See the blue and yellow blossoms
Fl-Ri9:63
Wi-Ci:99

This is my garden
Cr-Fi:35
Fl-Ri9:64
Gr-Le:46

HAWAII *See:* United States—
Hawaii
HEAD *See:* Body Parts—Head
HEARING *See:* Body Parts—
Ears; Senses—Hearing
HELPING
The dishes need washing
Wi-Ci:103
Wi-Ev:37
*He runs for Daddy's
slippers*
Fl-Ri9:55
*I have two hands to work
with*
Cr-Fi:14#
HELPING (continued)
*I help my family by
sweeping the floor*
Wi-Ev:164
I help my mother
Fl-Ri9:40
*I like to help my dad a
lot*
Wi-Ci:110
*I make my bed, I get the
broom*
Ka-Fa:13#
*This is the way I pound
a nail*
Cr-Fi:80
*This little girl does
nothing but play*
Gr-Le:82
HENS *See:* Birds—Chickens
HIBERNATION
*The bear crawls out of
his cave*
Mo-Pr:155#
*Here is a cave, inside is
a bear*
De-Ch:37
*Here is the cave and here
is the bear*
Fl-Fi:18
*Into their hives the busy
bees crawl*
Sc-Rh:120
*A little ground hog lived
cozy and snug*
Fl-Fi:32
HIDE AND SEEK *See:* Games—
Hide and Seek
HIGH AND LOW *See:* Con-
cepts—High and Low
HINDI *See:* Foreign Lan-
guages—Hindi
HIPPOPOTAMUS *See:* Ani-
mals—Hippopotamus
HISTORY—GOLD RUSH
*In the mountains was a
man*
Do-Mo:66#

HISTORY—PILGRIMS
*Five little Pilgrims on
Thanksgiving Day*
De-Ch:76
Sc-Rh:62
*Pilgrim children did not
play*
Sc-RhL:80
*The Pilgrims sailed the
stormy sea*
Cr-Fi:63
*To see what he could see,
a little Indian climbed
a tree*
Le-Fi:99
Wake up, little Pilgrims
Cr-Fi:64
Sc-Rh:63
*When the pilgrims came
to this new land*
Cr-Fi:64
HOBOS
*Herbert the Hobo, he
hopped on a train*
Do-Mo:79#
HOLIDAYS—APRIL FOOL'S
DAY
*The big round sun in an
April sky*
Fl-Ri9:3
Wi-Ci:88
*Little bears have three
feet*
Fl-Ri9:3
Mc-Fi:31
Wi-Ci:88
HOLIDAYS—CHANUKAH *See:*
Holidays—Hanukkah
HOLIDAYS—CHRISTMAS *See
also:* Mythical Creatures—
Elves; Animals—Reindeer
1, 2, 3, 4, 5 little reindeer
Pe-Fi:17
Sc-Rh:69
Sc-RhL:88
Alisa was a little elf
Cr-Fi:68#
*A ball, a book, and a
tooting horn*
Mc-Fi:27
Wi-Ci:51
Bells at Christmas ring
El-FP:68
*Christmas is a-coming,
the geese are getting fat*
Gr-Le:92
Th-Ca
*Christmas is a happy
time*
De-Ch:80
*Coming downstairs,
well, what do we see?*
Sc-RhL:93

*Down the chimney dear
Santa Claus crept*
Gr-Le:92
Le-Fi:104
*Eight little reindeer
playing in the snow*
Cr-Fi:67
*Eight tiny reindeer
pawing in the snow*
Sc-Rh:68
*The first little reindeer
went to the market to
buy some Christmas
trees*
Cr-Fi:67
First we mix and mix it
Ov-Le:24
*Five bright stars on a
Christmas Night*
Ro-Mi:71
Sc-Rh:65
*Five children dreamed of
Christmas day*
Sc-Rh:64
*Five Christmas stockings
were hanging in a row*
Sc-RhL:92
*Five Christmas trees in a
forest green*
Ro-Mi:71
*Five little bells, hanging
in a row*
Cr-Fi:67
El-Fi:71
El-Fi:72#
Fl-Ri9:27
Le-Fi:102
Pe-Fi:16
Wi-Ci:51
*Five little bells ring with
a chime*
Ro-Mi:69
*Five little reindeer
standing in a row*
De-Ch:81
*Five merry bells at
Christmas time*
De-Ch:81
*Five red stockings heard
the fire roar*
Ro-Mi:72
*Hear the merry Christ-
mas bells*
Gr-Le:92
*Here is a chimney deep
and wide*
Cr-Fi:66
*Here is a great tall
Christmas tree*
Sc-RhL:88

*Here is a window in a
Christmas Toy Shop*
Sc-Rh:66
*Here is Bobby's Christ-
mas tree*
Cr-Fi:67
Here is old Santa
De-Ch:79
*Here is the chimney.
Here is the top*
Be-We:59
Gr-Le:94
Le-Fi:102
Ov-Le:24
Pe-Fi:9
Wi-Ci:51
Here is the toy shop
De-Ch:81
*Here's Santa, jolly and
gay*
Cr-Fi:66
Here's the chimney
De-Ch:79
Fl-Ri9:81
*Here stands a lovely
Christmas tree*
Gr-Le:93
I know so many secrets
Sc-RhL:91#
I'm a Christmas tree
Cr-Fi:67#
*I'm a Fairy Doll on the
Christmas Tree*
Ma-Ga:54*
*I'm a little Christmas
bell*
Cr-Fi:67
*I'm a little Christmas
tree*
Le-Fi:105
*If I could find old Santa,
I'd ask him for a ride*
Cr-Fi:66
*In Santa's workshop far
away*
Sc-Rh:67
*Isn't it the strangest
thing that Santa is so
shy?*
Pe-Fi:15
*Mary rocks Him gently,
so*
Vo-Ac:24
*My Christmas tree is
nice and bright*
El-FP:34
Pe-Fi:15
*Mysterious boxes under
the tree*
Sc-RhL:91#

HOLIDAYS—HALLOWEEN
(continued)
Five little goblins on a Halloween night
Br-Ha:12
Fl-Ri9:30
Ro-Mi:63
Sc-Rh:61
Five little pumpkins sitting on a gate
Cr-Fi:61
De-Ch:75
Gl-Ey:40*
Gr-Le:95
Le-Fi:94
Mo-Pr:151
Pa-Gi:80
Ro-Mi:64
Wi-Ci:32
Five little pumpkins were standing in a row
El-Fi:78
El-Fi:79#
Five little witches on Halloween night
Ro-Mi:65
Sc-RhL:75#
Four big jack o'lanterns made a funny sight
Sc-RhL:73
Friendly ghosts are on their flight
Le-Fi:96
A ghost in white, on Halloween night
Ka-Fa:19
Goblin, goblin, green and gooey
Ov-Le:19
Halloween will soon be here
Sc-RhL:70
Have you seen the Ghost of Tom?
Wi-Mu:179#
Here is a pumpkin, big and round
El-Fi:58
El-Fi:60#
Here is a witch's tall black hat
Sc-RhL:73
Here's a pumpkin big and yellow
Mo-Pr:151
Here's a witch with a tall, tall hat
Fl-Ri9:38
Here's my pumpkin big and orange
Ov-Le:19

Ho! Ho! Little folks
Cr-Fi:60
I am a pumpkin, big and round
Br-Ha:10
Cr-Fi:61
Fl-Ri9:50
Mc-Fi:25
I am the witch's cat
Gr-Le:96
I carved a pumpkin, orange and round
Ka-Fa:19
I laugh at my jack-o-lantern
Wi-Ci:33
I made a Jack-o'-lantern for Halloween night
El-FP:20
I put on a hat
Ga-Bu2:68
I'll pretend on Halloween
De-Ch:74
I'm a friendly ghost— almost!
Gr-Le:97
I'm a scary ghost. See my big and scary eyes?
Le-Fi:97
I've a jack-o'-lantern
Gr-Le:95
I've got a pumpkin with a great big grin
Ov-Le:18
I've made a funny false face
Cr-Fi:58
If I were a witch, I'd ride on a broom
Gr-Le:98
Le-Fi:97
Wi-Ci:33
It was the finest pumpkin that you have ever seen
Fl-Ri9:95
Sc-Rh:59
Wi-Ev:92
A little witch in a pointed cap
De-Ch:74
Fl-Ri9:58
Mr. Pumpkin! Well, hello!
Do-Mo:54
My head is round, and so are my eyes
Sc-RhL:72
October time is pumpkin time
Cr-Fi:60

An old witch laughed, "Hee, hee, hee, hee!"
Sc-RhL:75#
On Halloween, just take a peek
Cr-Fi:58
El-FP:30
On my Jack-o'-lantern
De-Ch:73
Once I had a pumpkin
Ov-Le:18
Once there was a pumpkin
Cr-Fi:61
Fl-Ri9:68
One jack o'lantern that I see
Sc-RhL:71#
One little, two little, three little witches
Gr-Le:95
Le-Fi:95
Sc-Rh:61
Sc-Rhl:72
Wi-Ci:32
One witch is riding on a broom
Sc-RhL:74
Pumpkin red, pumpkin yellow
Wi-Ci:33
Scarecrow, scarecrow, turn around
Wi-Ci:32
See my big and scary eyes
De-Ch:3
Gr-Le:97
See my pumpkin round and fat
Gr-Le:97
The sky was dark but a moon was seen
Sc-RhL:74#
Sometimes big and sometimes small
Be-We:55
Le-Fi:98
Ten little goblins dancing in a ring
Fl-Ri9:89
Ten little pumpkins all in a line
Sc-Rh:60
There is a ghost who lives in a cave
Ov-Le:21
There once was a witch who lived in the town
Sh-Rh:8#

This is a very nice jack-o'-lantern
Gr-Le:97
This little pumpkin was taken to market
Cr-Fi:61
Three little pumpkins, laying very still
Fl-Ri9:94
Three little pumpkins sitting on a wall
Ha-Cl:18
A very old witch was stirring a pot
Ca-Li:57#
We have a pumpkin, a big orange pumpkin
Cr-Fi:61
"What makes you run, my little man?"
Cr-Fi:61
When goblins prowl
Fl-Ri9:38
A witch once went for a ride on her broom
Fl-Ri9:38
A witch, she went a-shopping
Fl-Ri9:69
The witches are riding tonight!
Le-Fi:95
Would you shake? Would you quake?
Pa-Gi:80
HOLIDAYS—HANUKKAH
Dredel, dredel, dredel— see the spinning top
Ro-Mi:68
Hanukkah is the Feast of Lights
Cr-Fi:65
Hanukkah tells of a struggle
Cr-Fi:65
Menorah, Menorah, your candles we will light
Cr-Fi:65
One light, two lights, three lights, and four
Sc-Rh:70
See the candle shine so bright
Cr-Fi:65
HOLIDAYS—MAY DAY
Five May baskets waiting by the door
Ro-Mi:59

SUBJECT INDEX

MUSICAL RHYMES (continued)

Gonna jump down, turn around, pick a bale of cotton
Gl-Ey:62*#

Good Mother Hen sits here on her nest
Po-Fi:18*

Ha! Ha! This-a-way
Gl-Do:28*#

Have you ever, ever, ever in your long-legged life
Co-Pl:53#
Gl-Do:72*#

Have you seen my dolly?
Ma-Ga:56*

Have you seen the little ducks
Ma-Ga:81*#
Po-Da:50#

Head and shoulders baby, 1-2-3
Sh-Rh:18*#

Head and shoulders, knees and toes
Be-We:46*#
Fl-Ri9:39#
Fo-Sa:46#
Gl-Do:30*#
Le-Fi:16#
Ma-Ga:125#
Ma-Re:48#
Mo-Pr:145#
Po-Da:63#
Pu-ABC:14#
Sc-RhL:36#
Sh-Sh:12#
Ta-Wi:13#
Wi-Ev:17#

Hello! Take off your hat
Gl-Do:31*

Help me wind my ball of wool
Ma-Ga:32*#

Here comes a policeman riding on a bicycle
Ma-Ga:71*

Here's a baby birdie; he's hatching from his shell
Be-We:40*#

Here's a tree with trunk so brown
Ma-Ga:93*#

Here stands a lovely Christmas tree
Gr-Le:93

Here we go Looby Loo
Fo-Sa:18*#
Gl-Do:33*#
Ko-Da:20*#
Mo-Pr:164#

Here we go round the mulberry bush
Cr-Fi:5#
Fo-Sa:16*#
Gl-Ey:50*#
Ko-Da:4*#
La-Ri:19#
Ma-Ga:45#
Mo-Pr:165#
Oa-Ch:26#
Po-Da:6#
Sh-Sh:14#
Wi-Ev:21#

Hickory, dickory, dock
Be-We:13*
Ca-Li:21
Cr-Fi:95
De-Ch:39
Gl-Ey:32*
Gl-Mu:61*
Gr-Le:31
Ha-St:15
Ka-Fa:19
Ke-Hi
La-Ri:40
Mo-Pr:152
Mo-Th:22
Pe-SP:94
Po-Da:29
Sh-Sh:94
Wi-Ro:26
Yo-La:8*

Hippety hop to the candy shop
Ma-Ga:139*#

Hoppa, hoppa Reiter
Sc-La:72*

How does a caterpillar go?
Ma-Ga:44*

Hush little baby, don't say a word
Gl-Ey:33*
Sh-Sh:91*

I am a fine musician
Gl-Ey:52*
Gr-Le:87

I am special, I am special
Ov-Le:36

I can dance upon my toes
Ma-Ga:141*#

I can knock with my two hands
Ma-Ga:119*

I had a bird and the bird pleased me
Gl-Ey:10*

I had a little brother, his name was Tiny Tim
Th-Ca
Wi-Mu:24*#

I had a little engine
Ma-Ga:70*

I had a little nut tree, nothing would it bear
Gl-Do:41*

I had a little rooster and the rooster pleased me
Gl-Do:44*

I have lost the "do" of my clarinet
Gl-Do:46*

I have made a pretty nest
Ma-Ga:155*

I know a little pussy
Ma-Ga:94*

I like one friendly puppy because
Sc-RhL:170*

I love the mountains
Gl-Do:48*

I love to row in my big blue boat
Ma-Ga:111*#

I point to myself
Gl-Do:50*#

I travelled over land and sea
Gl-Do:16*#

I went to school one morning and I walked like this
Ma-Ga:145*#

I'm a Fairy Doll on the Christmas Tree
Ma-Ga:54*

I'm a little flower pot mom put out
Ov-Le:36

I'm a little teapot short and stout
Be-We:42*#
Co-Ee:20*#
Cr-Fi:106#
De-Ch:60#
Fl-Ri9:87#
Fo-Sa:106#
Gl-Ey:36*#
Gl-Mu:52*#
Gr-Le:82#
Ha-St:16#
Ke-Im#
La-Ri:24#
Ma-Ga:31*#
Or-Rh#
Pa-Gi:24#
Pe-SP:99*#
Po-Da:60#
Ta-Ju:80#
Tw-Rh#
Wi-Ev:146#
Wi-He#

Wi-Ro:44#
Yo-La:12*#

I'm a stegosaurus, short and stout
Yo-La:12*

I'm an acorn small and round
Gl-Do:54*

I'm bringing home a baby bumble bee
Fl-Ri9:4
Ka-Le:41

I'm looking for a friend to take a walk with me
Ka-Le:19

I'm stretching very tall
Be-We:38*#

If a bird you want to hear
Ka-Le:4

If I could have a windmill, a windmill, a windmill
Ma-Ga:84*#

If I were a little bird, high up in the sky
Ma-Ga:153*#

If you're happy and you know it, clap your hands
Co-Ee:42*#
Fl-Ri9:47#
Fo-Sa:44*#
Gl-Do:52*#
Ka-Le:8#
Pe-SP:110*#
Ta-Ju:91*#
Wi-Ci:13#
Wi-Ev:36#

If you were a beech tree
Ma-Ga:96*

In Frisco Bay, there lived a whale
Gl-Do:91*

Itisket, Itasket
Gl-Do:55*#

Jack and Jill went up the hill
Be-We:16
Be-We:46*
Cr-Fi:94
De-Ch:40
Gl-Ey:22*
Gr-Le:52
Ka-Fa:20#
Mo-Pr:152
Sh-Sh:26*
Wi-Ev:146

Jack-in-the-box is out of sight
Wi-Mu:20*#

MUSICAL RHYMES *(continued)*
See the soldiers in the street
  Ma-Ga:163#
See us go round and round
  Ka-Le:20
She waded in the water and she got her feet all wet
  Gl-Do:93*#
Shoo fly, don't bother me
  Gl-Mu:54*#
Sing a song of popcorn
  Cr-Fi:106
Six little snails
  Ma-Ga:48*
Slowly, slowly walks my Granddad
  Ma-Ga:172*#
Snow piled up will make a hill, make a hill, make a hill
  Cr-Fi:29
Swim, little fish, in water clear
  Ma-Ga:112*
Ta ta ta li
  Sc-La:63*
Tall shop in the town
  Ma-Ga:66*#
  Po-Da:51#
  Wi-Ro:33#
A tall thin man walking along
  Ma-Ga:168*#
Tape tape petites mains
  Sc-La:58*
Tete, epaules, genoux et pieds
  Sh-Sh:12#
There's a little white duck sitting in the water
  Gl-Ey:46*
There was a farmer had a dog
  Fo-Sa:91*
  Gl-Ey:13*
  Mo-Th:100
  Sh-Rh:34*
  Ta-Ju:94*
There was a tailor had a mouse
  Gl-Ey:70*
There were five in the bed
  We-Fi2:17
  Wi-Mu:22*

This is my little house
  Ma-Ga:29*
This is the way we walk to school
  Wi-Ci:13#
This is the way we wash our clothes
  Gr-Le:84*#
  Ma-Ga:37#
  Mo-Ca:14#
  Oa-Ch:27#
  Sc-Rh:85#
This old man, he played one
  Ba-On
  Co-Ee:46*#
  De-Ch:56#
  Gr-Le:68*#
  Ko-Th
  Mo-Th:31
  Sh-Sh:59*#
Three blind mice
  Ka-Le:38
Three crows sat upon a wall
  Gl-Do:98*
Three jelly fish, three jelly fish
  Ma-Ga:110*
Three little angels all dressed in white
  Gl-Do:100*
Three little leopard frogs
  Fl-Ri9:93#
To and fro, to and fro
  Ma-Ga:42*#
Tommy Thumb, Tommy Thumb
  Ma-Ga:169*
  Wi-Ro:35
The train is carrying coal
  Ma-Ga:69*
Trot, trot, trot
  Ma-Ga:17*
  Sc-La:71*
Two little boats are on the sea
  Ma-Ga:115*#
Up I stretch on tippy toe
  Ma-Ga:142*#
Wait, wait, wait a bit
  Cr-Fi:99
We are going to plant a bean
  Ma-Ga:48#
We are soldiers marching along
  Ma-Ga:140*

We are woodmen sawing trees
  Ma-Ga:92*#
What does the clock in the hall say?
  Ma-Ga:38*
What shall we do when we all go out?
  Sh-Sh:20*#
What will we do with the baby-o?
  Gl-Mu:51*#
The wheels of the bus go round and round
  Co-Ee:34*#
  Fl-Ri9:102#
  Gl-Ey:16*#
  Gr-Le:25#
  Ha-St:10#
  Ka-Le:28
  Ma-Ga:73*#
  Pe-SP:105*#
  Po-Da:38#
  Wi-Ci:15#
  Wi-Ev:194#
When all the cows were sleeping
  Ma-Ga:86*#
When Billy Boy was one
  Wi-Mu:14*
Where is thumbkin? Where is thumbkin?
  Be-We:17*
  Br-Fi:10
  Cr-Fi:2
  De-Ch:25
  Fl-Ri9:104
  Gl-Ey:88*
  Gl-Mu:66*
  Gr-Le:6
  Ka-Le:9
  Le-Fi:28
  Pe-SP:106*
  Sc-La:110*
  Sh-Sh:19*
  We-Fi2:33
  Yo-La:18*
Willum he had seven sons
  Ma-Ga:167*#
Wind the bobbin up
  Ma-Ga:122*
With my little broom I sweep, sweep, sweep
  Ka-Le:10
  Ma-Ga:33*#
  Tw-Rh
Yankee Doodle came to town
  Mo-Th:85

You and me, we're gonna be partners
  Gl-Do:10*#
You put your right foot in
  Co-Pl:44#
  Gl-Do:35*#
Zoom! Zoom! Ain't it great to be kooky
  Gl-Mu:1*#
Zum Gali, Gali, Gali
  Gl-Do:103*
MUSICAL SCALE
Here's a baby birdie; he's hatching from his shell
  Be-We:40*#
I know a little pussy
  Ma-Ga:94*
MUSKRATS *See:* **Animals—Muskrats**
MYTHICAL CREATURES—BROWNIES
Do you suppose a giant
  Fl-Ri9:86#
This little elf likes to hammer
  Fl-Ri9:8
MYTHICAL CREATURES—CENTAURS
Chester Centaur saw a rabbit
  Cr-Fi:103#
I am called a centaur
  Cr-Fi:103
There once was a centaur named Frank
  Cr-Fi:103
MYTHICAL CREATURES—DRAGONS
Little Huey Dragon counts to three
  Cr-Fi:98#
Today I was in my sandbox
  Cr-Fi:98
MYTHICAL CREATURES—ELVES
Alisa was a little elf
  Cr-Fi:68#
Five little elves met one autumn day
  Sc-RhL:196
Here is a giant who is tall, tall, tall
  Sc-Rh:98#
In Santa's workshop far away
  Sc-Rh:67
Little Elf sat up in her rose petal bed
  Pe-SP:111#

PLANTS—LEAVES (continued)

To and fro, to and fro
Ma-Ga:42*#

When autumn comes, the leaves that were green
Cr-Fi:24#

When the leaves are on the ground
Cr-Fi:23
Fl-Ri9:103

The wind blows the leaves
Ga-Bu2:55

PLANTS—MUSHROOMS

The mushroom is an umbrella
Fl-Fi:14

PLANTS—PEAS

Five fat peas in a pea-pod pressed
Co-Ee:40
Ha-Cl:19
Wi-Ro:29

PLANTS—PUSSY WILLOWS

I know a little pussy
Ma-Ga:94*

Now put away your sled
Wi-Ci:82

PLANTS—SEEDS

Dance, little raindrops
Sc-RhL:107#

Dear little seed, so soft and round
Sc-RhL:62#

Dig a little hole
Le-Fi:92
Wi-Ci:83

Dig! Dig! Dig! Rake just so
Fl-Ri9:59

Eat an apple
Do-Mo:84#

First the farmer plows the ground
Fl-Ri9:24#

First the farmer sows his seeds
De-Ch:62#

First the plow he takes in hand
Fl-Fi:8

Five little seeds a-sleeping they lay
Ma-Ga:133

Five little seeds, five little seeds
Sc-RhL:118

Here I have a little bean
Cr-Fi:54#

Here's a tree in summer
Fl-Ri9:71

I am a little seed in the earth so low
Ka-Le:4#

I dig, dig, dig
Fl-Ri9:45
Wi-Ci:113

I had a little cherry stone
Ma-Ga:46
Sc-RhL:117

I'm a little brown seed in the ground
Cr-Fi:33#

I put some little flower seeds down in the warm soft ground
Le-Fi:93

I take my little shovel
El-FP:78

I took a little seed one day
Wi-Ev:118

I work in my garden
Cr-Fi:33

In a milkweed cradle
Fl-Ri9:5

In my little garden bed
Cr-Fi:35
De-Ch:11
Po-Fi:22*

In the heart of a seed
De-Ch:13
Fl-Ri9:56

In their little cradles, packed in tight
Fl-Ri9:54

Lao gua piao, loa gua piao (Thistle-seed, thistle-seed)
Sc-La:88

A little seed so soft and round
El-Fi:74
El-Fi:76#
Pe-Fi:24

Once I found a cherry stone
Wi-Ro:46

See the farmer plant the seeds
Cr-Fi:35#

See the little seed I bought
Mc-Fi:31

Seeds stick, seeds fly
Ka-Fa:11

Some little seeds have parachutes
El-FP:70
Pe-Fi:10

Take the little seed so hard and round
De-Ch:15

Ten brown seeds lay in a straight row
Sc-RhL:112#

There was a field that waiting lay
Po-Fi:62*

We are going to plant a bean
Ma-Ga:48#

PLATYPUS See: Animals—Duckbill Platypus

PLAYGROUNDS

Climb the ladder, down we slide
Fl-Ri9:33#
Sc-Rh:133#

Climb up the ladder
Fl-Ri9:51

Climbing, climbing up the ladder
Fl-Ri9:48#

Hold on tightly as we go
Gr-Le:77

See-saw, see-saw, up and down we go
Fl-Ri9:81#
Sc-Rh:133#

The seesaw goes up
Gr-Le:78

Up and down, and up and down
Fl-Ri9:88

PLAYING BALL See: Activities—Playing Ball
PLAYING See: Activities—Playing
PLEASE & THANK YOU See: Behavior—Manners
PLUTO See: Solar System
POLAR BEARS See: Animals—Polar Bears
POLECATS See: Animals—Skunks
POLICE OFFICERS See: Community Helpers—Police Officers
PONIES See: Animals—Horses
POODLES See: Animals—Dogs
POPCORN See: Food—Popcorn
PORCUPINES See: Animals—Porcupines
PORPOISES See: Marine Life—Porpoises
POSSESSIONS See: Belongings
POSSUMS See: Animals—Possums

POSTMEN See: Community Helpers—Mail Carriers
PRAYERS

Now I lay me down to sleep
Le-Fi:43, D.S.L.

Now let us clasp our little hands
Fl-Ri9:72

Thank you for the world so sweet
Le-Fi:100

What do the farmers do all day?
Vo-Ac:11#

PRESENTS

Listen! Listen! Close your eyes!
Do-Mo:113

Mysterious boxes under the tree
Sc-RhL:91#

This little present goes to Mary
Sc-Rh:70

PRETENDING See: Activities—Pretending; Imagination
PUMPKINS

Cinco calabacitas sentadas en un porton
Fl-Ri9:14

Cut into a pumpkin
Cr-Fi:59
Fl-Ri9:74

Did you know that jack o'lanterns are of Indian breed?
Sc-RhL:73

A face so round
Fl-Ri9:101

The first yellow pumpkin said, "Oh, my!"
Sc-RhL:81

First you take a pumpkin
Cr-Fi:59

Five little pumpkins sitting on a gate
Cr-Fi:61
De-Ch:75
Gl-Ey:40*
Gr-Le:95
Le-Fi:94
Mo-Pr:151
Pa-Gi:80
Ro-Mi:64
Wi-Ci:32

Four big jack o'lanterns made a funny sight
Sc-RhL:73

SEASONS—AUTUMN (continued)

The leaves are green, the nuts are brown
Cr-Fi:24

The little gray squirrel makes a scampering sound
Le-Fi:60
Sc-RhL:66

Little Jack Frost must have come last night
Fl-Fi:42

The little leaves are falling down
Gr-Le:47
Fl-Ri9:55

The little leaves are whirling round, round, round
Gr-Le:47

Little leaves fall gently down
Fl-Ri9:35
Mo-Pr:148#
Sc-Rh:119
Wi-Ci:21

Many leaves are falling down
Gr-Le:47

The month is October
Gr-Le:47

Not all trees wear autumn colors
Cr-Fi:24

One leaf and two leaves tumbling to the ground
Sc-RhL:67

One leaf of gold, two leaves of brown
Sc-RhL:67

These are the brown leaves fluttering down
Fl-Ri9:83
Wi-Ci:21

Three little oak leaves, red, brown and gold
Sc-Rh:119
Sc-RhL:65

Wear a warm coat for fall is here
Sc-RhL:67

When autumn comes, the leaves that were green
Cr-Fi:24#

When the birds fly south
Cr-Fi:24

When the leaves are on the ground
Cr-Fi:23
Fl-Ri9:103

Who comes creeping in the night
Fl-Ri9:49

SEASONS—SPRING See also: Growth; Holidays—Easter; Holidays—May Day; Holidays—St. Patrick's Day; Plants—Flowers; Plants—Seeds; Toys—Kites; Weather—Rain

The big round sun in an April sky
Fl-Ri9:3
Wi-Ci:88

Bright colored butterfly looking for honey
Cr-Fi:36
Ja-Fi:33
Wi-Ev:80

A caterpillar crawled to the top of a tree
Br-Ha:28
Fl-Ri9:11
Wi-Ci:83

Dance, little raindrops
Sc-RhL:107#

Drip, drop, drip, Spring rain has come no doubt
Le-Fi:110

Five little May baskets waiting by the door
Sc-Rh:128

Five little snowmen, happy and gay
El-Fi:41
El-Fi:42#
Fl-Ri9:32
Ol-Fi
Pe-Fi:25

Flowers tall, flowers small
Pe-Fi:9
Sc-Rh:127

Here are two apple buds growing on a tree
Wi-Ev:99

Here is the cave and here is the bear
Fl-Fi:18

Here's a green leaf
Cr-Fi:38
Fl-Ri9:33
Le-Fi:90
Sc-Rh:126

Here's a tree in summer
Fl-Ri9:71

I dig the ground and plant the seeds
Pe-SP:103

In the heart of a seed
De-Ch:13
Fl-Ri9:56

A little ground hog lived cozy and snug
Fl-Fi:32

Now put away your sled
Wi-Ci:82

Pitter, patter falls the rain, on the roof and window pane
Fl-Ri9:72
Wi-Ci:82

Pitter-patter, raindrops
Fl-Ri9:77
Sc-Rh:125

See the kite away up high
Cr-Fi:34

Skates we bring
Ja-Fi:27

Spring is here, it must be so
Ka-Fa:10

Spring is here! Spring is here!
Sc-RhL:110

The sun comes out and shines so bright
El-FP:12

Ten little leaf buds growing on a tree
Cr-Fi:32
Fl-Ri9:52
Sc-RhL:112

This is the way the flowers sleep
De-Ch:16

The winds of March begin to blow
Sc-Rh:124

SEASONS—SUMMER

In the summer I'm a runner
Do-Mo:61#

A little boy went walking one lovely summer day
De-Ch:9
Fl-Ri9:53
Le-Fi:59
Mo-Pr:150
Po-Fi:30*
Wi-Ci:113

SEASONS—WINTER See also: Activities—Sledding; Hibernation; Snowmen; Weather—Snow

The clouds are dark and in our town
Sc-RhL:100

The day is cloudy. The wind is bold
Sc-RhL:101#

Down the hill on sleds we go
Vo-Ac:13#

Five little snow men, standing in a row
De-Ch:48
Gr-Le:48

Five little snowmen, happy and gay
El-Fi:41
El-Fi:42#
Fl-Ri9:32
Ol-Fi
Pe-Fi:25

Five little snowmen standing round my door
Ro-Mi:53

Gather snow and make a ball
Cr-Fi:27

Hat and mittens keep us warm
Ka-Fa:11#

Hello, Mr. Snowman. How are you today?
Cr-Fi:28

Here comes the month of January
Sc-RhL:100

Here is brown bulb, small and round
De-Ch:17

Here is the cave and here is the bear
Fl-Fi:18

Here's a great big hill
Fl-Ri9:7
Gr-Le:23
Le-Fi:112
Wi-Ci:46

I am a snowman, cold and white
Fl-Ri9:44#
Sc-Rh:123#

I built a snowman, fat and round
Le-Fi:113

I hab a terrible code id my head
Cr-Fi:29

I have two red mittens
Sc-RhL:102#

I made a little snowman
Fl-Fi:36

I made a little snowman with hat and cane complete
Cr-Fi:28

TOYS—KITES

Blow, little wind, on my kite
Le-Fi:82

The first little kite that was sailing by
Sc-RhL:114#

Five little kites flying high in the sky
Ro-Mi:55

Here's a kite for Monday
Sc-RhL:114

"I can go higher than you," boasted a dragon-shaped kite
Mc-Fi:40

I have a little kite—the best I've ever seen
Vo-Ac:7

See the kite away up high
Cr-Fi:34

When winds blow hard, we fly a kite
Ga-Bu2:43

The winds of March begin to blow
Sc-Rh:124

TOYS—PIANOS

See my piano
Ja-Fi:23

TOYS—SOLDIERS

Five wooden soldiers standing in a row
Fl-Ri9:32
Sc-Rh:130

Wooden soldiers, red and blue
Fl-Ri9:107
Wi-Ci:118

TOYS—TEDDY BEARS

One little teddy bear, finding things to do
Ro-Mi:21

Round and round the garden
Ha-Cl:27
Ha-Ro
Ke-Ro
La-Ri:11
Ma-Ga:14
Mo-Th:19
Oa-Ch:8
Po-Da:14
Ra-Tr
Sc-La:99
Th-Ca
Tw-Rh
Wi-He
Wi-Ro:6

Teddy bear, teddy bear, turn around
Co-Pl:76#
Cr-Fi:106#
De-Ch:59#
Fl-Ri9:87#
Fo-Sa:49#
Pe-SP:101#
Sh-Rh:40*#
We-Fi1:23#
Wi-Ev:182#
Wi-Mu:191#

This is a cuddly teddy bear
Ga-Bu2:37

TOYS—TOPS

Five little tops were spinning on the floor
Sc-RhL:95#

I am a top all wound up tight
Fl-Ri9:44
Ka-Le:46
Pe-Fi:18
Sc-Rh:130

I have a top
Fl-Ri9:95
Gr-Le:27

Wind the top
Fl-RI9:95

TOYS—YO-YOS

Three pretty yo-yos are made for play
Sc-RhL:94

TRAFFIC COPS *See:* **Community Helpers—Police Officers**

TRAINS

Choo, choo, choo, the train runs down the track
Gr-Le:22
Le-Fi:85
Pe-SP:97

Clickety-clack, wheels on the track
Ka-Le:28
Th-Ca

Down by the station, early in the morning
Be-We:23*
Gl-Ey:21*
Gr-Le:22
Ha-St:12#
Ka-Le:22
Ma-Ga:67
Mo-Th:80
Yo-La:20*

The great big train goes up the track
Gr-Le:22

Herbert the Hobo, he hopped on a train
Do-Mo:79#

Here is an engine
Fl-Ri9:20

Here is the engine on the track
Fl-Ri9:41
Ka-Le:28
Ro-Mi:16
Sc-Rh:20

I go on a train that runs on the track
Wi-Ev:190

I had a little engine
Ma-Ga:70*

If I were a choo-choo train
Cr-Fi:85

The little train coming down the track
Ov-Le:35

Oh, a peanut sat on a railroad track
Co-Ee:43*

One is the engine, shiny and fine
Sc-Rh:20

One red engine puffing down the track
Ma-Ga:69

Piggy on the railway
Ma-Ga:68
Wi-Ro:12

Puffer train, Puffer train
Ma-Ga:109*#

This is a choo-choo train
Cr-Fi:85
De-Ch:35
Fl-Ri9:12
Gr-Le:23

The train is carrying coal
Ma-Ga:69*

The train's big wheels go clickety-clack
Cr-Fi:85

TRANSPORTATION *See also:* **Activities—Horseback Riding; Airplanes; Automobiles; Bicycles; Boats; Buses; Motorcycles; Trains; Wagons**

Here comes a big red bus
Ma-Ga:74#

Here comes a policeman riding on a bicycle
Ma-Ga:71*

How do I get from here to there?
Cr-Fi:86

I had a little engine
Ma-Ga:70*

I'm the policeman, yes I am
Ka-Le:24

Wheels, wheels, wheels go around, around
Sc-RhL:191

TRAVEL

I think I'll go to Tim-buc-tu
Do-Mo:71#

Mr. Pickett bought a ticket
Do-Mo:79#

TREATS *See:* **Food—Treats**

TREES

As I was walking down a lane I saw an apple tree
Mc-Fi:47

Away up high in the apple tree
Co-Ee:15#
Cr-Fi:22#
De-Ch:63#
Fl-Ri9:3#
Gr-Le:48#
Le-Fi:91
Pa-Gi:50#
Pe-Fi:24#
Pe-SP:104#
Sc-Rh:119#
We-Fi2:25#
Wi-Ci:25
Wi-Ev:99#

Elm trees stretch and stretch so wide
Fl-Ri9:97#
Wi-Ci:97
Wi-Ev:121

Flowers grow like this
Ma-Ga:43
Po-Da:18

Here is a tree so tall and strong
Mc-Fi:30

Here is a tree with its leaves so green
Ma-Ga:46
Wi-Ci:25
Wi-Ev:99
Wi-Ro:11
Ya-Fi

Here is an oak tree, straight and tall
Fl-Ri9:67
Wi-Ci:97
Wi-Ev:121

WEATHER—RAIN (continued)
Ha-Cl:16
Ha-In
Ko-Da:24*
La-Ri:25
Le-Fi:52
Ma-Ga:156*
Mo-Pr:149
Mo-Th:52
Oa-Ch:14
Pe-SP:98*
Po-Da:27
Sc-Rh:91
Sh-Rh:39
Sh-Sh:61*
Ta-Ju:82
Wi-He
Wi-Ro:17
Yo-La:14*
First I see a big gray cloud
Ga-Bu2:52
The first umbrella is red
Sc-RhL:111
Five little flowers standing in the sun
Fl-Ri9:79
Pe-Fi:10
Sc-Rh:126
Wi-Ci:99
Fletcher the Weatherman says it will rain
Do-Mo:58
Four little raindrops sat upon a cloud
Sc-RhL:108
From big black clouds
Wi-Ev:130
Get your rain coat
Ka-Fa:8
Here are little Jim and Jane going for a walk
De-Ch:32
Here's my umbrella on a rainy day
Pu-ABC:20
I hear thunder, I hear thunder
Ha-St:21#
Ma-Ga:60#
Sh-Sh:56*#
Wi-Ro:37
I listen to the raindrops fall
Fl-Ri9:77
I put on my raincoat
Sc-RhL:110
I sit before the window now
Cr-Fi:49
It drizzles, it rains
De-Ch:15

It's raining, it's raining, it's pouring from the sky
Ka-Fa:14
Jiggle on the doorknob!
Do-Mo:102
Mr. Pocatella had a leaky um-ber-ella
Do-Mo:68#
Oh! Where do you come from, you little drops of rain
Cr-Fi:34
One little white cloud played tag in the breeze
Sc-RhL:108
One puddle, two puddles, made by the rain
Sc-RhL:115
One sunny, summer morning, a fluffy cloud sailed by
Pe-Fi:20
Pitter-pat, pitter-pat, oh so many hours
Co-Ee:14
Gr-Le:46
Pitter, patter falls the rain, on the roof and window pane
Fl-Ri9:72
Wi-Ci:82
Pitter, patter goes the rain, splash, splash go my feet
Ca-Li:49#
Pitter-patter, raindrops
Fl-Ri9:77
Sc-Rh:125
Pitter, patter, scatter! See the raindrops on the wall
Do-Mo:58
Pray open your umbrella
Ma-Ga:62*
Rain is falling down, rain is falling down
Gr-Le:47
Rain on green grass
Fl-Ri9:77
Ha-St:18#
Wi-Ci:82
Raindrops are such funny things
El-FP:80
Raindrops, raindrops! Falling all around
Fl-Ri9:23
Pe-Fi:29
Sc-Rh:125

Slip on your raincoat
Fl-Ri9:78
Wi-Ci:83
Wi-Ev:130
Softly, softly falling so
Ma-Ga:60
Some little raindrops come quietly down
El-Fi:44
El-Fi:46#
Squish, squash says the mud
Ka-Fa:15
The sun is gone
Sc-RhL:44#
Ten little raindrops dancing on the walk
De-Ch:16
There's a rain cloud in the sky
Sc-RhL:111
This is the sun, high up in the sky
Fl-Ri9:57
Wi-Ev:146
The trees and sky are overhead
Fl-Ri9:73
Two tiny bunnies hopped down the land
El-FP:22

WEATHER—RAINBOWS
One day the sun was shining bright
Cr-Fi:32
Purple, blue, green, yellow
Le-Fi:111
Rainbow, rainbow, way across the sky
Pu-ABC:19

WEATHER—SNOW
A chubby little snowman had a carrot nose
Cr-Fi:27
Fl-Ri9:13
Wi-Ev:134
The clouds are dark and in our town
Sc-RhL:100
Down the hill on sleds we go
Vo-Ac:13#
Five little snow men, standing in a row
De-Ch:48
Gr-Le:48
Five little snowmen, happy and gay
El-Fi:41
El-Fi:42#
Fl-Ri9:32

Ol-Fi
Pe-Fi:25
Five little snowmen standing round my door
Ro-Mi:53
Gather snow and make a ball
Cr-Fi:27
Hello, Mr. Snowman. How are you today?
Cr-Fi:28
Here comes the month of January
Sc-RhL:100
Here is brown bulb, small and round
De-Ch:17
Here's a great big hill
Fl-Ri9:7
Gr-Le:23
Le-Fi:112
Wi-Ci:46
I am a snowman, cold and white
Fl-Ri9:44#
Sc-Rh:123#
I am a snowman made of snow
Sc-RhL:98#
I made a little snowman
Fl-Fi:36
I made a little snowman with hat and cane complete
Cr-Fi:28
I made a snowman in my yard today
El-FP:55
I will build a snowman
Fl-Ri9:9
Let's go walking in the snow
Fl-Ri9:101#
Wi-Ev:134
"Let's put on a warm coat and zip it up to the chin"
Mo-Pr:157#
Let's put on our mittens
Fl-Ri9:107
Wi-Ci:46
Make a ball of soft, white snow
Fl-Ri9:59
Wi-Ci:46
Many little snowflakes falling through the air
Wi-Ev:134
Merry little snowflakes
Br-Ha:17#
Cr-Fi:26#
Sc-Rh:122#

FIRST LINE INDEX

Clothes on fire, don't get
scared
Wi-Ev:28
The clouds are dark and
in our town
Sc-RhL:100
The clouds are floating
through the sky
Pe-Fi:31
Clouds are swiftly floating
by
Fl-Ri9:85
Ja-Fi:43
A clown you can tell by the
look of his clothes
Do-Mo:73#
Cluck, cluck, cluck, cluck,
good morning, Mrs.
Hen
Ka-Le:31
Coal-black cat with
humped-up back
Gr-Le:98
Cobbler, cobbler, mend my
shoe
Ba-On
Co-Pl:93#
Fl-Ri9:15
Fo-Sa:100
Gl-Ey:69*
Gr-Le:18
Ma-Ga:174*
Mo-Th:100
Sh-Sh:46
Tw-Rh
Wi-Mu:28*
Wi-Ro:28
The cobbler, the cobbler,
makes my shoes
De-Ch:30
Coca Cola went to town
Wi-Mu:194#
Cock-a-doodle-doo! My
dame has lost her shoe
Mo-Th:88
Come follow, follow,
follow
Gr-Le:9
"Come little children,"
calls Mother Hen
Fl-Ri9:66
"Come my bunnies, it's
time for bed."
Cr-Fi:70
Fl-Ri9:94
Come, pet my pony
Do-Mo:17#
Come play with me at my
house
Ka-Fa:8

Come see my small
garden, how sweetly
they grow
De-Ch:12
Coming downstairs, well,
what do we see?
Sc-RhL:93
Con esta mano derecha
Fl-Ri9:2
Con las manos
Sc-Rh:44
Sc-RhL:149
Conejito que corre
Sc-Rh:41
Conejo, conejo, salta, salta
Sc-RhL:145
Cover your face
Ga-Bu2:28
The cow bows her head
and gives a big moo
Co-Zo:16#
Cow, cow, her tail goes
swish
Pu-ABC:12
A cowboy wears a western
hat
Cr-Fi:107
Cows and pigs and sheep
make up
Cr-Fi:55
The cows on the farm go,
moo-oo, moo-oo
Cr-Fi:46
Creep, little mouse, creep,
creep, creep
Ka-Le:38
Creep, little mousie, come
along to me
Ma-Ga:152
Creep mouse, creep mouse,
all around town
Wi-Pl
Creeping, creeping
De-Ch:8
Creeping, creeping,
creeping
Br-Ha:27
Cr-Fi:70
Fl-Ri9:16
Creepy, crawly, creepy,
crawly
Sc-Rh:33
The cricket does chirp by
rubbing his wings
Co-Zo:16
Criss, cross, applesauce
Co-Pl:103
"Croak, croak," said Mr.
Frog as he was sitting
in the sun
Cr-Fi:38

Croak said the frog, with
his golden eyes
Ka-Fa:14
A crocodile could walk a
mile
Do-Mo:50#
Crooked heels and scuffy
toes
Wi-Ci:15
The crossing guard keeps
us safe as he works
from day to day
Cr-Fi:82
The crow flies around and
makes a loud noise
Co-Zo:17
Crunch, crunch went the
caterpillar
Cr-Fi:37
Currants for my eyes
Ka-Fa:16
Cut into a pumpkin
Cr-Fi:59
Fl-Ri9:74
Cut up the vegetables, put
them in a pot
Ga-Bu2:31

La da ju (We push the big
saw)
Sc-La:89
Daddy and I bake a cake
Ga-Bu2:30
Daddy and I went to the
park
Ga-Bu2:63
Daddy has a moustache
Ga-Bu2:21
Daddy's foot is a fly-away
horse
Wi-Pl
Dairy products are food
from the farm
Cr-Fi:55
Dance a baby diddy
Mo-Th:35
Dance and twirl together
Ca-Li:50#
Dance, little raindrops
Sc-RhL:107#
Dance, Thumbkin, dance
Mo-Ca:11
Mo-Th:49
Sc-Rh:104
Dance to your daddie, my
bonnie laddie
Mo-Th:86
Davy, Davy, Dumpling
Co-Pl:102
Dawn and Dave hid in a
cave
Cr-Fi:101

The day before Thanksgiv-
ing, as quiet as could
be
Sc-RhL:79
The day is cloudy. The
wind is bold
Sc-RhL:101#
Dear little seed, so soft
and round
Sc-RhL:62#
Dear Little Stranger, born
in a manger!
Ja-FPL:12
Derry, down Derry, and
up in the air
Sc-La:79
Detras de dona Pata
Fl-Ri9:82
Dewey was a captain at
Manila bay
Gl-Do:20*
Did you feed my cow?
Fl-Ri9:18
Did you know that jack
o'lanterns are of Indian
breed?
Sc-RhL:73
Diddle, diddle, dumpling,
my son John
Mo-Th:41
Diddle-me-diddle-me—
dandy-O!
Mo-Th:38
Dig a little hole
Le-Fi:92
Wi-Ci:83
Dig! Dig! Dig! Rake just
so
Fl-Ri9:59
DING! DONG! Tell me,
did the school bell ring?
Do-Mo:100
The dinosaurs live long
ago
Cr-Fi:48
Dirt comes in colors
Wi-Ev:114
Dirty hands are such a
fright
Cr-Fi:5
The dishes need washing
Wi-Ci:103
Wi-Ev:37
Dive, little goldfish one
Sc-RhL:57
Dive, little tadpole, one
Sc-Rh:92
Do you know that this is?
Yes, a heart. Pretend
it's mine
Mc-Fi:29

Esta es la mama gordita y bonita
    Fl-Ri9:23
Este compro un huevo
    Fl-Ri9:15
    Gr-To
Este era un pollito
    Fl-Ri9:22
Este es un rey honrado
    Sc-Rh:44
Este ninito compro un huevito
    Sc-Rh:41
Este payasito tan alegre y gordo
    Fl-Ri9:21#
Este se hallo un huevito
    Fl-Ri9:21
Esther passed her sister. Was her sister running faster?
    Do-Mo:95#
Every day when we eat our dinner
    Cr-Fi:63
    Gr-Le:94
    Pe-Fi:23
    Sc-Rh:62
Every morning at half past eight
    Gl-Do:26*#
Every morning, I dream at dawn
    Gr-To
Everybody do this, do this, do this
    Ka-Le:12#
Everybody out the door! All aboard for Singapore!
    Do-Mo:64#
Everybody—say your name
    Ga-Bu2:6
Everyone knows a buffalo grows
    Do-Mo:49#
Eye Winker, Tom Tinker
    Fl-Ri9:22
    Gl-Ey:24*
    Gr-Le:11
    Ma-Re:15
    Mo-Ca:19
    Or-Rh
    Sc-La:54
    Sh-Sh:12
Eyes, ears, nose and mouth
    Ka-Le:10
Eyes to see with
    Fl-Ri9:23
    Wi-Ev:23

A face so round
    Fl-Ri9:101
The family all come home at night
    Ga-Bu2:23
A family of rabbits lived under a tree
    Sc-Rh:75
The famous King of France See: THE NOBLE DUKE OF YORK
"The farmer and the miller have worked," the mother said
    Po-Fi:70*
The farmer in the dell
    Pu-ABC:13
The farmer plants the seeds
    Fl-Ri9:24#
A farmer went trotting
    Ca-Li:48#
    Ma-Ga:19#
    Sc-La:69#
A fat bunny rabbit with ears so tall
    Fl-Ri9:25
    Wi-Ci:91
Father and Mother and Uncle John, went to market, one by one
    Mo-Th:83
    Or-Rh
Father bought a feather duster
    Do-Mo:104
February second
    Sc-RhL:106
Fee, Fi, Fo, Fum, Measure my arm, measure my nose
    Mo-Pr:147#
Fee, fie, foe, fum, see my finger, see my thumb
    Fl-Ri9:25
    Gr-Le:5
    Ma-Re:19
    Ov-Le:31
Feetikin, feetikin, when will you gang?
    Mo-Th:41
A fellow named Niece had a bucket of bolts
    Do-Mo:110#
A fence is tall
    Pe-Fi:19
The ferris wheel goes up so high
    Wi-Ev:196

A few is not so many
    Do-Mo:122
Find a foot and hop, hop, hop!
    Fl-Ri9:43#
The finger band has come to town
    Be-We:23#
    Fl-Ri9:25#
    Gr-Le:86#
    Wi-Ci:106#
    Wi-Mu:150#
Fingers, fingers everywhere
    Fl-Ri9:26
    Ka-Le:3
    Sc-RhL:24
Fingers, fingers here and there
    Sc-RhL:26
Fingers like to wiggle, waggle
    Ma-Ga:120*
The fingers went to walk one day
    Sc-RhL:29
Finnerty Haggerty bought a fur hat
    Do-Mo:76
The fire station's empty
    Wi-Ev:177
Fire will warm us and cook with its heat
    Cr-Fi:50#
The firefly gives a flash of his light
    Co-Zo:21
Firman the Fireman! I need you!
    Do-Mo:73#
The first girl / boy said, "It's a very dark sky."
    Sc-RhL:75
The first groundhog digs a home in the fall
    Sc-RhL:105
The first hat is mine. I wear it for fun.
    Sc-RhL:156
First he walks upon his toes
    Ma-Ga:146*#
First I get my black crayon out
    Cr-Fi:59
First I loosen mud and dirt
    Fl-Ri9:82
    Gr-Le:19
    Wi-Ev:173

First I see a big gray cloud
    Ga-Bu2:52
First I take two pieces of bread
    Ga-Bu2:32
First is the father, who brings us our bread See: This is the father, who brings us our bread
The first little cricket played a violin
    Sc-RhL:187
The first little frog stubbed her toe
    Sc-RhL:180*#
The first little ghost floated by the store
    Sc-RhL:71
The first little kite that was sailing by
    Sc-RhL:114#
The first little pig danced a merry, merry jig
    De-Ch:52
The first little pig squeals and squeals
    Sc-RhL:164#
The first little rabbit went hop, hop, hop
    Sc-RhL:120#
The first little reindeer went to the market to buy some Christmas trees
    Cr-Fi:67
The first one is little and quite fat
    Sc-RhL:23
First the farmer plows the ground
    Fl-Ri9:24#
First the farmer sows his seeds
    De-Ch:62#
First the plow he takes in hand
    Fl-Fi:8
The first umbrella is red
    Sc-RhL:111
First we mix and mix it
    Ov-Le:24
First we take a tiny seed and put it in the ground
    Ga-Bu2:54
The first yellow pumpkin said, "Oh, my!"
    Sc-RhL:81
First you push him out of sight
    De-Ch:28

Five little ducks swim-
ming in the lake
  Ol-Fi
Five little ducks that I
once knew
  Br-Ha:22
  Co-Ee:10*
  Fl-Ri9:75
  Ka-Le:29
  Wi-Ci:83
  Wi-Ev:69
Five little ducks went in
for a swim
  Gr-Le:36
  Sc-RhL:168
Five little ducks went out
to play
  Fl-Ri9:75
  Ka-Le:29
  Sc-RhL:166
Five little ducks went
swimming one day
  Gl-Ey:26*
  Ma-Ga:136*
  Ro-Mi:30
  We-Fi1:29
Five little Easter eggs
lovely colors wore
  Fl-Ri9:27
  Pe-Fi:26
  Sc-Rh:73
Five little Easter rabbits
  Sc-Rh:74
Five little elephants
rowing toward the
shore
  Fl-Ri9:28
  Wi-Ev:76
Five little elves met one
autumn day
  Sc-RhL:196
Five little Eskimos by the
igloo door
  Fl-Ri9:28
Five little farmers woke
up with the sun
  De-Ch:22
  Fl-Ri9:29
  Wi-Ev:168
Five little firemen sit very
still
  Fl-Ri9:29
  Ka-Le:21
  Ro-Mi:45
  Sc-Rh:25
Five little firemen stand-
ing in a row
  Ka-Le:23
Five little fishes were
swimming near the
shore
  Fl-Ri9:30

Five little fishies swim-
ming in a pool
  Be-We:19
  Ja-Fi:37
  Pa-Gi:28
  Ro-Mi:31
  Sh-Sh:55#
Five little flags were
waving in the breeze
  Cr-Fi:84
Five little flowers stand-
ing in the sun
  Fl-Ri9:79
  Pe-Fi:10
  Sc-Rh:126
  Wi-Ci:99
Five little froggies sat on
the shore
  Gr-Le:62
  Le-Fi:56
Five little froggies sitting
on a lily pad
  Cr-Fi:44
Five little froggies sitting
on a well
  Ma-Ga:132
  Ro-Mi:34
Five little froggies stand-
ing in a row
  We-Fi1:15
Five little ghosts dressed
all in white
  Cr-Fi:58
Five little ghosts went out
to play
  Ro-Mi:62
Five little girls woke up in
their beds
  Gr-Le:20
  Ro-Mi:44
Five little goblins on a
Halloween night
  Br-Ha:12
  Fl-Ri9:30
  Ro-Mi:63
  Sc-Rh:61
Five little Indians, on a
nice fall day
  El-Fi:48
  El-Fi:49#
Five little Indians running
through a door
  Gr-Le:61
Five little jack-o-lanterns
sitting on a gate **See**:
Five little pumpkins
sitting on a gate
Five little Jinny birds,
hopping by my door
  Ro-Mi:25

Five little kites flying high
in the sky
  Ro-Mi:55
Five little kittens in the
house
  Ga-Bu2:59
Five little kittens on a
summer day
  Ka-Le:39
Five little kittens playing
on the floor
  Sc-Rh:31
Five little kittens sleeping
on a chair
  Br-Ha:24
  Fl-Ri9:51
Five little kittens standing
in a row
  Co-Ee:33
  Gr-Le:64
Five little ladies going for
a walk
  Ma-Ga:134
Five little leaves in the
autumn breeze
  Ro-Mi:61
Five little leaves so bright
and gay
  Ma-Ga:89
Five little leprechauns
were dancing on the
shore
  Sc-RhL:195#
Five little letters lying on
a tray
  Cr-Fi:81
  Mc-Fi:10
Five little May baskets
waiting by the door
  Sc-Rh:128
Five little mice came out
to play
  Fl-Ri9:30
  Ma-Ga:131
  We-Fi1:19
Five little mice looked for
something to eat
  Sc-RhL:169
Five little mice on the
pantry floor
  Br-Fi:16
  De-Ch:8
  Po-Fi:42*
  Ro-Mi:39
  Sc-Rh:89
Five little mice ran
around the house
  Sc-RhL:177
Five little mice ran out to
the farm
  Sc-RhL:169#

Five little mice went out to
play
  Ka-Le:38
  Sc-RhL:53
Five little mice were
hungry as could be
  Cr-Fi:47
Five little milkmen got up
with the sun
  El-Fi:11#
  El-Fi:9
  Pe-Fi:9
Five little monkeys
jumping on the bed
  Co-Ee:38
  Fl-Ri9:30
  Ro-Mi:38
  Sh-Rh:32*
  Wi-Ev:41
Five little monkeys sitting
in a tree
  Fl-Ri9:61
  Ro-Mi:37
  We-Fi1:25
  Wi-Ev:42
Five little monkeys walked
along the shore
  Ma-Ga:99
Five little peas in a pea-
pod pressed
  Ma-Ga:43
  Po-Da:32
  Sh-Sh:73
  Th-Ca
Five little pennies—I took
them to the store
  Ro-Mi:40
Five little pigs were eating
corn
  Sc-RhL:52
Five little Pilgrims on
Thanksgiving Day
  De-Ch:76
  Sc-Rh:62
Five little Pixies decided
to have tea
  Sc-RhL:194
Five little polar bears
playing on the shore
  Cr-Fi:78
Five little polliwogs swam
near the shore
  Sc-RhL:179
Five little ponies all
dapple gray
  Fl-Ri9:31
Five little pumpkins
sitting on a gate
  Cr-Fi:61
  De-Ch:75
  Gl-Ey:40*

Four little jack-o'-lanterns on a window sill
Mc-Fi:25

Four little raindrops sat upon a cloud
Sc-RhL:108

Four little turkeys lived in a pen
El-FP:11
Pe-Fi:22

Four scarlet berries
Ma-Ga:96

Four young frogs were swimming in a pond
Sc-RhL:179

A fox in the henhouse! O run for your life!
Do-Mo:101#

The fox on the rock keeps open one eye
Co-Zo:22#

Franklin, Franklin! Can't you see?!
Do-Mo:90

Fred had a fishbowl
Sc-Rh:53
Wi-Ev:71

Frere Jacques, Frere Jacques
Sc-La:109*

A friendly frog lives in our pond
Do-Mo:8#

Friendly ghosts are on their flight
Le-Fi:96

Friends, I have quite a few
Wi-Ci:68

The frog leaps along
Co-Zo:22#

A frog on a log in a cranberry bog
Do-Mo:11

Frogs jump. Caterpillars hump.
Fl-Ri9:51#

From big black clouds
Wi-Ev:130

The funny, fat walrus sits in the sea
Cr-Fi:78

Fuzzy little caterpillar
Cr-Fi:36
Po-Fi:34*

Fuzzy wuzzy caterpillar
Fl-Ri9:35
Wi-Ev:60

Gather snow and make a ball
Cr-Fi:27

Gee up, my horse, to Buddleigh Fair
Mo-Th:79

Gee up, Neddy, to the fair
Mo-Ca:16

Georgy Porgy pumpkin pie
Wi-Mu:178#

Get well, get well, little frog tail
Gr-To

Get your baseball. Get your cap.
Ka-Fa:14

Get your rain coat
Ka-Fa:8

A ghost in white, on Halloween night
Ka-Fa:19

The Giraffe's long neck
Co-Zo:23#

Go to rest while I count one: One
Sc-RhL:48

Go to sleep now, little bird
El-Fi:15
El-Fi:16#

The goat has long horns
Co-Zo:23#

Goblin, goblin, green and gooey
Ov-Le:19

God made the big round sun
Ja-FPL:5

God's birdie built a nest of twigs
Ja-FPL:23

God took blue from His skies
Ja-FPL:24

Going to the circus to have a lot of fun
Gr-Le:100

Golden fishes swimming, swimming
Gr-Le:35

Gonna jump down, turn around, pick a bale of cotton
Gl-Ey:62*#

Good day, everybody!
Fl-Ri9:36
Wi-Ci:11

Good little mother, how do you do?
Gr-Le:40

Good morning, good morning
Ka-Fa:17

Good morning, good morning, good morn-ing, now we'll say
Gr-Le:80

Good morning, merry sunshine
Fl-Ri9:36

Good morning, Mr. Sunshine
Wi-Ev:212

Good morning to you, Valentine
Gr-Le:99

Good Mother Hen sits here on her nest
Po-Fi:18*

The goose moves his beak to make a big hiss
Co-Zo:24

The gorilla sits and looks over all
Co-Zo:24#

The grand old Duke of York See: *The noble Duke of York*

Grandfather, Grand-mother Tat
De-Ch:66#

Grandma Moon, Grandma Moon, You're up too soon!
Le-Fi:76

Grandma's baked a cake for me
Po-Da:58

Grandmother, Grandfa-ther, do come in
Wi-Ci:17
Wi-Ev:37

Grandmother Thee Thee That
Sc-Rh:81

Grandpa lost his glasses
Ka-Le:43

Grandpa, my Grandpa, he plays ball with me
Pu-ABC:14

Grandpa's barn is wonderful
Mc-Fi:8#

The grasshopper jumps, he's easy to catch
Co-Zo:25#

Gray squirrel, gray squirrel, swish your busy tail
Fl-Ri9:37#
Wi-Ci:20

A great big ball
Co-Ee:23
Gr-Le:64

Great big teeth, chomp, chomp, chomp, chomp
Co-Tw:18

The great big train goes up the track
Gr-Le:22

Green, green, green, green, who is wearing green today?
Wi-Ci:80

The green leaves are turning
Cr-Fi:23

Gregory Griggs, Gregory Griggs, had twenty-seven different wigs
Sh-Rh:17#

Guang-guang cha (Pat-a-cake)
Sc-La:57

Ha! Ha! This-a-way
Gl-Do:28*#

Ha ke yoi (Japanese wrestling rhyme)
Sc-La:87

Habia una Viejita
Gr-To

Hag Hogaga Wa Bat Allah
Sc-La:72

Halloween will soon be here
Sc-RhL:70

Hammer, hammer, hammer
Cr-Fi:108

Hana, hana, hana, kuchi
Sc-Rh:47
Sc-RhL:150

Hand on myself
Cr-Fi:9#

Hands are blue. Hands are green
Ka-Fa:13

Hands can lift a box or chair
Ka-Le:9#

Hands on hips; now turn around
Sc-RhL:43#

Hands on shoulders, hands on knees
Fl-Ri9:10#
Gr-Le:13#
Ka-Fa:17#
Ka-Le:6#
Le-Fi:23#
Ma-Re:49#
Mo-Pr:147#
Pe-Fi:12#
Pe-SP:93#
Ta-Ju:76

219

Here is a house built up high
  Ka-Le:16
  Ma-Ga:25
  Sc-La:107
Here is a house for Jimmy
  Pa-Gi:75
Here is a house with two little people
  Ma-Ga:27
Here is a kitty
  Ol-Fi
  Pe-Fi:30
  Sc-Rh:32
Here is a leaf, it is yellow and brown
  El-FP:18
Here is a little crocus, I plant it in the earth
  Ka-Fa:9
Here is a nest for the robin [Mr. Bluebird]
  Cr-Fi:31
  De-Ch:35
  Fl-Ri9:44
  Le-Fi:74
  Pe-SP:100
  Sc-Rh:86
  Wi-Ev:80
Here is a piggie, fat and round
  Sc-RhL:165
Here is a pumpkin, big and round
  El-Fi:58
  El-Fi:60#
Here is a roof on top of a house
  Sc-RhL:162
Here is a round, sweet lollipop
  Sc-RhL:35#
Here is a starfish
  Sc-RhL:126
Here is a steamroller, rolling and rolling
  Ma-Ga:65
Here is a tall, straight tree
  Pe-Fi:13
Here is a tree so tall and strong
  Mc-Fi:30
Here is a tree with its leaves so green
  Ma-Ga:46
  Wi-Ci:25
  Wi-Ev:99
  Wi-Ro:11
  Ya-Fi

Here is a turkey with his tail spread wide
  De-Ch:76
  Fl-Ri9:41
Here is a window in a Christmas Toy Shop
  Sc-Rh:66
Here is a witch's tall black hat
  Sc-RhL:73
Here is a yellow daffodil
  Pe-Fi:19
  Sc-Rh:126
Here is an airplane flying about
  Mo-Pr:146
Here is an engine
  Fl-Ri9:20
Here is an oak tree, straight and tall
  Fl-Ri9:67
  Wi-Ci:97
  Wi-Ev:121
Here is an ostrich straight and tall
  Sc-RhL:189#
Here is Baby's tousled head
  Cr-Fi:108
  Sc-Rh:79
Here is Bobby's Christmas tree
  Cr-Fi:67
Here is brown bulb, small and round
  De-Ch:17
Here is hungry Piggie Snout
  Fl-Ri9:67
  Sc-Rh:27
Here is Mr. Bluebird
  Mc-Fi:10
Here is my little garden
  Sc-RhL:112#
Here is my little garden bed
  Sc-RhL:122
Here is my pretty mother
  Sc-Rh:78
Here is old Santa
  De-Ch:79
Here is the barn so big, don't you see?
  Fl-Ri9:16
  Wi-Ev:65
Here is the beehive, where are the bees?
  Be-We:11
  Br-Ha:14
  Ca-Li:19
  Co-Ee:37

  Cr-Fi:36
  Cr-Fi:46
  De-Ch:50
  Fl-Ri9:6
  Ha-Cl:12
  Ka-Le:41
  Le-Fi:55
  Ma-Ga:43
  Ma-Re:19
  Ov-Le:32
  Pe-Fi:13
  Po-Fi:54*
  Ro-Mi:23
  Wi-Ci:113
  Wi-Ro:34
Here is the Bible!
  Ja-FPL:11
Here is the cave and here is the bear
  Fl-Fi:18
Here is the chimney. Here is the top
  Be-We:59
  Gr-Le:94
  Le-Fi:102
  Ov-Le:24
  Pe-Fi:9
  Wi-Ci:51
Here is the church
  Be-We:18
  Br-Ha:31
  Co-Ee:28
  Co-Pl:18
  Cr-Fi:110
  De-Ch:2
  Fl-Ri9:13
  Fo-Sa:103
  Gl-Ey:30*
  Gl-Mu:53*
  Gr-Le:52
  Ha-Cl:6
  Le-Fi:36
  Ma-Ga:65
  Mo-Ca:9
  Mo-Th:58
  Oa-Ch:10
  Pe-Fi:28
  Po-Da:52
  We-Fi2:29
  Wi-Ro:41
  Yo-La:10
Here is the engine on the track
  Fl-Ri9:41
  Ka-Le:28
  Ro-Mi:16
  Sc-Rh:20
Here is the little puppy
  Ca-Li:37

Here is the ostrich straight and tall
  Le-Fi:68
  Ma-Ga:101
  Wi-Ro:13
Here is the sea, the wavy sea
  Ma-Ga:112
Here is the toy shop
  De-Ch:81
Here's a baby birdie; he's hatching from his shell
  Be-We:40*#
Here's a ball, and here's a ball
  Cr-Fi:91
  De-Ch:12
  Fl-Ri9:42
  Le-Fi:87
  Pe-Fi:21
  Sc-Rh:131
  We-Fi2:19
  Wi-Ci:51
  Wi-Ev:46, 182
Here's a ball for baby
  Cr-Fi:18
  De-Ch:10
  Fl-Ri9:1
  La-Ri:18
  Le-Fi:86
  Ma-Ga:51
  Ma-Re:18
  Mo-Th:53
  Sc-La:114
  Wi-He
  Wi-Ro:39
  Ya-Fi
Here's a ball I keep on the shelf
  Fl-Ri9:6
Here's a ball of yarn
  Pu-ABC:21
Here's a bowl of milk
  Ja-Fi:9
Here's a cup, and here's a cup
  Co-Ee:21
  De-Ch:7
  Fl-Ri9:16
  Gr-Le:83
  Pa-Gi:24
  Pe-Fi:20
  Pe-SP:97
  Sc-Rh:85
  Ta-Wi:100
Here's a donut
  Wi-Ev:46
Here's a great big hill
  Fl-Ri9:7
  Gr-Le:23

I am a cat, orange and white
Ka-Fa:18#

I am a clown and I don't care a bit
Sc-RhL:141#

I am a cobbler
Fl-Ri9:44
Ha-Cl:7

I am a fine musician
Gl-Ey:52*
Gr-Le:87

I am a funny hoppity toad
Pe-Fi:12

I am a great big floppy clown
Sc-RhL:48#

I am a little seed in the earth so low
Ka-Le:4#

I am a little toad
Ca-Li:30
Cr-Fi:45
Sc-Rh:93

I am a popcorn kernel
Wi-Ev:107

I am a pumpkin, big and round
Br-Ha:10
Cr-Fi:61
Fl-Ri9:50
Mc-Fi:25

I am a snowman, cold and white
Fl-Ri9:44#
Sc-Rh:123#

I am a snowman made of snow
Sc-RhL:98#

I am a tall tree
Fl-Ri9:97
Wi-Ev:121

I am a top all wound up tight
Fl-Ri9:44
Ka-Le:46
Pe-Fi:18
Sc-Rh:130

I am an elephant so big and strong
Le-Fi:68#

I am called a centaur
Cr-Fi:103

I am called a mermaid
Cr-Fi:104#

I am called a Pegasus
Cr-Fi:101

I am called a unicorn
Cr-Fi:104

I am glad as glad can be, that I am no one else but me
Ka-Le:2

"I am going to work," said Mister Thumb
Sc-RhL:24

I am making cookie dough
Fl-Ri9:59

I am packing my lunch
Sc-RhL:61

I am ready for my bath tonight
Wi-Ev:146

I am so happy that I am me
Ka-Le:9

I am special, I am special
Ov-Le:36

I am the witch's cat
Gr-Le:96

I brush my teeth sparkling clean—up and down, up and down
Ga-Bu2:20

I build big towers with my blocks
Ga-Bu2:47

I built a snowman, fat and round
Le-Fi:113

I came to Sunday school today
Ja-FPL:10

I can be an airplane flying in the air
Sc-RhL:43#

I can count. Want to see?
Cr-Fi:92

I can dance upon my toes
Ma-Ga:141*#

I can dive. I can swim.
Ka-Fa:15#

I can do a trick like a funny clown
Cr-Fi:16#

I can feel all over my skin
Cr-Fi:51

"I can go higher than you," boasted a dragon-shaped kite
Mc-Fi:40

I can knock with my two hands
Ma-Ga:119*

I can make a hammock
Cr-Fi:110
Mc-Fi:17

I can make letters with my fingers
Sc-RhL:27

I can make myself get smaller, smaller, smaller
Mo-Pr:148#

I can raise my right hand
Sc-RhL:34#

I can reach high, I can reach low
Pe-Fi:27#

I can spin just like a top
Sc-RhL:35#

I can stand away up tall
Cr-Fi:4#

I can stretch upon my toes
Sc-RhL:142#

I can tie my shoe lace
Or-Rh
Wi-Ro:32

I can walk from here to there
Ga-Bu2:14

I can wiggle my fingers just like this
Ga-Bu2:10

I can, you can, he can, she can!
Do-Mo:106

I carved a pumpkin, orange and round
Ka-Fa:19

I clap my hands, I touch my feet
Fl-Ri9:44#

I dig, dig, dig
Fl-Ri9:45
Wi-Ci:113

I dig the ground and plant the seeds
Pe-SP:103

I eat my food up every day
Ka-Fa:12#

I eat my peas with honey
Fl-Ri9:45
Po-Da:30
Sh-Sh:72

I found a great big shell one day
Fl-Ri9:67
Wi-Ev:60

I found a hole
El-FP:56

I go on a train that runs on the track
Wi-Ev:190

I go to the bus stop each day
Cr-Fi:86

I go to the seashore
Sc-RhL:127

I go to the seashore every day
Fl-Fi:21

I hab a terrible code id my head
Cr-Fi:29

I had a bird and the bird pleased me
Gl-Ey:10*

I had a little balloon
Fl-Ri9:53

I had a little brother, his name was Tiny Tim
Th-Ca
Wi-Mu:24*#

I had a little cherry stone
Ma-Ga:46
Sc-RhL:117

I had a little engine
Ma-Ga:70*

I had a little husband, no bigger than my thumb
Mo-Th:51

I had a little manikin
Mo-Th:51

I had a little monkey
Ca-Li:62#

I had a little monkey, his name was Slimsy Jim
De-Ch:62#
Ka-Le:40

I had a little nut tree, nothing would it bear
Gl-Do:41*

I had a little pig and I fed it in a trough
Ka-Le:39

I had a little pony, his name was Dapple-Gray
Ka-Le:39

I had a little poodle
Fl-Ri9:45

I had a little rooster and the rooster pleased me
Gl-Do:44*

I had a little tea party
Ka-Le:3

I had an Easter bunny
Sc-RhL:121

I had one candle on my cake
Sc-RhL:132

I have a ball, it is big and round
El-FP:60

I have a cat
Wi-Mu:182

I have a dog
El-FP:50

I have a little apple, red and round
Ov-Le:17

I have a little cuckoo clock
Ma-Ga:36#

I have a little kite—the best I've ever seen
Vo-Ac:7

I make my bed, I get the
broom
Ka-Fa:13#

I make my cheeks as fat as
a pig
Ga-Bu2:13

I met a turkey gobbler
Fl-Ri9:97
Wi-Ci:37

I play my horn with a toot,
toot, toot
Ga-Bu2:44

I point to myself
Gl-Do:50*#

I pour it in a glass and I
think
Ga-Bu2:34

I put my arms up high
Fl-Ri9:46#

I put my finger in the
woodpecker's hole
Mo-Th:72

I put on a hat
Ga-Bu2:68

I put on my raincoat
Sc-RhL:110

I put some little flower
seeds down in the
warm soft ground
Le-Fi:93

I rake the leaves when
they fall down
Sc-RhL:66#

I rarely have soup when
I'm eating at noon
Do-Mo:88

I rode my bike down
Downer's hill
Do-Mo:99

I saw a child at play today
Wi-Ev:33

I saw a little bird go hop,
hop, hop
Gr-Le:37
Sc-La:104

I saw a little lady bug
flying in the air
Ro-Mi:36

I saw a little rabbit come
Hop, hop, hop!
Ca-Li:51#

I saw a puppy yawn and
yawn—ow—oop!
Sc-RhL:47

I saw a rabbit, I said
"Hello"
Ov-Le:30

I saw a slippery, slithery
snake
Ma-Ga:102

I saw eight magpies in a
tree
Ba-On

I saw one hungry little
mouse
Sc-RhL:177

I saw two cats, two, two,
two
Sc-RhL:174

I say "Hello," to friends at
Storyhour
Fl-Ri9:33
Wi-Ci:11

I see me, I see me
Ka-Le:12

I see one kitten
Fl-Fi:10

I see something fat and
furry
Do-Mo:59#

I see three—one, two, three
Fl-Ri9:47
Sc-Rh:51

I shut the door and locked
it tight
Gr-Le:81

I sit before the window
now
Cr-Fi:49

I squeeze a lemon just like
this
Mc-Fi:18

I started my life
Cr-Fi:11

I stretch it. I pound it.
Ka-Fa:13

I stretch my fingers away
up high
Cr-Fi:3
Sc-Rh:117

I stuck my head in a little
skunk's hole
Ka-Le:37
Wi-Ev:23

I take my little shovel
El-FP:78

I think I'll build a little
house
Fl-Fi:34

I think I'll go to Tim-buc-
tu
Do-Mo:71#

I think when a little
chicken drinks
Gr-Le:36

I tiptoe here and I tiptoe
there
Sc-RhL:51#

I took a little seed one day
Wi-Ev:118

I toss the kites up in the
sky
Sc-RhL:97

I touch my hair, my lips,
my eyes
Le-Fi:16

I travelled over land and
sea
Gl-Do:16*#

I try to listen and obey
Cr-Fi:13

I want to be a carpenter
and work the whole day
long
Sc-RhL:159#

I want to be as kind as I
can be
Cr-Fi:13

I watch my table manners
Cr-Fi:13

I watch the stars come out
at night
Fl-Ri9:85
Wi-Ev:138

I went to Nantucket to fill
my bucket with sand
Do-Mo:62

I went to school one
morning and I walked
like this
Ma-Ga:145*#

I wiggle my fingers
Fl-Ri9:66
Ka-Le:14
Ka-Le:45
Le-Fi:39
Ma-Re:50
Sc-Rh:117

I will build a snowman
Fl-Ri9:9

I will make a little house
Fl-Ri9:43

I wish I had a pair of
specs
Co-Tw:27

I wish I may, I wish I
might
Wi-Ci:60

I wish I were a circus
clown
Fl-Ri9:47

I wish I were an octopus
Fl-Fi:25#

I work in my garden
Ja-Fi:45
Cr-Fi:33

I would like to go to the
zoo
Pu-ABC:22

I'd like to be a baker
Ka-Le:27

I'd like to be a circus
clown
Cr-Fi:76

I'd like to be a doctor
Ka-Le:27

I'd like to be a fireman
with a ladder and a
hose
Ka-Le:22

I'd like to be a flower
Ka-Fa:10

I'd like to be a spaceman
Ka-Le:25

I'd rather be a bird, flying
all around
Ka-Fa:9#

I'll pretend on Halloween
De-Ch:74

I'll put my hand in my lap
Fl-Ri9:22#

I'll touch my hair, my
eyes, my chin
Ka-Le:10#

I'm a bear—hear me
growl!
Fl-Ri9:73#

I'm a big spider
De-Ch:64#

I'm a cat—hear me Me-
ow!
Ol-Fi

I'm a Christmas tree
Cr-Fi:67#

I'm a duck—I quack,
quack, quack
Le-Fi:65

I'm a Fairy Doll on the
Christmas Tree
Ma-Ga:54*

I'm a floppy, floppy rag
doll
Cr-Fi:108#
Fl-Ri9:77#
Mo-Pr:147#

I'm a friendly ghost—
almost!
Gr-Le:97

I'm a funny little puppet
clown
Fl-Ri9:48#
Sc-Rh:132#
Sc-RhL:47#

I'm a great, tall pine tree
Sc-RhL:34#

I'm a limp rag doll with
no bones at all
Sc-RhL:39#

I'm a little brown seed in
the ground
Cr-Fi:33#

FIRST LINE INDEX

231

Two tiny bunnies hopped
   down the land
   El-FP:22
Two wheels, three wheels
   on the ground
   Wi-Ev:29

Ug-u-ly, bug-u-ly, og-u-ly
   eyes!
   Do-Mo:31#
Ulu, uauau, tulivae
   tamatamivae (Head,
   shoulders, knees and
   toes)
   Sc-La:106
Un, deux, trois, j'irai dans
   le bois
   Sc-Rh:40
   Sc-RhL:149
Un elefante se balanceaba
   Fl-Ri9:20#
Un elephant se balancait
   Co-Pl:20#
Una boquita para comer
   Fl-Ri9:99
Uncle Fumble Bumble Bee
   began to buzz around
   Do-Mo:12#
Uncle Henry bought a car
   Do-Mo:98#
Under a stone where the
   earth was firm
   Ma-Ga:149
Under a toadstool, there
   sat a wee elf
   Sc-Rh:99
Under the spreading
   chest-nut-tree
   De-Ch:57#
Under the water, under
   the sea
   Sc-La:85
Une poule sur un mur
   Sc-La:102
United States has a
   birthday
   Le-Fi:106
Uno, dos, amarrate los
   zapatos
   Sc-RhL:145
Uno, dos, tres, cho-
   Fl-Ri9:80
   Gr-To
Uno, dos, tres, cuatro,
   cinco, cogi una mari-
   posa de un brinco
   Sc-Rh:46
   Sc-RhL:149
Uno, dos, tres, cuatro y
   cinco
   Fl-Ri9:15

Uno, dos, tres, uno, dos,
   tres
   Fl-Ri9:99
Uno, uno, contar es
   divertido
   Sc-RhL:146
Up a step, and up a step,
   and up a step and up
   Gr-Le:79
Up and down again, on
   the counterpane
   Mo-Th:35
"Up and down" and "all
   around." That's the
   way I brush my teeth
   Mc-Fi:29
Up and down and round
   and round
   Cr-Fi:5
   Fl-Ri9:8
Up and down, and up and
   down
   Fl-Ri9:88
Up and down the market,
   selling penny buns
   Mo-Th:39
Up goes the ladder to the
   side of the wall
   Sc-RhL:151
Up I stretch on tippy toe
   Ma-Ga:142*#
Up in the tower there's a
   carillon of bells
   Mc-Fi:27
Up in the tree
   Ja-Fi:19
Up on the mountain where
   the pine tree grows
   Ka-Fa:13
Up the candlestick he ran
   De-Ch:34
Up the steps, one, two,
   three, four
   Sc-RhL:113#
Up the steps we will go
   Gr-Le:78
Up the tall white candle-
   stick
   Ma-Ga:35
Up to the ceiling, down to
   the floor
   Co-Ee:26
Up, up, very slowly
   Sc-RhL:50#
Upon each hand a little
   band
   De-Ch:50
Upstairs, downstairs,
   quiet as a mouse
   Sc-RhL:50#

Use your eyes, use your
   eyes
   Fl-Ri9:100
   Wi-Ev:23

Vacation time went by on
   wings
   Mc-Fi:28
The valentine Dad gave to
   Mom
   De-Ch:69
A valentine for you
   Gr-Le:99
Valentines, valentines,
   how many do you see?
   Sc-Rh:71
Valentines, valentines,
   red, white and blue
   Fl-Ri9:100
   Wi-Ci:68
¡Veo, veo, veo!
   Sc-Rh:45
   Sc-RhL:148
A very old witch was
   stirring a pot
   Ca-Li:57#
"Vroom!" says the engine
   Cr-Fi:86

Waddle, waddle, waddle
   duck
   De-Ch:62#
Wahad etnen talatah
   Sc-La:60
Wait, wait, wait a bit
   Cr-Fi:99
Wake up, little fingers, the
   morning has come
   Fl-Ri9:101
   Sc-Rh:109
Wake up, little Pilgrims
   Cr-Fi:64
   Sc-Rh:63
Walk very slowly, hands
   by your sides
   Sc-RhL:31#
Walk, walk, softly—
   slow—This is the way
   the tigers go
   Sc-RhL:137#
Walking through the
   jungle
   Ma-Ga:100
Warm hands warm
   Cr-Fi:8
   Gr-Le:55
   Sc-La:57
Wash my hands
   Ja-Fi:7
Wash my hands, wash my
   face
   Ja-FPL:14

Wash your face, comb your
   hair
   Ka-Fa:12#
Watch me jump, watch me
   hop
   Ka-Fa:9#
The watch on my arm
   makes a little click
   De-Ch:63#
'Way last summer, when
   the corn grew tall
   Do-Mo:60#
Way up high in the apple
   tree See: Away up high
   in the apple tree
We are baby robins in a
   nest
   Sc-RhL:46#
We are brave police
   officers standing in a
   row
   Pa-Gi:62#
We are going to plant a
   bean
   Ma-Ga:48#
We are having a Fourth of
   July parade
   Sc-RhL:130#
We are little soldiers
   Sc-Rh:22#
We are soldiers marching
   along
   Ma-Ga:140*
We are ten little snow-
   flakes
   El-Fi:69
   El-Fi:70#
We are woodsmen sawing
   trees
   Ma-Ga:92*#
We can jump, jump, jump
   Fl-Ri9:101#
We can play a color game
   Cr-Fi:110
We have a birthday to
   celebrate
   Cr-Fi:74
We have a pumpkin, a big
   orange pumpkin
   Cr-Fi:61
We'll hop, hop, hop like a
   bunny
   Cr-Fi:47#
   Sc-Rh:88#
We love our flag
   Cr-Fi:72
We play a lot of games
   Sc-RhL:62
We're going on a bear hunt
   See: Let's go on a bear
   hunt

FIRST LINE INDEX

Where, oh where did my
puppy go?
Vo-Ac:21#

While the band is playing
Fl-Ri9:94

Whirlee, twirlee, look at
the squirrel
Ka-Fa:11

Whisky, frisky, hoppity
hop
Br-Fi:25
De-Ch:24
Fl-Ri9:83
Ka-Le:34
Ma-Ga:90
Pe-SP:101

The whistle blows at the
factory
Wi-Ev:177

White sheep, white sheep,
on a blue hill
Ha-St:19#

Whittle on a broomstick!
Do-Mo:106

Whizzin' frisbee in the air!
Do-Mo:111

Who comes creeping in the
night
Fl-Ri9:49

Who feels happy at school
today?
Sc-RhL:35#

Who feels happy, who feels
gay?
Gr-Le:76
Ka-Le:12
Ta-Ju:77#
Wi-Ci:68
Wi-Ev:33

Who is coming down the
chimney tonight
De-Ch:78

Who is it that wears a
smile
Fl-Ri9:105

Who lives in a nest high
up in a tree?
Vo-Ac:17

Who's that little boy
sitting in the seat?
Sh-Rh:13

Who's that tapping at my
window?
Fl-Ri9:105

"Who's that tickling my
back?" said the wall.
Sc-La:96
Th-Ca

Who stole the cookie from
the cookie jar?
Fl-Ri9:105
We-Fi2:9

Wi-Ev:59
Wi-Mu:170

A whooping crane came
walking
Sc-RhL:137#

Whose little pigs are these,
these, these?
Mo-Th:16

Wickware climbed up the
stair
Do-Mo:123#

Wiggle, wiggle, fingers
Fl-Ri9:105

A wiggle wiggle here
Sc-RhL:23#

Wiggle your fingers
Ga-Bu2:26

Wiggly, wiggly, wiggly
worm
Ka-Le:41

Will you have a cookie, or
a piece of pie
Fl-Ri9:36
Ha-Cl:18

Willum he had seven sons
Ma-Ga:167*#

The wind blows the leaves
Ga-Bu2:55

The wind came out to play
one day
Fl-Ri9:106
Pe-Fi:11
Sc-Rh:125
Wi-Ev:142

The wind comes in from
way out here
Ga-Bu2:56

The wind is a friend when
it's at rest
Cr-Fi:50#

The wind is full of tricks
today
Fl-Ri9:106
Wi-Ci:88
Wi-Ev:142

Wind the bobbin up
Ma-Ga:122*

Wind the top
Fl-RI9:95

Wind, wind, I can't see
you
Pu-ABC:21

Wind, wind, wind the
bobbin
Gr-Le:78

The winds of March begin
to blow
Sc-Rh:124

The windshield wipers on
our car are busy in the
rain

Gr-Le:24

Winking, blinking,
winking, blinking
De-Ch:5

The wise old owl
Fl-Fi:11

Witch, old witch, how do
you fly?
De-Ch:75

A witch once went for a
ride on her broom
Fl-Ri9:38

A witch, she went a-
shopping
Fl-Ri9:69

The witches are riding
tonight!
Le-Fi:95

With a "Cock-a-doodle-do,
cock-a-doodle-do,"
Ga-Bu2:64

With a net I go hunting to
catch a butterfly
Ka-Le:41

With a tick and a tock
Fl-Ri9:15

With arms out wide, when
there's a wind
Vo-Ac:9#

With clowns that play
Wi-Ev:199

With icicles hanging in
nice, little rows
Do-Mo:56

With my hands I clap,
clap, clap
Sc-RhL:149

With my little broom I
sweep, sweep, sweep
Ka-Le:10
Ma-Ga:33*#
Tw-Rh

With my little scissors I
cut some paper strips
Mc-Fi:32

With two hands and
fingers, count to ten
Vo-Ac:6

The wolf gives a howl
that's scary to hear
Co-Zo:46#

Won't you join our band
and play?
Wi-Ev:207

The woodchopper chops
down an old oak tree
Sc-Rh:52

Wooden soldiers, red and
blue
Fl-Ri9:107
Wi-Ci:118

A woodpecker pecked on
the front of my door
Do-Mo:102

The woodpecker pecks all
over the tree
Co-Zo:46

Woolly, woolly caterpillar
Ga-Bu2:49

Worms and germs and
rainy days
Wi-Ev:186

Would you shake? Would
you quake?
Pa-Gi:80

Xiao yan-er kan jjingzhier
Sc-La:53

Xylophone strike
Pu-ABC:21

The yak has long hair
under it I'll hide
Co-Zo:47#

Yankee Doodle came to
town
Mo-Th:85

The yellow giraffe is tall
as can be
Cr-Fi:78
Wi-Ev:76

Yesterday I went to the
field
Gr-To

You and me, we're gonna
be partners
Gl-Do:10*#

You can hear the jingle-
jangle of the parrots in
the jungle
Mc-Fi:38

You can take your dirty
clothes
Wi-Ev:168

You get a present in the
mail
Cr-Fi:11

You have ten fingers
Sh-Rh:5#

You lovely white swan
Ja-Fi:25

You put your right foot in
Co-Pl:44#
Gl-Do:35*#

You see me in the sky
above
Wi-Ev:130

You twiddle your thumbs
and clap your hands
Ma-Ga:123

You walk into a little
room
El-Fi:29
El-Fi:31#

First Line Index

KEY TO THE SOURCES INDEXED

Ba-On Barnes-Murphy, Rowan. *One, Two, Buckle My Shoe: A Book of Counting Rhymes.* New York: Simon & Schuster, 1987.

Be-We Beall, Pamela Conn, Susan Hagen Nipp & Nancy Klein. *Wee Sing: Children's Songs and Fingerplays.* Los Angeles: Price/Stern/Sloan, 1979.

Br-Fi Brown, Marc Tolon. *Finger Rhymes.* New York: Dutton, 1980.

Br-Ha Brown, Marc Tolon. *Hand Rhymes.* New York: Dutton, 1985.

Ca-Li Carlson, Bernice Wells. *Listen! And Help Tell the Story.* New York: Abingdon Press, 1965.

Co-Ee Cole, Joanna. *The Eentsy, Weentsy Spider: Fingerplays and Action Rhymes.* New York: Mulberry Books, 1991.

Co-Pl Corbett, Pie. *The Playtime Treasury: A Collection of Playground Rhymes, Games & Action Songs.* Garden City, NY: Doubleday, 1989.

Co-Tw Cope, Wendy. *Twiddling Your Thumbs: Hand Rhymes.* Boston: Faber & Faber, 1988.

Co-Zo Colville, M. Josephine. *The Zoo Comes to School: Finger Plays and Action Rhymes.* New York: Teachers Publishing Division, Macmillan, 1973.

Cr-Fi Cromwell, Liz & Dixie Hibner. *Finger Frolics: Fingerplays for Young Children.* Livonia, MI: Partner Press, 1983.

De-Ch Delamar, Gloria T. *Children's Counting-Out Rhymes, Fingerplays, Jump-Rope, and Bounceball Chants and Other Rhythms.* Jefferson, NC: McFarland, 1983.

Do-Mo Dowell, Ruth I. *Move Over, Mother Goose: Finger-Plays, Action Verses and Funny Rhymes.* Mt. Rainier, MD: Gryphon House, 1987.

El-Fi Ellis, Mary Jackson. *Finger Play Approach to Dramatization.* Minneapolis: T.S. Denison, 1960.

El-FP Ellis, Mary Jackson & Frances Lyons. *Finger Playtime.* Minneapolis: T.S. Denison, 1960.

Fl-Fi Fletcher, Helen Jill. *Finger Play Poems and Stories.* Darien, CT: Teachers Publishing Corp., 1958.

Fl-Ri9 *Ring a Ring O' Roses: Finger Plays for Pre-School Children.* Cynthia Stilley, comp. Flint, MI: Flint Public Library, Ninth Edition. 1988.

Fo-Sa Fowke, Edith. *Sally Go Round the Sun: Three Hundred Children's Songs, Rhymes and Games.* Garden City, NY: Doubleday, 1971.

Ga-Bu2 Gawron, Marlene E. *Busy Bodies: Finger Plays and Action Rhymes.* Second Edition. Orlando, FL: Moonlight Press, 1985.

Ga-Ov Galdone, Paul. *Over in the Meadow: An Old Nursery Counting Rhyme.* Englewood Cliffs, NJ: Prentice-Hall, 1986.

Gl-Do Glazer, Tom. *Do Your Ears Hang Low? Fifty More Musical Fingerplays.* Garden City, NY: Doubleday, 1980.

Gl-Ey Glazer, Tom. *Eye Winker, Tom Tinker, Chin Chopper: Fifty Musical Fingerplays.* Garden City, NY: Doubleday, 1973, 1978.

Gl-Mu Glazer, Tom. *Music for Ones and Twos: Songs and Games for the Very Young Child.* Garden City, NJ: Doubleday, 1983.

Gr-Le Grayson, Marion & Weyl, Nancy. *Let's Do Fingerplays.* Washington, DC: Robert B. Luce, Inc., 1962.

Gr-To Griego, Margot C. *Tortillitas Para Mama, and Other Nursery Rhymes / Spanish and English.* New York: Henry Holt, 1981.

Ha-Cl Hayes, Sarah. *Clap Your Hands: Finger Rhymes.* Boston, New York: Lothrop, 1988.

Ha-In Hawkins, Colin & Jacqui. *Incy Wincy Spider.* New York: Viking Kestrel, 1985.

Ha-Ni Hayes, Sarah. *Nine Ducks Nine.* New York: Lothrop, Lee & Shepard, 1990.

Ha-Ro Hawkins, Colin & Jacqui. *Round the Garden.* New York: Viking Kestrel, 1985.

Ha-St Hayes, Sarah. *Stamp Your Feet: Action Rhymes.* Boston, New York: Lothrop, 1988.

Ha-Th Hawkins, Colin & Jacqui. *This Little Pig.* New York: Viking Kestrel, 1985.

He-Th Hellard, Susan. *This Little Piggy.* New York: Putnam, 1989.

Ja-Fi Jacobs, Frances E. *Finger Plays and Action Rhymes.* Boston, New York: Lothrop, 1941.

Ja-FPL Jackson, Janet. *Finger Plays for Little Folks.* Elgin, IL: David C. Cook, 1985.

Ka-Fa Kahle, Gratia Underhill. *Favorite Fingerplays and Action Rhymes.* Minneapolis: T. S. Denison, 1987.

Ka-Le Karay, Hanne. *Let's Learn With Finger Plays: A Collection of Finger Plays, Action Verses, and Songs for Early Childhood.* Bowling Green, KY: Kinder Kollege Press, 1982.

Ke-Hi Kemp, Moira. *Hickory Dickory Dock.* New York: Dutton, 1991.

Ke-Im Kemp, Moira. *I'm a Little Teapot.* Toronto: Kids Can Press, 1987.

Ke-Kn Kemp, Moira. *Knock at the Door.* Los Angeles: Price/Sloan/Stern, 1987.

Ke-Ov Keats, Ezra Jack. *Over in the Meadow.* New York: Four Winds Press, 1971.

Ke-Pa Kemp, Moira. *Pat-a-Cake, Pat-a-Cake.* Toronto: Kids Can Press, 1987.

Ke-Ro Kemp, Moira. *Round and Round the Garden.* Toronto: Kids Can Press, 1987.

Ke-Th Kemp, Moira. *This Little Piggy.* New York: Dutton, 1991.

Kn-Ti Knight, Joan. *Tickle-Toe Rhymes.* New York: Orchard Books, 1989.

Ko-Da Kohn, Michael. *The Dandelion Book of Nursery Games.* New York: Dandelion Press, 1979.

Ko-Th Koontz, Robin. *This Old Man: The Counting Song.* New York: Dodd, Mead, 1988.

La-Ov Langstaff, John. *Over in the Meadow.* Harcourt, Brace & World, 1957.

La-Ri Lamont, Priscilla. *Ring-a-Round-a-Rosy: Nursery Rhymes, Action Rhymes and Lullabies.* Boston: Little, Brown, 1990.

Le-Fi Leighton, Audrey Olson. *Fingerplay Friends: Action Rhymes for Home, Church, or School.* Valley Forge, PA: Judson Press, 1984.

Le-Te Leydenfrost, Robert. *Ten Little Elephants.* Garden City, NJ: Doubleday, 1975.

Ma-Ga Matterson, Elizabeth. *Games for the Very Young: Finger Plays and Nursery Games.* New York: American Heritage Press, 1969.

Ma-Re Mahoney, Ellen & Leah Wilcox. *Ready, Set, Read: Best Books to Prepare Preschoolers.* Metuchen, NJ: Scarecrow Press, 1985.

Mc-Fi McGuire, Maybelle B. *Finger and Action Rhymes.* Dansville, NY: Instructor Publications, 1973.

Mc-In McNally, Darcie, adapt. *In a Cabin in a Wood.* New York: Dutton, 1991.

Mo-Ca Mother Goose. *The Calico Mother Goose Book of Games, Riddles and Tongue Twisters.* Chicago: Calico Books, 1989.

Mo-Pr Moore, Vardine. *Pre-School Story Hour.* Metuchen, NJ: Scarecrow Press, 1972.

Mo-Th Montgomerie, Norah, comp. *This Little Pig Went to Market: Play Rhymes.* New York: Franklin Watts, 1967.

Oa-Ch Oakley, Ruth. *Chanting Games.* New York: Marshall Cavendish, 1989.

Ol-Fi Oldfield, Margaret. *Finger Puppets and Finger Plays.* Minneapolis: Creative Storytime, 1982.

Or-Rh Ormerod, Jan. *Rhymes Around the Day.* New York: Lothrop, Lee & Shepard, 1983.

Ov-Le Overholser, Kathy. *Let Your Fingers Do the Talking.* Minneapolis: T.S. Denison, 1979.

Pa-Gi Patrick, Jenett. *Gingerbread Kids: Super Easy Activities to Help Young Children Learn.* Livonia, MI: Partner Press, 1987.

Pe-Ba Peek, Merle. *The Balancing Act: A Counting Song.* New York: Clarion, 1987.

Pe-Fi Peek, Don. *Finger Plays That Motivate: A Collection of Tested and Novel Action Verses.* Minneapolis: T.S. Denison, 1975.

Pe-SP Peterson, Carolyn Sue & Brenny Hall. *Story Programs: A Source Book of Materials.* Metuchen, NJ: Scarecrow Press, 1980.

Pe-St Pellowski, Anne. *The Story Vine.* New York: Macmillan, 1984.

Po-Da Pooley, Sarah. *A Day of Rhymes.* New York: Knopf, 1988.

Po-Fi Poulsson, Emilie. *Finger Plays for Nursery and Kindergarten.* New York: Dover, 1971.

Pu-ABC Pugmire, Mary Carolyn Weller. *ABC Way to an Effective Fingerplay.* Rexburg, ID: Ricks College, 1980.

Ra-Tr Ra, Carol F. *Trot, Trot, to Boston: Play Rhymes for Baby.* New York: Lothrop, 1987.

Ro-Mi Roberts, Lynda. *Mitt Magic: Finger Plays for Finger Puppets.* Mt. Rainier, MD: Gryphon House, 1985.

Ro-We Rosen, Michael. *We're Going on a Bear Hunt.* New York: McElderry Books, 1989.

Sc-La Scott, Anne Leolani. *The Laughing Baby: Remembering Nursery Rhymes and Reasons.* South Hadley, MA: Gergin & Garvey, 1987.

Sc-Rh Scott, Louise Binder. *Rhymes for Fingers and Flannelboards.* St. Louis: Webster, 1960.

Sc-RhL Scott, Louise Binder. *Rhymes for Learning Times: Let's Pretend Activities for Early Childhood.* Minneapolis: T.S. Denison, 1983, 1984.

Sh-Rh Shotwell, Rita. *Rhythm & Movement Activities for Early Childhood.* Sherman Oaks, CA: Alfred Publishing, 1984.

Sh-Sh Sharon, Lois & Bram Staff. *Sharon, Lois & Bram's Mother Goose: Songs, Finger Rhymes, Tickling Verses, Games, and More.* Boston: Atlantic Monthly Press, 1985.

Si-Im Sivulich, Sandra. *I'm Going on a Bear Hunt.* New York: Dutton, 1973.

St-Th Stobbs, William. *This Little Piggy.* London: Bodley Head, 1981.

Ta-Ju Tashjian, Virginia A. *Juba This and Juba That: Story Hour Stretches for Large or Small Groups.* Boston: Little, Brown, 1969.

Ta-Wi Tashjian, Virginia A. *With a Deep Sea Smile: Story Hour Stretches for Large or Small Groups.* Boston: Little, Brown, 1974.

Th-Ca Thompson, Brian. *Catch It If You Can: Nursery Rhymes Compiled by Brian Thompson.* New York: Viking Kestrel, 1989.

Tw-Rh Twinn, Colin. *Rhyming Games.* London, New York: Frederick Warne, 1989.

Vo-Ac Vogels, Mary Prescott. *Action Plays for Little Hands.* Minneapolis: T.S. Denison, 1971.

We-Fi1 Weimer, Tonja Evetts. *Fingerplays and Action Chants, Volume One: Animals.* Pittsburgh: Pearce-Evetts Publishing, 1986.

We-Fi2 Weimer, Tonja Evetts. *Fingerplays and Action Chants, Volume Two: Family and Friends.* Pittsburgh: Pearce-Evetts Publishing, 1986.

We-Pe Westcott, Nadine Bernard. *Peanut Butter and Jelly: A Play Rhyme.* New York: Dutton, 1987.

Wi-Ci Wilmes, Liz & Dick. *The Circle Time Book.* Dundee, IL: Building Blocks, 1982.

Wi-Ev Wilmes, Liz & Dick. *Everyday Circle Times.* Dundee, IL: Building Blocks, 1983.

Wi-He Williams, Jenny. *Here's a Ball for Baby: Finger Rhymes for Young Children.* New York: Dial Books for Young Readers, 1987.

Wi-Mu Wirth, Marian & Verna Stassevitch. *Musical Games, Fingerplays and Rhythmic Activities for Early Childhood.* West Nyack, NY: Parker, 1983.

Wi-Pl Wilkin, Esther. *Play with Me.* New York: Golden Press, 1988.

Wi-Ro Williams, Sarah. *Round and Round the Garden: Play Rhymes for Young Children.* Oxford; New York: Oxford University Press, 1983.

Wo-Pi Wood, Audrey & Don. *Piggies.* New York: Harcourt Brace Jovanovich, 1991.

Ya-Fi Yamaguchi, Marianne. *Finger Plays.* New York: Holt, Rinehart & Winston, 1970.

Yo-La Yolen, Jane, ed. *The Lap-Time Song and Play Book.* San Diego: Harcourt, Brace, Jovanovich, 1989.

INDEX

Compiled by Janet Perlman